The Forge of Tubal Cain

The Forge of Tubal Cain

by
Ann Finnin

Pendraig Publishing, Los Angeles

© 2008 Ann Finnin. All rights reserved. No part of this publication may be reproduced, stored in a retrieval system or transmitted in any form or by any means, electronic, mechanical, photocopying, recording or otherwise without the prior written permission of the copyright holder, except brief quotations used in a review.

Roebuck logo created by Sandy Penney
Used by permission of
Roebuck Tradition and the Ancient Keltic Church

Pendraig Publishing, Sunland, CA 91040
© Ann Finnin 2008. All rights reserved.
Published 2008.
Printed in the United States of America

ISBN 978-0-9796168-3-9

Contents

Foreword by Ed Fitch	6
Introduction	8
We Learned It From Our Grandmother	12
The Saga of 1734	22
The Founding Of The Roebuck	30
The Forge of Old Tubal	38
The Journey Across The Pond	52
The Spiral Staircase	62
The Magical Mystery Tour	76
The Wolf Pack	86
The Two-Edged Sword	96
Death, Transformation and Rebirth	104
Roebuck 101	**114**
Magical Mental Training	120
Invocation Techniques	126
Casting The Castle	136
Pathworking Techniques	140
Trance State Induction	146
Quarter Pathworkings	154
The Path To Initiation	158
The Magical Mindset	180
The Roebuck Way	196
Appendix I - Castle of the East	218
Appendix II - Castle of the South	222
Appendix III - Castle of the West	226
Appendix IV - Castle of the North	230
Appendix V - The Spiral Castle	234
Appendix VI - The Forge of Old Tubal	236
Appendix VII - The Black Goddess	238
Index	242

Foreword

Dave and Ann Finnin were easily the very best students that I've ever taught. We originally met in an historical re-enactment group ... then our casual conversations led by degrees into a mutually rewarding investigation into the deeper meanings of the nature of reality, of magic, and of the Gods. For my good friends it has been an investigation that has lasted now for more than a third of a century, and (as with any true quest for fundamental Truths) shows no sign of ever concluding.

This book which Ann has written is in two parts actually, and both are a totally original approach to what one will find in other volumes now on the market. First, she explains in detail how the tradition that would come to be called "Roebuck" was started, originally with close guidance from me, as I gave them the benefit of my own years of historical, folkloric, and magical research. Then increasingly, Dave and Ann struck out on their own, to seek out and refine the lore which quite likely would otherwise have been lost forever.

The history of their search is fascinating in that it covers not only their long quest to uncover ancient Mysteries that have been hidden for centuries, but also many of the intrapersonal and organizational problems that are encountered when one seeks to lay out, organize, and develop an operating Mystery tradition in our modern world. It's never easy.

Of particular importance are the discussions of the various types of people who come to covens and lodges asking to be trained and to become members, then how to separate the worthwhile ones from the ones driven by ego, greed or other psychological problems and how to handle them.

Then she goes into the second part of this fascinating book, and one that deserves close study from all who are interested in the Craft. Ann describes in detail exactly how to go far beyond the ritual techniques used by most magical traditions, and how to safely contact the highest Powers ... be they Gods, archetypes, group minds, or whatever one chooses to name them ... and to gain valid, totally new lore from them.

The course of training demanded by the Roebuck mystery tradition is a stern and taxing one, and not something that can be gained easily or in a weekend of formal ritual. There are no "words of power" or "names of power" that will grant instant enlightenment, or rituals of magic that will automatically give one the powers of a near-demigod. Roebuck is not for everyone; it is demanding and exacting, and takes a lot of work ... but it is quite likely the best and most effective magical and Mystery tradition existing!

Yet even so, the training and working techniques given in this book can provide invaluable guidance to anyone involved with the Old Religion. What Ann describes are not formulas, spells, and rites that have been quoted and re-quoted over and over again by dozens of occult authors: the contents of this book are totally _new_, and totally _original_!

The reader is encouraged to study Ann's writing over and over, and to experiment with the approaches she has discussed, one at a time. By all means, read over the basic (if often quite dry) texts that she recommends. Using what is in this book will take lots of work, but the results will be immensely rewarding. Read on. You won't regret it!

Ed Fitch
Orange County, California
February 2008

Introduction

More than any other time in known history, books on Witchcraft flood the bookshelves of major bookstores. This book is one more of those. Most books either describe the Craft the way it was, the way it is, or the way it ought to be, according to the writer's social and political biases. This book is one more of those as well. However, most books describe a Craft tradition, whether past, present or future, as a complete and fully formed entity, having sprung full-grown like Athena from the brow of Zeus.

This book is different.

It attempts to tell the story of one group's attempt at the reconstruction of an Anglo-Celtic hereditary Craft tradition called the Clan of Tubal Cain and its transplantation to American soil as the Roebuck Tradition. In it, I try to present not only the final product as it is now, but describe the process by which the product was achieved along with all the glorious folly that accompanied it – the mistakes, wrong turns and failed experiments along with the breakthroughs and achievements.

I also try to portray how such a tradition is actually lived and worked by ordinary modern people who lead ordinary modern lives – along with possible solutions to problems that our ancestors couldn't have dreamed of, as well as some which they, no doubt, suffered from as much as we.

The story begins back in 1965. An American from Kansas City named Joe Wilson placed an ad in the short-lived but lively British Journal "Pentagram" edited by Gerald Noel in the late 1960s for someone to correspond with him regarding traditional Craft. The ad was answered by a man calling himself Robert Cochrane, (real name, Roy Bowers) a self-described Witch, blacksmith, mystic and poet who had written several articles in the magazine and had some very unusual ideas about what the Craft really should be.

In a series of five letters written between December of 1965 and his tragic death in June of 1966, Cochrane outlined a mysterious Craft tradition totally unlike anything that had appeared in the States up until then. It revolved around a group called the Clan of Tubal Cain and a dark and unnamed Goddess known only as the 1 in 7 wisdom, or 1734. There were no spells, no scripted full moon or sabbat rituals, no magical formulae, no bells, books or candles. There were only visions, mystical philosophy, a severe, no-nonsense creed and an intense devotion to a Goddess whose only name was Fate.

Was <u>this</u> really Witchcraft? And if it was, what were the bell, book and candle crowd actually doing?

Serious scholars have for the most part agreed that modern Witchcraft, or Wicca, is a twentieth-century reconstruction of a religious and devotional way of life that hasn't been practiced in nearly fifteen hundred years. It disappeared not only because of Christian and Moslem religious persecution, and political upheavals but also advances in education, technology and other cultural factors which made many of its more urgent rituals unnecessary for physical survival.

A very small part was preserved in a fragmentary state by a few rare manuscripts outlining myths and stories as well as simple recipes and charms – all brutally edited and expurgated of any religious and philosophical content by the monks that transcribed them. Centuries later, these fragments were collected, edited, enlarged upon, even fabricated out of whole cloth by amateur antiquarians for whom, even as early as the 16th and 17th centuries, such things were hopelessly out-of-date and old-fashioned.

They, too, attempted a reconstruction of the material. However, unlike our modern attempts, theirs was often presented as past history, something quaint and curious that a modern person might enjoy studying, but certainly would not consider practicing, especially if it meant abandoning the religious and social conventions of the day in order to do so.

The sad part of all of this is that all too often, it is their reconstruction - with all of its cultural and religious bias - rather than the original material that forms the basis of our own reconstructions. In order to get closer to the way in which the Craft was actually practiced by real people, one has to examine many other different and often unrelated sources - painstakingly peeling away the surface bias, whether religious, scientific or political to see if and how it all fits together. This process is particularly difficult for Americans, since many of the books, manuscripts, folklore and other resources are either out of print or otherwise unavailable here.

Adding to the confusion is the controversy that continues to rage on both sides of the Atlantic as to whether or not a tradition of this kind even belongs in America in the first place. Even Dion Fortune advised Americans to try the contacts of the Aztecs or Mayans rather than try to work a British system. This well meaning but short sighted advice ignores the basic complexity of the American psyche. The basic cornerstone of all shamanic traditions, traditional Craft included, is to establish a connection with the ancestral spirits of the tribe. The problem is that for the vast majority of Americans, the Aztec, Maya or any of the Native American tribes simply are not our ancestors.

A true story will illustrate this problem. Back in 1974 when we first began to study the Craft, we had a friend who wanted to be a shaman. Determined to find a Native American medicine man to study with, he traveled to an obscure corner of northern California and hung around for several years, doing odd jobs and going to as many Native American gatherings as he could. Eventually, he found his medicine man and humbly made his request. The medicine man refused him, saying in essence, "You are not of our people. Our Gods are not your Gods. We couldn't teach you our medicine even if we tried. You must go and find the medicine of your own people."

The medicine of our own people. This presents a major problem. Just who <u>are</u> 'our' people? For most of those attracted to traditional Craft, their ancestors are immigrants who came over here from England, Scotland,

Ireland, France, Germany, Scandinavia and eastward to Poland, Hungary, Czechoslovakia and Russia. Celtic. Teutonic. Northern European.

In my case, three of my four grandparents came from Europe or Britain. However, even those who have bloodlines from other parts of the world haven't escaped the melting pot and it's a good bet that anyone who has been here more than a couple of generations shares that bloodline to some degree or other. Do we in America have less of a right to this tradition than those still in Europe who are also a mixture of cultures and bloodlines?

For thousands of years, our northern European ancestors migrated across Europe and Asia, bringing their ancestral Gods with them. After all that time, it seems strange that those ancestral Gods of ours would sever ties with us just because we crossed the Atlantic. Does it make that much of a difference if we perform the ancient dances and rituals on a hilltop in Somerset or Los Angeles? Mother earth is still the same. The stars above our heads, the dragon lines beneath our feet, the sun, the wind and the rain are still the same no matter where we are. Everything else, we carry with us as we've always done – even to the shores of a new continent.

All over the world, there are cultural traditions - folk souls if you will - that some people are drawn to and others not, no matter what country they live in or who their parents were. Nationality is arbitrary and transitory. Cultural and racial purity is a cruel fiction. The folk soul of a particular tradition calls to who it will, no matter where they live on this earth. The ancestors embrace their own and don't demand a pedigree or birth certificate first.

The medicine of our people.

Here is one group's attempt to find it.

We Learned It From Our Grandmother

All modern Craft traditions, despite the often-elaborate mythology surrounding them, come from somewhere. The research into mythology and ancient folk practices is done by someone, the rituals written by someone and the training organized and conducted by someone. Furthermore, traditions are rarely linear. Most craft leaders have been influenced by and even received initiations, ordinations or other credentials, from a variety of teachers. Then, by means of research, trial-and-error, a sprinkling of intuition and a large dollop of common sense, put the pieces together to form a coherent and workable whole which can be passed down to another generation.

The Roebuck is no exception.

In February of 1974, we began weekly journeys to the center of the San Bernardino County Bible Belt in Redlands, California, to study with a man who would, himself, become a Craft folk hero. We originally met Ed Fitch, a former Air Force officer and a 3rd degree Gardnerian Priest, through the local chapter of the Society for Creative Anachronism (SCA). Ed held weekly classes at his home, which several other members of the SCA group also attended. We joined this group along with them.

It's worth noting that the SCA itself exerted a great deal of influence on us in those early days. Part historical recreation group and part fantasy role playing game, the SCA (and various other related groups which work renaissance fairs all over the country), provided an important cultural and social backdrop for the fledgling craft in the late 60's and early 70's. It attracted into its membership mostly well-educated, literate young people who shared an interest in myth, folklore, ancient and medieval history - a kind of counter-culture intelligentsia with romantic ideals much like the Romantic Movement a century earlier.

Such people found in the SCA, with its tournaments, banquets, wars and revels, a social outlet and alternate lifestyle which often lasted for years. They often married within the SCA and looked upon other members as a surrogate family of like-minded people with whom they could discuss such topics as J.R.R. Tolkein, Star Trek, Ancient Egyptian myths and Arthurian legend without being thought weird by the Brady Bunch popular culture which surrounded them in the so-called 'mundane' world. In the effort to make their events more historically accurate, many SCA members engaged in extensive research into a variety of cultural topics - art, music, literature, dance, costume, social customs and so on. It isn't surprising, then, that in such an environment, those people who were religiously and spiritually minded would experiment with reconstructions of ancient Pagan faiths and rituals.

Consequently, a number of reconstructed Pagan faiths, particularly Celtic and Norse, flourished under the aegis of 'historical recreation' and recruited from the ranks of the SCA members who would meet outside of an SCA event for rituals and training. It was in this context that Gardnerian Witchcraft, particularly in California, landed upon fertile ground.

The SCA and similar organizations took the Craft out of the realm of the Occult or even the New Age and allied it more closely with the Science Fiction and Fantasy community. Writers such as Marion Zimmer Bradley, Andre Norton and others following in the footsteps of J.R.R. Tolkein, wrote frankly Pagan stories featuring characters which used magic and interacted with Pagan Gods as both mentors and adversaries. These books were marketed as fantasy and as such, were considered far more socially acceptable than if they had been considered works of the 'occult' - even though certain classic occult sources, particularly old grimoires obtained from the British Museum, were employed extensively as research

Ann with Ed Fitch

material. In addition, the introduction of Celtic, Norse, Greek and Egyptian magical themes in these stories helped immensely to popularize them and induce readers to explore them further.

There has been criticism - some of it justified - leveled at the SCA and related groups for "romanticizing" and "whitewashing" the Craft and ignoring the darker aspects of the tradition, rendering it superficial and irrelevant to the problems encountered in a person's actual daily life. It treated Pagan religion as a kind of Dungeons and Dragons role playing game in which people donned elaborate costumes, employed a variety of beautifully made tools, such as swords and chalices, and engaged in elaborate rituals in which fantastic Gods, mythical creatures and spirits were invoked and communed with.

For many people it was difficult, if not downright impossible, to translate this kind of religion into the real mundane world of job, finances, familial duties and community and civic issues. Some devotees adjusted to this problem by abandoning the mundane world altogether. They worked mindless, soul-less jobs only so much as necessary to buy the basic necessities of life and ignored anything else having to do with mundane reality. Every spare moment was spent going to circles and other gatherings trying desperately to pretend that the mundane world didn't exist until some job or family crisis made it impossible.

Others developed a kind of schizoid dual personality. One half (using their legal name) would work or otherwise function in the world as best they could and the other half (bearing another name altogether) would function within the Craft community in some capacity or other. This strategy, of course, eventually took its toll. A great deal of energy had to be spent keeping the two identities separate so that the friends and associates of one wouldn't find out about the other, particularly if the mundane identity had a job that would subject him or her to derision or ridicule in Craft circles. Drug and alcohol abuse was often the result of the strain on both psychic and physical resources.

However, despite the drawbacks, the alliance of the Craft and the Fantasy and Science Fiction community served the vital purpose of placing the Craft into its proper cultural and historical context - not as a rebellion against Christianity but as an ancestor of Christianity, albeit in the long-ago and far-away. If nothing else, this portrayal helped to ensure that the people coming into it would have positive motivations (eagerness to learn about the Goddess and the Old Gods) rather than negative ones (rebellion against authority or casting spells for money or power over others).

So, it was in Ed's outer court training coven, with its romantic trappings of cloaks, swords and courtly gallantry, we learned the beginnings of Craft ritual. In the beginning, this consisted of little more than following a written script. Although the Roebuck was to eventually abandon nearly all scripted rituals, the training-wheel function of working from scripts was invaluable in those early days. From scripted rituals, we learned what constitutes a ritual, how it is constructed, what the parts are and how they all fit together as a whole.

A script shows how words and gestures can be used to compliment each other and keep the ritual flowing rather than getting bogged down or stopping altogether. Furthermore, it encourages the participants to pay attention to what is being done and what the effect of each gesture or speech will have on both the performer and the other participants. And, last but not least, it enables the performers, especially ones new and inexperienced, to remember what comes next and not leave out anything important.

Ed's scripted rituals were beautifully written and very poetic. Still, he considered them to be guidelines rather than Holy Writ and he allowed the words to serve as inspiration for our own thoughts rather than insisting they be slavishly read verbatim. As our confidence grew, so did the ability to speak as the spirit moved when performing whatever ritual actions were required. Quarter invocations in particular were first read, then memorized, then ad-libbed. Then, gradually, as the ritual steps were engrained, entire speeches could be made up on the spot, as an inspired poem would be. Soon, nothing was actually read and the entire ritual would be ad-libbed, with only a short outline for reference.

Spell casting is also a useful way of learning how to construct rituals. Deciding what your purpose is, what symbols to use on the physical realm to correspond with what you want to do on the Astral, and how to "fix" the spell so that there is closure constitutes a mini-ritual in itself. With Ed, we created our own spells rather than using those out of a cookbook. These are not only much more effective, but more fun as well. Furthermore, we found the same techniques to be useful on a larger scale within a group in order to get everybody to focus on a physical symbol, like tying knots in a cord or burning something in a brazier, using jingles, short chants and other aids in the process.

On the more esoteric side, it was originally from Ed that we learned how to explore past lives and explore the nature of the link between the two of us and where we had been as individuals. Acceptance of reincarnation is a very important part of Craft training. It gives the student a feeling of continuity to his or her magical development - a sense of having done this before and picking up where one has left off in the past. It also is vital in teaching ethical responsibility and gives teeth to the three-fold law. If what you send out doesn't return to you three-fold in this lifetime, there's always the next lifetime, and the next. One isn't off the hook, so to speak, just because one sheds one's physical body.

There were many other things we learned from Ed that were less concerned with techniques and information and more with an attitude towards the Craft as a whole that would later guide the course of the Roebuck. It was while we were in Ed's training group that we first became aware of what we called the Gardnerian Myth of the Craft – originally gleaned from Gardner's books and later elaborated on by various other writers and Gardnerian apologists. Even though we heard it first from the Gardnerians, we soon discovered that even non-Gardnerians, especially newcomers, believed this story without question and passed it along to others. The story, as we heard it, went something like this:

The Craft as practiced by the Gardnerians consisted of a tradition of Goddess-worship that had continued unbroken for centuries, passed along in secret from High Priestess to High Priestess since the Middle Ages in the form of a sacred Book of Shadows. This Book was given into the hands of Gerald Gardner who had been initiated by a High Priestess named Old Dorothy in the New Forest. This book had, in turn, been entrusted to Ray and Rosemary Buckland who were authorized to bring it to the United States. This Book of Shadows could not be altered in any way, even to correct obvious grammar mistakes and must be transmitted only to properly initiated Gardnerians within a magic circle.

The upshot of this myth was that only people who could trace their initiatory lineage to Ray and Rosemary were considered 'real' Witches by many American Gardnerian covens. Anyone else, no matter what their tradition or training, was considered beyond the pale and were treated as outsiders. Members of certain Gardnerian circles were in some cases actually forbidden to participate in anybody else's rituals and often stood outside the circle during public gatherings in order to watch the proceedings.

It must be pointed out that it wasn't all Gardnerians who promulgated this story and insisted on exclusionary circle practices. In fact, many Gardnerians on both sides of the Atlantic have worked long and hard to dispel this myth and uncover the true antecedents of both Gardner and Old Dorothy. Many covens have since updated their Books of Shadows, making corrections as well as adding and deleting material that they have discovered doesn't work, isn't authentic, might be harmful and so on.

Over the years, it seems to have been primarily one particular line of American Gardnerians, founded by a couple in New York, who promoted this particular story and who tended to attract and keep people who had a psychological need to be a part of the one true right and only Craft tradition. This caused a problem when it came time for us to be initiated. At the time there was only one Gardnerian coven of this lineage in the Los Angeles area. We either had to join this particular Gardnerian coven or none at all.

Ed, although a <u>bona fide</u> third-degree Gardnerian of the New York line, did not, at the time, have a third-degree High Priestess. Therefore, he was not authorized to run a legitimate Gardnerian coven, nor could he use actual Gardnerian rituals. All he could do, according to Gardnerian regulations, was run an "outer court." He couldn't initiate us, or anybody else for that matter, into the Gardnerian tradition and have them recognized as such by the Gardnerian establishment.

There was, however, an alternative. A coven that practiced something called the American Tradition, now called the Mohsean Tradition, was located not far away. The couple that ran this group, Bill and Helen Mohs, had connections to a group in Cincinnati, Ohio that practiced a combination of Alexandrian and Gardnerian Craft. The coven they ran was large, open, colorful and friendly. Furthermore, they were willing to accept us at face value and were willing to give us an "inner court" First Degree initiation on Ed's recommendation alone.

Bill & Helen Mohs

On Lammas, 1974, we were given a First Degree initiation in a ritual which we later discovered was virtually identical to that of a Gardnerian First Degree. However, it was not altogether clear at the time just what that initiation meant. We were still not accepted by the local Gardnerians as legitimate, nor were we allowed to attend initiates' only circles.

This seemed particularly unfair since the couple who ran this coven had themselves been initiated by Bill and Helen only a few months before we were. The woman had then traveled to New York and received the Gardnerian three degrees over the course of a weekend. She returned to Los Angeles and founded the Gardnerian coven with not a whole lot more experience and training than we had.

When we expressed our dismay at this state of affairs, the High Priestess in question put pressure on Ed to stop training us. Not wanting to cause trouble for Ed, we agreed to stop attending his circles. Ed, who by this time had a young family to care for, referred a couple of his other students to us for training. Bill Mohs gave us an American Trad Second Degree and we sallied forth on our own to see what fate awaited us.

We didn't stay adrift long. Other teachers appeared to guide us even farther along the path of Traditional Craft. Fred and Martha Adler had been members of the Alexandrian/Gardnerian coven in Cincinnati and had originally initiated Bill and Helen Mohs. Having since retired from running their own coven, the Adlers took us under their wing and not only taught us further lore, but encouraged us to forget about trying to join somebody else's coven and go start our own. They served as Godfather and Goddessmother to our first coven in 1975 – called by the accurate but singularly uninspiring name of The Pasadena Training Coven. Eventually, the Adlers gave us an American Tradition Third Degree.

We soon became active within the local Craft community. We helped coordinate public rituals with a group called the Quintella and signed the original charter of the Covenant of the Goddess as the Pasadena Training Coven in 1975. During the course of all this community work, we discovered that there were several covens in our area that worked quite happily outside the Gardnerian hierarchy. We attended several of their rituals, often two or three a week. From them, we learned not only what to do when we eventually put together our own circle but, in several cases, the equally valuable lesson of what not to do as well.

Even though we were shut out of most of the inner workings of the Gardnerian system, we learned a great deal of worth from them all the same. For all of their dogma and rigidity, the Gardnerians had a structure and a circle discipline that ensured that the tradition they practiced remained more-or-less consistent from coven to coven. Once a Gardnerian was given a First Degree initiation, he or she could travel from one coven to another and feel pretty much at home with what was being done in the ritual. The way the circle was cast, the methods for raising power, the god and Goddess names and so on would be familiar, enabling the initiate to participate in the magic as fully as if the person was in his or her home coven.

The often politically-based Gardnerian hierarchy, much as we chafed beneath it, served a useful purpose. It insured that some semblance of consistency and accountability was maintained within each coven and between covens. In a Gardnerian circle, there was one person - usually the High Priestess - who was in charge. Every member of her coven knew who initiated her and where her training and information came from. They also knew they could, theoretically at any rate, call upon her initiator in the event of a possible dispute or problem.

In other, more eclectic traditions, each coven did whatever they pleased, answered to no one but themselves and left a member with no recourse in a dispute. This lack of uniformity and accountability while encouraging creativity and innovation, led to a variety of abuses, particularly in the area of training and credentials. If one claimed to be a Gardnerian, one could prove it with lineage papers. Such credentials said nothing about one's character or knowledge, but they did say that one had, even if it was only rudimentary, training in the Gardnerian tradition and had been acknowledged as such by somebody.

In the eclectic traditions, anybody could claim anything with no proof other than their word. And, if they found students who were willing to believe them, they could teach all manner of odd things in the name of the Craft. This led to a variety of self-appointed Witch gurus who would read several books on the subject and set themselves up as teachers, telling prospective students that they had learned it from their grandmothers. This practice became so common that "learning it from your grandmother" became a cliché. The only ones who didn't find it funny were the unfortunate students who bought into it and found out later that they'd been had.

Ed's material, in particular, was used in this fashion. He had written his Outer Court Grimoire and Book of Shadows to be disseminated, via the magazine Crystal Well, to anybody who requested it. However, since it was years before it was actually published, it was not readily available to anyone unfamiliar with the Crystal Well. An unscrupulous teacher could (and, in at least two cases, did) get a hold of it and, since his students would not be able to find it in a bookstore, easily make outrageous claims about where it came from.

Indeed, over the years, we hosted several people from a variety of different groups who recognized Ed's Outer Court material as the "secret" Book of Shadows that their teacher had claimed to have inherited from his grandmother. We decided that since Ed was everybody else's grandmother, he would be ours as well.

The Saga of 1734

As we left the Gardnerian tradition behind, there was nothing else to do but to return to the American Trad and explore that avenue further. Upon closer scrutiny, we discovered that the American Trad had at its core the same basic Book of Shadows as the Gardnerians had. But, since they were under no compunction to refrain from altering the rituals, many interesting variations and practices had been added.

Over the years, Bill and Helen had done a great deal of research on their own exploring a variety of magical traditions - herbal lore, Cabala, Ceremonial Magic and Demonology. They had also gleaned a great deal of information from other, less secretive traditions than the Gardnerian one. Their Book of Shadows, unlike the relatively spare Gardnerian book, was voluminous - containing rituals, lore, poems, invocations, spells, jingles, chants, rules and regulations that we had never learned from Ed.

Very little of it was annotated as to where it originally came from. Some things were fairly standard such as the herb lore and some things obviously taken *verbatim* from the Gardnerian Book of Shadows or various ceremonial magic books. But we noted other bits and pieces of a mystery tradition that we had never seen before, strange mystical teachings that hinted at a view of the craft very different than what the Gardnerians were practicing.

Part of this mystery tradition involved discovering the secret name of, and thereby communing with, the dark or wisdom aspect of the Goddess and thereby transcend one's own fate. This secret name was contained in a glyph made up of four numbers: 1, 7, 3 and 4. By solving the riddle of "1734," one could discover the nature of this Goddess and enlist Her aid in mastering one's own spiritual destiny.

It was this mysterious secret - buried deep within the American Trad Book of Shadows – that drew us like a magnet. It pointed to a path very different from anything we had encountered before, a spiritual path of personal devotion, philosophical principles and visionary experiences rather than spells, sabbat rituals and dogmatic rules.

As we began the task of untangling and sorting out this hodge-podge of material, we learned that there was another Craft influence in the States, other than the Gardnerians. Bill and Helen had worked with a man in the Midwest who had been active in the craft, both teaching and writing, for as long as any of the local Gardnerians had. The strange mystical lore that we had discovered in their Book of Shadows had come from him. His name was Joseph Wilson.

Joe, a brilliant but iconoclastic character, wasn't recognized by the official Gardnerian establishment either, but managed to function quite successfully outside the pale anyway, authoring rituals, newsletters and teaching correspondence classes. In the ten years since he had first corresponded with Robert Cochrane, Joe had established a tradition that was completely separate from the Gardnerian one. It consisted of his own researches and material from several other British groups as well as his letters from Cochrane and from another British Crafter named Norman. He called it "1734."

Ed introduced us to Joe and we started to attend circles that he and his wife Mara were holding at their home in a nearby mountain community called Tujunga. Finally, we discovered the source of all the interesting bits scattered throughout Bill and Helen's Book of Shadows. Our task now was to follow them to their source. From Joe, we learned that there were other Craft traditions that had issued forth from England about the same time as the Gardnerian tradition did.

After the repeal of the Witchcraft laws in England in 1951, a number of people calling themselves "Hereditary" Witches began to come out of the woodwork and also began writing books and articles. These folks, we discovered, claimed to belong to "Witch" families who had kept certain Craft practices preserved in secret for generations. It was this tradition of "Witch" families which constituted the source of the common practice of questionable Craft gurus - first in England, and then the States - to claim that their tradition came from their Grandmother.

Latent psychic ability, commonly called "The Sight" often manifests as a family trait. Like many family traits, it will often skip a generation and will be passed on and encouraged by the grandparents to the grandchildren, bypassing the parents entirely. In this way, the family tradition is passed along to a new generation. For the most part, the only way to belong to one of these family traditions was to either be born into the family or marry into it. It became clear to us that the material in Cochrane's letters reflected the fact that he had been working in one of these hereditary traditions.

Ann & Joe Wilson

Along with the letters from Cochrane, Joe had in his possession a collection of essays and letters which appeared in Pentagram in which Robert Cochrane and someone calling himself "Taliesin" took on the Gardnerians in a no-holds-barred debate regarding the authenticity of their practices and the wisdom of the publicity they sought in the press. For the first time, we learned that not everybody on the other side of the Atlantic thought that Gardnerian Craft was the one true right and only way either.

In the August 1965 issue of Pentagram, Cochrane describes Modern Witchcraft, particularly the Gardnerian movement as "civilized sophisticates running round behaving like simple peasants ... headed by a deity [described by one old fellow] 'who is the sweetest woman, everyone loves her.'" Taliesin was considerably less tactful. "...sweetness and light," was the way he described "Gardnerianism" in the March, 1965 issue, "coupled with good clean fun, all under the auspices of a Universal Auntie."

Many Hereditary Witches denounced the fact that a Gardnerian could learn all there was to learn in a few short months, go through three theatrical performances and be qualified to run a coven. The quest for knowledge, they maintained, which marked a true "Witch" was distinctly lacking. They preferred to remain in, as Taliesin put it, "their little house that GBG built".

Where Gerald Gardner obtained his tradition still remains a matter of controversy. However, at the time, what interested us was the realization that there existed paths to becoming a Witch that didn't involve either submitting to local Gardnerian autocracy or taking one's chances amid spurious and sometimes downright fraudulent groups with dysfunctional lifestyles. "1734" was one such path.

The allure of 1734 was undeniable, particularly for Americans who have a fondness for rebelling against established authority. Since the founding of the Long Island hierarchy in the late 1960's, the Gardnerians had established themselves as the One True Craft. By the mid 1970's when we came on the scene, the only way one could be a "real" Witch was to have an initiation from that hierarchy. And since that hierarchy was only initiating people that fit their criteria and were willing to obey their rules, a lot of people, particularly the black-sheep type, were left out in the cold.

There were several ways around this situation. One way, as mentioned above, was to get a hold of a couple of books, invent a grandmother, and set oneself up as a hereditary Witch. This was fairly easy to do. By the mid-1970s, nearly all of the Gardnerian Book of Shadows had been published in one form or another. A version out of England had seen print under the name of Rex Nemorensis in a publication called Earth Religion News, edited by the late Herman Slater. Still another version published by Llewellyn Books appeared under the title, 'Lady Sheba's Book of Shadows'.

Back in England, a colorful character who called himself King of the Witches, Alex Saunders, put together his own version of the Craft – based on Gardner's version but with more Ceremonial Magic thrown in – called the Alexandrian Tradition. Saunders was the subject of several books that described his rituals and lore in enough detail that it wasn't hard to filter out the lurid bits (or not, as one chose) and put together a reasonable facsimile of an Alexandrian coven. Some covens, like the Cincinnati coven that Fred and Martha Adler were part of, had both Alexandrian and Gardnerian lineages and combined the two traditions. And, of course, there were people who could trace their lineage back to old Alex himself, like Stuart and Janet Farrar, who were running their own groups.

Consequently, tradition after tradition sprang up all over the country like mushrooms. Some were little more than Gardnerian clones. Others, however, took the basic Gardnerian circle structure, laws, rituals, etc. and added further material gleaned from research, psychic experiences and myths and folklore from a variety of cultures, particularly Egyptian, Greco-Roman and Celtic.

All of these traditions had their sincere adherents and it wasn't long before they began to be passed down from High Priest/ess to High Priest/ess for several "generations." As long as nobody bothered to look too deeply into the antecedents of either the material or the teachers, everything went well. However, there were always the few who dared to question the veracity and authenticity of that which they had been taught. Almost without fail, what they found at the core was some version of the Gardnerian Book of Shadows.

Except for 1734, that is. Since the 1734 Corpus had never been published by any publishing house, the only way to get a hold of it was to study with someone who, at one time, had contact with Joe Wilson. However, since the material was seldom marked with the sources from which it came, the people who inherited it from their initiators often felt free to add things they liked, subtract things they didn't like, annotate the letters with interesting but spurious references from other sources, supply various explanations and commentary on what Cochrane *really* meant in such-and-such a passage, and otherwise try to 'beef up' the material with other things that might have been interesting and worthy but didn't belong in the Corpus.

This made it easy for the second or third generation recipients, out of ignorance or ego, to promulgate the idea of a secret tradition passed down from group to group by the chosen few. That meant if you were somehow privileged to get a hold of the Corpus, you were one of those chosen few. It didn't matter that that Gardnerian establishment didn't recognize you or that your teacher started with nothing but a bogus grandmother and a copy of Lady Sheba. You were now 1734 - whatever that meant.

The sad truth was that, in practice at least, it meant very little. The 1734 Corpus, as inspiring and informative as it was, contained very little in the way of workable rituals. You couldn't pick it up and follow a script the way you could with the Gardnerian rituals. Cochrane's tradition, being extremely mystical and visionary, depended on a great deal of experience in trance work and out-of-body journeying of the kind one learns by training with a shaman. And, things being what they were at that time, extremely few of the people who obtained this information had such training.

Therefore, the 1734 material proved virtually useless for any kind of practical application for the vast majority of the people who got a hold of it. As Joe himself commented, "many of them, once they got the written material, chose to ignore the purpose and context for which it was developed, and instead ran off with it, hoarding it like some prized secret, deluding themselves by thinking that because they had these writings they were now authentic Witches". They refused to stay around and to learn the oral tradition which this was meant to supplement, or to understand the training that goes along with it." *(Flags Flax and Fodder website, Joe Wilson, 1999)*

Consequently, most people tucked the material into their Book of Shadows and did very little with it, save for using a few of the invocations, phrases, bits of lore and buzz-words that it contained. An excellent example of this was the famous and distinctive benediction "FFF" that Cochrane used in the closing of his letters to Joe. This benediction was short for Flags (water), Flax (air) and Fodder (earth), and constituted a wish for all the good things in life. Those people who were 1734 would often use this benediction rather than the Gardnerian "Blessed Be" as a kind of recognition code, since only those folks who had the Corpus would know what it meant.

In the course of putting together their own version of 1734, Joe and Mara added something to the mixture that finally rendered the whole system workable. Joe spent some years studying with a local clinical psychologist who had a background in both hypnotism and magic. This proved to be a powerful combination. Joe began using hypnotic techniques in his rituals, particularly trance state induction and post-hypnotic suggestion.

This, perhaps more than any one thing, proved to be the key that opened the gates of the tradition. An induction of an altered state of consciousness, or trance, is vital to any kind of shamanic work. But research into such trance states usually reveals the use of hallucinogenic substances or other techniques that involve threats to physical health and well-being. And while these techniques are highly effective, they simply are not suitable for a person practicing magic in a highly technological and demanding culture. There had to be a way to induce a trance deep enough to allow meaningful and intense psychic work and allow the person in question to drive home safely after the ritual was over.

Hypnosis fit the bill nicely. Using self-hypnosis techniques, coven members could easily train themselves to enter a deep trance easily and safely then bring themselves out of it quickly, free from drowsiness and other unwanted side effects. Then, by use of appropriate post hypnotic suggestions, dreams and other visionary experiences could be remembered clearly and the trance state entered into again the next time with far more ease.

At last, we felt ourselves on our proper path.

A third and final thing we learned from the Gardnerians was the importance of lineage. As much as we poked fun at the 'pedigreed Gardnerians,' we gradually realized that initiatory lineage carried with it an importance that went beyond who was 'legitimate' and who wasn't. A valid initiation will psychically mark the initiate as a member of a particular tradition and it doesn't much matter if anybody else in that tradition approves of it or even knows about it.

It seems that the otherworld guardians of a tradition know their own and call to them. The people who are drawn to that tradition are answering that call. For whatever reason, we didn't belong with the Gardnerians. The guardians of that tradition knew it and wisely denied us entry – on more than one occasion. In handing us over to Bill and Helen for initiation rather than initiating us himself, Ed had in some deep and fundamental way allied us with the scattered and obscure lineage of 1734 rather than the more organized and orthodox Gardnerian one. This was our true path and the guardians knew it.

So does that mean anybody who inherits a Book of Shadows with the 1734 material in it is automatically a member of the tradition? Not necessarily. Since there was no standardized 1734 initiation, any and all ritual forms could be used to bring people into the tradition. There was no hierarchy, so there was no way of verifying that an initiator was 'authorized' to bring anyone else into the tradition. And since the material was scattered thither and yon, just inheriting the Corpus didn't mean that you actually inherited the tradition that went with it. There is far more to *any* tradition than a stack of papers with writing on them.

This isn't to say that everybody who thought they were initiated into the 1734 tradition isn't real or genuine. Of the 1734 people that we have met and worked with over the years, some have inherited the tradition and done nothing with it. A few have used it as a personal power trip or as a weapon to wield against anyone who disagreed with them. But the vast majority have answered the call of the guardians with sincerity and have used the material to further their own spiritual growth and that of their students to the best of their ability. And that's really all the guardians can - and do - ask of any of us.

Our work in an actual 1734 coven ended abruptly in January of 1976 when the marriage between Joe and Mara broke up, shattering their group into smithereens. There was nothing for us to do then but to continue with our own group and carry on the work ourselves. Armed with a copy of the 1734 Corpus, Joe's hypnotic techniques and Graves' *The White Goddess*, we began our own reconstruction of Cochrane's mysterious hereditary tradition and changed the name of our group.

We called it the Roebuck.

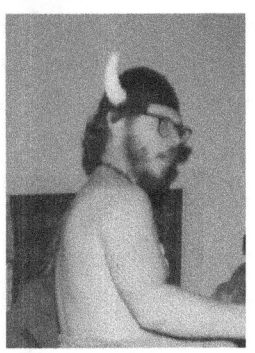

Joe Wilson

The Founding of the Roebuck

By December of 1976 when we officially founded the Roebuck, we had been in the Craft for two years. During that time, we had worked on and off with no less than five different groups, often attending two circles a week and more than that on Sabbats. We had run training groups, coordinated open festivals, participated in workshops and done extensive networking with groups outside the Southern California area. With this intense introduction into the neo-Pagan community, it wasn't long before we noticed many things that we didn't like.

Sexual exploitation was the biggest problem. In some groups, prospective members were expected to have sex with the other members of that group in order to join and were branded "not really Pagan" if they didn't want to. This condemnation was particularly virulent if the prospective members were legally married and wanted to remain faithful to their spouses. Candidates were most often expected to submit to sexual practices as a part of their Initiation rituals - usually during the course of the Great Rite part of the Third Degree, but we witnessed abuses during First Degree initiations as well.

Substance abuse was another issue. Some groups actually employed illegal substances in their rituals and were always one step ahead of the cops. But, even when the substances were not actually illegal, sometimes the leaders and other members were alcoholics or prescription drug abusers and had a tendency to conduct rituals while intoxicated. New members were subjected to pressure to partake in those substances or put up with the chaos resulting from their use and suffered emotional abuse if they refused.

Both of the above problems were serious enough to ruin the lives, health and finances of the members of a group and thankfully many of the worst of these practices have since been discredited and discontinued. Still, joining a group in those early days was still fraught with problems that ranged from annoying to downright painful and all served to prevent any serious spiritual or magical development from being accomplished. Nearly all of them stemmed from the fact that there was almost no accountability among the leaders of the various groups for their behaviors.

Consequently, many succumbed to the temptation to cloak their personal problems and dysfunctional lifestyles in the aura of magical tradition and foist them off on their unsuspecting students. Most of these problems were no worse than one would find in a similar group of highly creative and unorthodox people. However, passing such things off as Magic served to give them credibility they didn't deserve and questioning them took on the taint of sacrilege and blasphemy. Such students were often told that by disapproving of the group leader's behavior, he or she was challenging the will of the Goddess herself. This led to a great deal of disillusionment and cynicism among thoughtful people who would have been an asset to the Craft as a whole.

With a few exceptions, however, the vast majority of the problems that occurred in these early groups were the result of insecurity or lack of training on the part of the people running them. In many groups, members did nothing but sit in circle, often for years, while the High Priest and/or High Priestess did all the work. Then, they were given a ceremony and told to go out and start their own group. Sometimes, they had little or no training at all in the parent group, save for having undergone an intensive week-end series of rituals designed to confer nothing but rank within the tradition. With a wave of the wand, these people were all of a sudden High Priests or High Priestesses with absolutely no idea of what to do.

Such people, faced with the awesome responsibility and challenge of running a magical group, tended to hide their ignorance and lack of experience behind demands for unquestioning obedience from their own members that they had not earned through demonstrated ability. Embarrassing questions about the tradition or the history thereof that the new leader found he or she didn't know would be answered with either elaborate secrecy or fabrications and anyone who challenged the veracity of the answers was summarily chastised or banished.

This practice resulted in some very bizarre practices turning up in people's Books of Shadows that nobody had any idea where they came from or what they were for. But for generations of initiates, these practices were faithfully passed along without anybody taking the initiative to find out just what they were supposed to accomplish. Not only were these practices not questioned, but any attempt to alter them to make them more practical was looked upon as some kind of sacrilege.

We were told a story once called the Sacred Ritual Dance Step. It seems that a fellow was taking initiation in a group and noticed that the High Priestess did a strange little hop as she approached the altar during the course of the ritual. Afterwards, he asked her what she was doing and why. His High Priestess replied that it was a Sacred Ritual Dance Step; her High Priestess had done it when she had been initiated and he wasn't of a high enough degree to know the reason why it was performed.

Some time later, he happened to meet the lady who had initiated his High Priestess. He asked her if he could finally learn about the Sacred Ritual Dance Step. The old lady laughed and said that it had never been a secret. What had happened was that she had just sewn a new robe for the initiation and hadn't had time to hem it properly. During the ritual, she tripped over the unfinished hem and barely avoided falling on her face in the circle.

Some group leaders also did questionable things like elevate their current lovers/spouses into positions of authority that they hadn't earned and expected the other members of the group, even those who had been around for a long time, to defer to them. Those who refused to go along with this were either tossed out of the group or left on their own. There might even be retaliation against the dissidents, especially if certain dirty laundry regarding the relationship was revealed to outsiders.

In cases where married couples were leaders of a group, one partner might have an affair with a group member and incur the wrath of the other partner. The couple would then break up and group members would be fought over as though they were pieces of furniture. Members were expected to take sides, choosing one partner over the other and shunning those members who sided with the other partner. The group would then split into two groups with each group slinging accusations of all sorts of dreadful things on the other group with very little evidence. Sometimes this even led to group members participating in an array of protection rituals against the "psychic attack" presumably coming from the other group.

Some leaders, confusing their own personal agendas with a mandate from the Gods, would form groups that met certain personal and social needs. Some were little more than private clubs in which only certain socially acceptable people were admitted, usually people with money or prestigious jobs. Their members were subject to being drop-kicked out of the circle as soon as they developed embarrassing personal problems or became otherwise inconvenient or bothersome to have around.

At the other extreme were groups which served as halfway houses run by good-hearted but naive people who took in lost souls and quickly found themselves overrun with moochers, drug and alcohol abusers and other dysfunctional people. Their troubled members often would move into the leaders' home, run up phone bills, eat the leaders out of house and home, break or steal personal belongings, then vanish without a trace, leaving the leaders with debts and damage.

Still others ended up being little more than Pagan prayer circles that attracted needy people who wanted spells and charms to solve personal problems. These groups would have a monthly "laundry list" of things that people wanted, usually spells for money, love or jobs. These groups tended to turn self-serving and mercenary very quickly. We were in a circle once in which we were expected to "charge" a sweepstakes ticket that could have won the group leaders a lot of money. What the participants themselves might expect to receive in exchange for their energy in this endeavor was never made clear. Needless to say, the sweepstakes ticket didn't win.

The Gardnerians had attempted to mitigate some of this chaos by both standardizing their tradition and imposing a hierarchical structure that insured some measure of accountability on the part of each coven. Like any franchise, you knew exactly what you were getting when you took initiation into a Gardnerian coven. The rituals were exactly the same, the coven structure was the same, and the rules were the same. And, if you suffered abuse at the hands of a particular High Priestess, you might be able to bring your complaint to her initiator and get some kind of redress.

However, this process could also backfire. Apart from publicly censoring the wayward High Priestess, there actually was little that her initiator could do in response to a complaint. A Third Degree couldn't be rescinded. The High Priestess in question was still a High Priestess. She could effectively thumb her nose at the Gardnerian hierarchy and continue to run a coven with whatever members might choose to remain with her. A disgruntled member had little recourse but to leave her coven and join another.

There was also the possibility that the High Priestess in question was herself the victim of personal and political abuse by her higher-ups. In many hierarchies, people who rise up in the pecking order often get there by being friends of their higher-ups rather than by earning their rank by hard work and talent. The Gardnerians were notorious for establishing covens by giving newcomers the three degrees over the course of a weekend and then setting them up as High Priests and Priestesses of their own covens who would owe personal loyalty to the people who elevated them. Any covener with a grievance would quickly discover that going to his High Priestess' superior would give him short shrift and might be just as bad if not worse than the High Priestess who abused him.

One of the advantages of not being part of the Gardnerian hierarchical structure was that it allowed us to insist on our autonomy and acknowledge no authority but our own. We could do whatever we wanted to with our own group - initiate whom we wished and establish whatever rules and regulations we desired. However, having been on the wrong end of some of the prevalent practices and witnessing the unhappiness and confusion caused by others, we found ourselves unable in good conscience to repeat any of the above scenarios in the Roebuck.

This was not for self-righteous, "moral" reasons. The reasons were entirely pragmatic. We had been exposed to enough groups to notice that the ones that continued certain practices simply didn't stay together very long. Nor did they seem to do much in the way of constructive magical rituals while they were together, producing instead little more than a series of personal dramas and energy draining emotional scenes of soap opera proportions. The abusive and exploitative, not to mention the downright illegal, practices were bad enough. But even those practices that were relatively benign and even altruistic proved to be counter-productive if the purpose of the group was to stay together, and perform constructive rituals in order to develop a magical tradition over time.

We found ourselves in the position of having to find a workable compromise between the very efficient but autocratic discipline of the Gardnerians and the unworkable and unproductive free-for-all of the eclectic groups we had encountered. We wanted to make the group work efficiently with a minimum of personal issues but not become heartless tyrants in the process. So, after much soul searching and brainstorming, we established the following ground rules for the emerging Roebuck. They remain unchanged to this day:

1. Circles were to be conducted with everyone at least partially clothed. We had discovered through experience that nudity was not only not required to do magic, often it was a distraction and a nuisance if you were cold or otherwise uncomfortable. Magic comes from what you are, not from what you wear or don't wear and we wished to avoid the sometimes sexually abusive situations that occur when people are required to be "skyclad". We also worked either out of doors or in drafty garage temples, so warm cloaks or robes became a garment that many people would choose out of necessity.

2. No ritual sex was to be practiced except in private between consenting adults. Despite all the rubbish about "Laws of Carnal Access" that were featured in our AmTrad Book of Shadows, Dave and I made the decision that we would both refrain from any sexual relationships with coven members under any circumstances. More covens shatter over the infidelity of one of the partners running it than for any other reason. If our purpose was to run a coven and develop a tradition rather than pursue our own self-gratification, self-discipline was the only practical answer. It had nothing to do with morality or prudery. It was just good sense.

3. Students would be chosen on the basis of sincerity and desire to learn, not on the basis of whether or not they had a pleasing personality, said all the right things in social situations, subscribed to a particular political viewpoint, or had a prestigious profession. In short, we trusted our guardian deities to choose who walked through our doors and we accepted anyone provided they were sincere and were willing to do the work we asked them to do. Their "suitability" and "worthiness" was to be something that they would demonstrate

over time, not some arbitrary whim on our part.

4. All students had to undergo an extensive period of training before they could be initiated. Traditionally, this training period was to last at least a year and a day, often longer. This training became more codified and elaborate as time went on. And, while the year-and-a-day rule was by no means arbitrary, we insisted that all of our prospective members, no matter how much magical experience they had beforehand, be trained in our methods and demonstrate skills that we required before they could formally join us.

5. All students were expected to be self reliant - financially and emotionally as well as magically. All personal rituals or spells such as those to get jobs, money, lovers, mates or other personal goals were to be done by the individuals themselves, not by the group. Healings were to be done only when the individual consented, or, ideally, showed up to the ritual in person. The purpose of the circle was to perform the magic needed to benefit the group and we didn't want people to turn up just to get the group to do their personal magic for them.

6. Finally, and most importantly, we decided to share our authority and responsibility with our initiates. Roebuck initiates would be trained specifically to run circles on their own and would be expected to come up with full moon, dark moon or festival rituals on a regular basis. Whoever had the responsibility for running a particular ritual, even if it was a student, had the authority to give everyone else instructions and tell everyone what to do during that ritual. That way, if they ever decided to hive off, they would know how to run a circle and a group.

So, from the very beginning, we decided that the Roebuck was going to be a mystery tradition dedicated to the pursuit of knowledge and magical and spiritual development, not a swingers club, kaffee-klatsch, or therapy group. The concept seemed so simple and so logical. Little did we suspect that we would one day catch hell for this.

The Forge of Old Tubal

Imagine for a moment that you want to put together a puzzle. You have a lot of strange-looking pieces scattered about. You have a vague idea of what the puzzle is supposed to look like, but there is no box with a picture of the finished puzzle to use as a guide. How do you begin putting it together?

That was precisely our dilemma in the winter of 1976 when we began the reconstruction of the "1734" tradition. What were we going to do in circle if not have sex, get drunk, do love and money spells or heal Aunt Edna's bunions? And how would we set up our circle, if not with the Gardnerian standard ritual? The circle casting rituals that we had learned up to that point were not only long, but were decidedly ponderous and took a lot of time and effort to perform.

We decided that there had to be a better way. So when we sat down with the rituals that we had from the Gardnerian and American Trads, starting from the Circle Casting, and dissected them. Using a variety of references, consultations with people who had worked the various traditions and a large dollop of common sense, we managed to identify and, in most cases, eliminate ritual practices that were unnecessary for the ritual form we were trying to reconstruct.

The first things to go were the obvious bits from Ceremonial Magic. These were particularly easy to identify from the reference books at our disposal. An example of this was the consecration of the salt and water, triple casting of the circle, warding with the elements and so forth. We had learned from our reading that these ritual elements were left over from the days when magic circles were cast preparatory for the summoning of demons. In such a working, it would obviously be imperative to use enough ritual in order to keep powerful negative forces out of the working area.

However, we were using the circle for an entirely different purpose – to contact powerful positive forces and keep them inside the ritual working area. In the tradition we were attempting to reconstruct, the circle was a sacred place where Gods and mortals could meet and commune, not a holding cell for antisocial spirits who had to be coerced into doing anything useful. Consequently, we found the vast majority of the ritual practices from ceremonial magic were superfluous, so we simply eliminated them. This cut down our circle casting time considerably and nobody was the worse for it.

The second thing to go was the scripted ritual. We originally learned how to "ad lib" our quarter invocations from Ed, and from that, we got to the point where we ad-libbed everything. Eventually, even the memorized bits, minuscule as they were, went away as well. For example, the circle casting ritual that we now recommend for students originally came from Joe Wilson, and it is given to students only as a model. As students become more comfortable at ad-libbing, they nearly always come up with their own words.

Once the circle was cast, then what? What could be done to develop the tradition between the circle being cast and broken? The purpose of a mystery tradition, after all, was to establish a relationship with Deity (or deities, depending upon your point of view) and enlist the aid of those deities in the process of spiritual and magical development. The way to do that would logically be: a) get in touch with the deity and establish a method of communication with him or her and b) establish enough of an altered state of awareness in which this was accomplished without undue risk.

At the time, few American Craft traditions did anything like this. Some did scrying exercises, using crystal balls or other media. A very few did 'aspecting' or what is known in the New Age community as channeling. In this practice, a Priest or Priestess became possessed by a god or Goddess much in the way a trance medium becomes possessed by the spirit of a departed person. These are time honored methods, but when we saw them performed it was by mostly untrained people in a rather haphazard fashion with no really reliable way of cross checking as to what was genuine and what was playacting. Again, we figured there had to be a better way. So, we abandoned our Craft training entirely and drew upon another source entirely.

In October of 1974, we met Carroll "Poke" Runyon and in 1975 we joined his magical lodge in Pasadena, called the Order of the Temple of Astarte. Originally carrying an OTO charter, the OTA had an important difference that set it apart from the usual Ceremonial Magical lodges such as the OTO or Golden Dawn. Dedicated to the Sumerian Goddess Astarte, the OTA was Pagan, rather than Judeo Christian and incorporated many of the philosophical tenets that distinguish a Pagan group from a strictly ceremonial one.

In choosing his magical methods, Poke made several key decisions. First, he used some of the same auto hypnotic techniques that Joe Wilson used to induce a safe and workable trance state in the participants in his rituals. Secondly, in the Goetia rituals he used, he invoked the original Sumerian Gods and Goddesses, particularly Baal and Astarte, and not the Judeo-Christian demonic forms that they later became.

It was from our work in the OTA that we learned how to have a god or Goddess manifest in the circle and enable people see them, hear them, talk to them and receive messages from them - either by means of scrying into a crystal or a black mirror, or through a person in a mediumistic trance. This was at its core little different from what we had seen in the various covens we visited, except for two major things.

The first was that the ritual was entered into with a definite purpose agreed upon beforehand by all parties involved. For example, the group might stipulate that their purpose was to contact a specific Goddess (say, Astarte) by utilizing a specific, standardized ritual (the dark mirror) and the medium is going to be a specific person (not necessarily the high Priest or Priestess) - and nobody else. Often, there were specific questions that people had for the deity regarding a particular topic, or those in attendance had personal questions that they sought answers to, from a deity with particular attributes.

Carroll "Poke" Runyon

The second thing proved to be more problematic. The ritual was performed as planned, then everyone assembled for a debriefing afterward. Did the operation work? If not, why didn't it? What went wrong? Did anyone else in the circle experience Astarte other than the chosen medium? Were the answers to the questions satisfactory? Did they make sense?

If this approach seems too structured and controlled, contrast it with a circle in which another ritual had been planned altogether. One woman suddenly drops unexpectedly to the floor, rolls her eyes back into her head, announces that she is a particular Goddess and proceeds to make pronouncements, give advice and make predictions, all unannounced, unasked for and totally unverifiable. The entire coven stands helpless until she decides she is finished. Then, she comes to, shaking and gasping and demands to be patted, pampered, coddled and generally paid attention to while the planned work of the evening goes out the window.

What is going on, here? Does this performance constitute a genuine oracle, or merely grandstanding on the part of the 'medium?' And even if the oracle was genuine, does it justify the interruption of someone else's ritual? And, perhaps more important, should the oracle's pronouncements and advice be taken to heart and followed as instructions from On High?

Spontaneous possessions, aspects and oracles do happen during the course of a circle. It even happened to me once in my very early days when I didn't know any better. The circle was not really a coven, but a haphazard collection of people who gathered for a full moon ritual. The High Priestess for the evening was a very inexperienced and emotionally troubled woman who was attempting to hold things together by virtue of an authority she didn't really have. A crusty old veteran - a man who had been in the craft more years than the woman had been alive and who had definite ideas on how things should be done - challenged her on some point. The two fell to arguing in the circle, putting the work of the evening on hold while they snapped back and forth regarding who was 'right' and who was 'wrong.'

Thoroughly uncomfortable with this state of affairs, and yet unable to do much about it, I found myself staring up at the moon overhead thinking what a terrible waste of a beautiful night all this brouhaha was. The next thing I remember was everyone staring at me as though I had just grown another head. I was told that for a brief moment, Someone or Something else stood in my body, looked out of my eyes, and spoke with my mouth saying something to the effect of 'how dare you argue in the sacred circle. Stop messing around and get on with it.'

The whole 'possession' (if such it was) lasted only a minute or two, then I was back with no discernable ill effects. Whether it was a Goddess, THE Goddess, or merely my own higher self, I have no idea. But it didn't seem to matter. It was something other than my inexperienced 22-year-old personality and the words, whatever they were, were taken to heart immediately. The two people in question immediately stopped arguing, actually apologized to each other (!) and the ritual proceeded to its conclusion.

Are such spontaneous 'possessions' genuine or not? It depends on the situation. Some are, some aren't. However, even if a genuine spontaneous possession does occur in a circle, it would seem to be an indication that something is going wrong in the ritual and otherworld intervention of some kind is necessary to sort it out.

This is not only risky magically and psychically, it is also hard on the medium who must channel a god-form with no warning and no preparation. And the emotional reactions to it from the other circle members distract them from any critical evaluation of the content of the message. Consequently, the task before us was to provide a means of a genuine, verifiable contact with the deities and leave enough latitude for the deities to speak as they would without the free-for-all which leads to grandstanding and other abuses.

Over the years, with additional training in hypnosis and psychotherapy, these techniques would become honed to a fine art. We have used black mirrors, incense smoke, shining blades, cauldrons filled with water and a variety of other scrying media to provide a manifestation that nearly everyone can perceive in one way or another. We also developed techniques by which any person can achieve some level of mediumistic ability and be able to bring anything from messages and images up to and including full assumption of godform possessions of some deity made manifest physically in the circle.

But who were the Gods to be invoked? The choice of these was pivotal since it would determine the eventual cultural mind set of the Roebuck. An Egyptian pantheon, say, would give an entirely different cultural underpinning from, say, a Greco-Roman one.

In the 1734 Corpus there was an odd three-page addendum, presumably from Norman outlining what appeared to be a circle setup. Each of the cardinal points were marked by a castle which had a ruler, a symbol and an elemental attribute as follows:

In the east, a castle surrounded by fire, ruled by Lucet.
In the south, a castle surrounded by trees, ruled by Carenos.
In the west, a castle beneath the depths of the sea, ruled by Nodens.
In the north, a castle built in the clouds, ruled by Tettans.

A little research soon revealed that Lucet was none other than Lugh Samildanach 'the many skilled' from Irish legend or Llew of the Long Hand from Welsh legend - both Apollonian solar warriors skilled in all forms of art and craft, particularly bardic poetry. There were also most likely Masonic associations with Lucifer in his role of Light Bringer, but we decided to abandon those in favor of concentrating on the Irish and Welsh form of the god. Since Lugh and Llew were almost identical, we decided to use them interchangeably.

Carenos, of course, was the Gaulish Cernunnos, the Stag-antlered god whose image graces the Gundustrup Cauldron. He is not only a Celtic fertility god, he is also Gwyn ap Nudd or Herne the Hunter, a god of animals, concerned with both breeding and hunting. While he is called in the south as Cernunnos when setting up the circle, his dark side is acknowledged during the festival of Hunters Moon in October when he leads the Wild Hunt to round up the souls of both animals and people who will not survive the cold winter ahead.

Nodens was a bit more obscure. He turned out to be a British sea god, specifically the god of the Great Deep, or Abyss. He had a temple at Lydney in Gloucestershire. People would invoke him for help with finding lost articles and hidden treasure, but there is also evidence that his temple was used to have oracular dreams that were interpreted by the Priests. He is also associated with Llawereint or "silver-handed," a term for the god Ludd, Nudd and the Irish Nuada, who also had a silver hand. He is mentioned in stories by Arthur Machen and H.P. Lovecraft.

Tettans was Teutates, or Toutoutes, another Gaulish god associated with thunderstorms. The Romans equated him with both Mars and Mercury, making him both a god of war and knowledge, much like the Norse Odin. He is also mentioned in a series of French comic books featuring characters from a small Gaulish village at the height of the Roman Empire. Throughout the dialog in the books, they swear "by Toutautes" as an educated Englishman of a later century would swear "by Jove." As far out as it seemed, that piece seemed to fit.

The emerging pattern was interesting to say the least. The most obvious feature was that the elemental associations were completely different from the ones used by both the Gardnerians and ceremonial magic. Air was in the north, balanced by earth in the south. Fire in the east balanced water in the west. Young warrior opposed old king, green man opposed wizened mage. Unorthodox as it was, it made magical, mythical and psychological sense. It formed a series of opposite archetypes that were arranged in the circle so that they balanced each other out.

This arrangement turned out to be similar to the system of Scottish Airts described by Doreen Valiente in her book *ABCs of Witchcraft* - the red spirits and grey, white spirits and black, fire opposing water, earth opposing air. We had inadvertently stumbled on a traditional Celtic pattern, rumored to have also been associated with ley lines, of elemental associations rather than the Golden Dawn inspired one used by the Gardnerians.

But the pattern was not yet complete. In the letters to Joe, Cochrane had hinted about the "queens of the wind Gods" or a system of quarter Goddesses that would complement the quarter Gods. Unfortunately, they were not named. Their identity was given to Joe to work out as an exercise, but at the time, Joe had never succeeded in working them out satisfactorily. We decided that in order to balance out the circle completely, there would have to be elemental Goddesses as well as Gods and that they would have to be invoked as well every time the circle was set up. From there, however, we were on our own.

With the help of Joe's ex-wife Mara, we began the search armed with two major assumptions. First, that the quarter Goddesses would not be "wives" or "consorts" to the quarter Gods. They would not even have to be necessarily from the same pantheon. They would be chosen as the "best fit" to a set of attributes irregardless of their mythological relationship to the Gods. For this, we decided to place the Goddesses at the cross-quarters, rather at the quarters, technically making it an eight-point circle rather than a four-point one. This would give each Goddess a festival and direction of her own, sharing nothing with the quarter god but a rather arbitrary elemental attribute.

The second thing we did, again a departure from ceremonial magic practice, was to have a Goddess associated with all the elements, including the traditionally "male" elements such as fire and air. Oddly enough, these vacancies proved to be the easiest ones to fill. The Irish had a fire Goddess in Bridget who traditionally presided over all the things that Lugh was famous for - bardic poetry, healing and smith craft. She was, in fact, so powerful that the Christians could not get rid of her. So they canonized her as Saint Bridget and kept her sacred fire still burning at Kildare for centuries. She was already associated with the Festival of Imbolc or Candlemas located at the wheel of the year at the north east point.

And then there was the Queen of Air and Darkness herself, the Irish battle Goddess Morrigan, flying over the battle fields in the form of a raven. There would be no more fitting Lady to preside over Samhain, the festival of the dead, when the herds of cattle and sheep were culled to make way for winter. As Morgan le Fey, she was also associated with sorcery and Samhain was a time when the veil between the worlds was the thinnest and divinations made to tell the fortune of the New Year.

South and west were more obscure and less obvious. A Goddess named Niamah, the sister of Tubal Cain and the inventor of the art of divination, had been suggested to us as a possible candidate for South. We found her similar to the Scottish Queen of Elfame and the Irish Niamh of the Golden Hair as well as the Arthurian Nimue. She was the lady who spirited the poet/mage away to the Otherworld, making him a slave of her love. She would preside not only over fertility of body but fertility of mind and spirit as well at the Festival of Beltaine.

The Lady of the West gave us the most trouble to find. Lammas, or Lugh's mass, was also the festival of Lugh's foster mother, Tailtiu, but we could find nothing on her that made any sense and she just did not feel right. We tried Maeve or Queen Mab, the lady of dreams and visions as described by Shakespeare, but she didn't work out either. It wasn't until we switched to the Welsh pantheon and considered the fact that Llew was also a bard. The Mother of Bards was Cerridwen. At that point, we knew we had hit it right. Cerridwen not only is the lady of the cauldron, the universal symbol of water, but was also associated with the Grail Queen. The grail, when stripped of its specious Christian symbolism, becomes the vessel of blood, the womb of the Great Mother, from which all partake of life. Since seawater is chemically almost identical to blood, this would also fit.

The circle was complete.

At this point, we departed from what was turning out to be a very Pan-Celtic circle pantheon and decided to keep the center god and Goddess form that we had been given in the Cochrane material. In the letters, Cochrane describes himself and his group as being the "people of Goda and the Clan of Tubal Cain." In order to ally ourselves with this tradition, we kept Goda as our Mother Goddess and Tubal Cain as our Father God and invoked them in the center at the casting of every circle. It would turn out later to be a wise decision.

The only reference we had to Goda was from the *White Goddess* where she is described as a particularly British form of the Lady who comes "neither clothed nor naked etc." hence her association with Lady Godiva of British folk tradition who, when challenged by her husband that if she appeared naked in the town square, he would rescind an onerous tax, rode through the streets of Coventry draped in her long hair. This poetic riddle is also found in a variety of folk songs which feature seemingly impossible tasks, the performance of which win access to the secrets of the Otherworld. This motif is very similar to a passage in the Mabinogian where Llew is describing to Blodewedd that he can only be killed "neither on land nor on water, etc." She asks him to solve the riddle and demonstrate the one and only position, then has her lover kill him with an arrow.

It was very obvious from the first that Goda was a title rather than a name (very probably from the Norse, Godia meaning Goddess or Priestess). The fact that She is invoked by Her title, rather than Her name, further identified Her with "1734," being both Love and Death, Black and White, the Rose from the Grave, the Creatrix and Destroyer. Her secret name, by which she can be called, is given to each seeker personally and is not to be revealed to anyone.

Tubal Cain was an enigma for a long time. In the *White Goddess*, he is described as a Semitic personage, the grandson of Cain, of Cain and Abel fame. However, Masonic lore has him as a semi-divine blacksmith who forges the things of this world, both things of usefulness as well as weapons of war, swords as well as plowshares. Several interesting poems written by British poets around the time of the First World War – including Kipling - describe Tubal Cain in this way.

The Coal Black Smith as the lover of the White Goddess is another figure which is featured in folk tales and folk songs. Certain medieval Sufic sects, especially in the British Isles, smeared their faces with coal soot and the Blacksmith as Magician as well as artificer is a particularly Celtic symbol. And, as Vulcan was lame in Roman myth, the Cochrane letters invokes the "twisted horned god." But why use Tubal Cain rather than Wayland or Goibniu or any other Celtic Blacksmith?

A scholar of no less renown than Isaac Asimov, in his commentary on the Bible, postulates that Tubal Cain, although mentioned in Genesis, is not Semitic at all. Tubal is an area in the Caucasus Mountains near the Black Sea. Cain means blacksmith or a worker in metal. So, Tubal Cain literally means the blacksmith of Tubal from an area where the Celts are said to originally come from before they migrated across Europe. If this is indeed the case, then the Old Man is literally great, great, great ... grandpappy, possibly the forger of the Celtic race.

And then, there is the Black Goddess, "1734" herself. This took a bit of unraveling. In the letters to Joe, Cochrane states: "Likewise the order of 1734 is not a date of an event, but a grouping of numerals that mean something to a 'Witch.' One that becomes Seven states of Wisdom - the Goddess of the Cauldron. Three that are the Queens of the elements ... Four that are the queens of the Wind Gods. The Jewish orthodoxy believe that whomever knows the Holy and Unspeakable Name of God has absolute power over the world of form. Very briefly, the Name of God spoken as Tetragrammaton ("I am that I am"), breaks down in Hebrew to the letters IHVH, or the Adom Kadomon (The Heavenly Man). Adom Kadomon is a composite of all archangels - in other words, a poetic statement of the names of the Elements. So what the Jew and the Witch believe alike, is that the man who discovers the secret of the Elements controls the physical world. 1734 is the Witch way of saying IHVH."

The solution to the puzzle turned out to be really quite simple. All we had to do was open our old yellow Faber edition of *The White Goddess* by Robert Graves to page 295. On that page is a table of correspondences between numbers and the letters of the old Druidic tree alphabet. It's all there. 3 - the elemental mothers. That's I. 4 - the queens of the wind Gods. That's O. Now, we have 1 and 7. That's A and P, right?

Unfortunately, no. Logic fails you at this point and you must rely on intuition. If you take 1 and 7 not as two numbers but as one, 17, the "one that becomes seven," then you are on the right track. But there is no correspondence for 17. The list ends at 16 - except for H, the letter with no number that was forbidden to utter. There is your seventeenth letter. Combine the three and you come up with H-I-O. Not profound, is it? It was certainly no name that we had ever heard of before. But we tried it anyway. We cast the circle with a woman serving as oracle. Then, we began to chant HIO like a mantra and waited to see what came through.

What came through was a shock.

"1734" turned out to be Hecate, Black Isis, Sophia, Kali and Erishkegal - every Dark Goddess that we had ever read about all rolled into one. This was definitely not the Lady that we originally encountered the books by Gardner, Crowther or Sheba - the "sweetest woman" who speaks in the Gardnerian Charge of the Goddess who has every act of love and pleasure as Her rituals. This Lady is the bringer of death and decay and all anguish and disillusion are Her rites. Why? Because that is how we learn life's lessons and forge our own destinies. No fun, frolic and fertility rituals here, folks. It's nose to the grindstone time. Reap only what you've sown. There is no free lunch. What goes around, comes around. No wonder Her name is kept secret. Too many people would curse it if they knew.

"In Her love," Cochrane wrote to Joe, "There is death - and she rends Her poets/lovers apart before finally making them all wise. ... Be careful throughout your life of Her traps - They will make you wise, but you will sing sweetly and sadly afterwards. She is Fate, the Creatoress and the Destroyer. You will understand why She destroys, but the destruction will bring its own sorrow. As the Goddess of Love, She humbles us all at some time - and that sorrow is perhaps Her greatest gift to the moonstruck poet."

The Black Goddess serves as the Guardian of the Portal to the world of manifestation. She is, if you wish, a personification of what has often been called Natural Law or the Laws of Nature - unbreakable and implacable rules and regulations which govern the material universe, particularly the law of Cause and Effect (called "Fate" in the west and "Karma" in the east.) This law states that any behavior, including the behavior of avoidance of action, produces a result or a consequence. This is not necessarily a linear process. Like a cue ball smashing into a rack of billiard balls, sending them in all directions, an action can produce a myriad of consequences which, in turn, serve as actions causing other consequences in an exponential fashion.

"In fate," Cochrane wrote, "and the overcoming of fate is the true Graal, for from this inspiration comes, and death is defeated ... Magic and religion are aids to overcome Fate, and Fate is a cradle that rocks the infant spirit."

This was why the Goddess is half white and half black.

Cochrane described the faith as having three mysteries, men's mysteries, women's mysteries and Priest/magician mysteries. By invoking what we believed was the secret name of the Goddess, we had stumbled onto the Priest/magician mysteries. This branch of the mysteries promotes the personal magical and spiritual growth of the individual, regardless of gender. It is geared for those men and women who wish to transcend the herd mentality, and the gender roles that go with it, and develop as individual souls.

This constituted the main difference between a fertility tradition and a mystery tradition. In a fertility tradition, gender roles, and the divinities that embody them (the source of the 'maiden,' 'mother,' 'crone' archetypes) are emphasized, since the function of men and women differ with respect to engendering offspring. However, in a mystery tradition, the devotion to the creative muse (the White Goddess) and the working out of karma (the Black Goddess) are essentially the same for both sexes. Age, marital status, or whether one has ever had children becomes immaterial.

The pieces were at last falling into place and the pattern began to emerge. However, one piece, and one alone, eluded us. There were two keys, or so said the Cochrane letters, that one needed to find in order to practice the tradition. One had to figure out the Goddess's secret name, hidden in the numbers "1734" and one had to figure out how to approach the altar, a ritual that was described very obliquely with lots of metaphor and little else. We had succeeded in discovering the Goddess's secret name and invoking Her aid. Now, we had to figure out how to Approach the Altar.

Robert Cochrane, in one of his letters, commented that the altar is "raised to every aspect you can think upon" but there is only one way to approach it, that is "with your back to it, and head turned right or left to regard the cross of the Elements and Tripod..." First, you "offer your devotions and prayers by bowing three times to the altar with arms crossed upon your chest and then turn about the altar ... the number of the Deity you are invoking or praying to."

We spent several months working out a ritual that that would meet the specifications described in the letters. Unfortunately, the instructions were vague (probably deliberately so). We figured out that one was supposed to spiral around some kind of central structure, gaze over one's shoulder at a focus point, and things were supposed to appear. But the logistics of how this was supposed to work remained a mystery.

Finally, after much pondering, we constructed an elaborate spiral dance affair in which one was supposed to spin around while circumambulating an illuminated central point. One Full Moon, we got everyone together and tried this ritual. It was far more difficult to do than we had thought. People were getting dizzy and dropping out. Our living room wasn't quite large enough and people were bumping into things. And all we got was a message strong enough to be picked up by everyone. We were close, but we still hadn't hit upon the secret. "Close," as someone said, "but no cigar".

About this time, it was becoming increasingly clear that we had just about reached the end of our resources. No book could guide us any farther and our intuition was circling in a dead end. We were stuck. We needed help from the Otherworld. But what kind of help did we need? And how should we go about asking for it?

The Journey Across the Pond

At first, we dismissed the idea of going to England. Both Joe and Mara had gone to England at two different times to try to find some of the people who had worked with Cochrane. They had some success but not very much. The only connection to the old group that either of them knew of was a man named Norman who had also corresponded with Cochrane.

Joe had contacted Norman in 1971 on his trip to England. Norman told Joe that Cochrane had ritually committed suicide in a circle before his entire coven after swearing them to secrecy and that he was the last remaining member of the group. He produced a stone that was supposed to have come from the Rollrights and conferred the right to pass on the 1734 tradition. This stone he solemnly bestowed upon Joe, claming that Joe was now the head of the tradition.

Mara also visited Norman on her trip to England in 1977. However, she came away with even less additional information about Cochrane's work. Norman, who lived in a small cottage with his mother, appeared to be more interested in taking photographs of her than telling her anything.

Mara ended the visit wondering if the information Norman gave to Joe was real or just a snow job designed to fool a gullible American.

When it came time for us to consider making the same journey, we were reluctant to be led down the garden path, like Joe and Mara had been. We needed to find someone who would tell us the truth about Cochrane and his group, but we knew of no other contact than Norman. We could think of only one alternative – ask the Old Ones to help us.

That turned out to be easier said than done. The only object we could use as a physical link was the stone that Norman had given Joe - the stone that was supposed to come from the Rollrights. Joe had given the stone to us after he founded his group, Temple of the Elder Gods, with his new wife Joey, who was more interested in Native American shamanism than "1734." We weren't even sure if the stone was really from the Rollrights, or if it actually was from someone's back garden. But, having no other choice, we decided to assume the stone was genuine and give it a try anyway.

Using the stone in the center of the circle, we invoked the Old Ones of the sacred places and stated our honest intentions to try to learn enough to revive the Old Ways. We asked them to guide us to the people who could (and would) help us, it didn't matter who or where they were. Then, we passed around a basket and everyone put in a coin to be tossed into the Chalice Well at Glastonbury to show our good faith. The coins were to be tied up in a silk pouch and carried with us on the plane.

During the course of the five week trip, we met a lady that had once been Norman's student. Norman, it seemed, was not a Witch but was more of a gypsy and had the reputation for being a trickster and a con artist. When we told her the story of the stone from the Rollrights, she laughed. She had been with Norman the night they scaled the fence around a group of stones called the Whispering Knights and grabbed a piece of the capstone, which had fallen. The stone that Norman had given Joe was a piece of this capstone. The rest of the stone they pilfered, did indeed reside in somebody's back garden.

However, Norman hadn't actually been a member of Cochrane's group, much less empowered to pass on his tradition. That, at any rate, was a complete fabrication. We had been right to be skeptical. The problem, then, was to find someone who actually worked with Cochrane and would be willing to talk to us. We met a number of people who knew Cochrane including a Gardnerian coven in London who had given him a

First Degree initiation. But none of them could tell us anything about his secret tradition.

We hadn't originally thought of writing to William G. "Bill" Gray, the author of many works on Ceremonial Magic and the Cabala. However, Bill had written one book, called The Rollright Ritual (now preprinted by Llewellyn as *By Elder Tree and Standing Stone*) which outlined some experimental work that he and several unnamed associates had done at the Rollrights. The ceremony described in The Rollright Ritual seemed to be more Craft-like than Ceremonial Magic, and it intrigued us. So, we wrote to Bill concerning the Rollright Ritual. His reply was very prompt, friendly and encouraging. He invited us to visit him at his home in Cheltenham. With this invitation in hand, we took off for London.

William Gray

As fate would have it, Bill Gray proved to be the contact with Cochrane's old group that we had so fervently asked for. We had no idea that Bill had anything to do with Cochrane. All of his previous books had been extremely critical of "Witchcraft," and especially Gardner's version. But we inquired about the background behind The Rollright Ritual anyway, saying that it was very close to what Cochrane wrote about in his letters. We told Bill about Joe Wilson's ad in Pentagram magazine, which Cochrane answered. We also produced copies of the letters. The Old Ones stepped in at this point.

Bill told us that he had worked with Cochrane for some years, attending his rituals and carrying on an extensive correspondence with him on a variety of topics. He even allowed us to make copies of this correspondence (part of which appears in the chapter entitled "Paganistic Principles" in his book *Western Inner Workings*, the first volume of his Sangreal series). He gave us Cochrane's cord and, perhaps the most valuable of all, wrote us a letter of introduction to Evan John Jones, the man who had been the Man in Black for Cochrane's old group. John now lived quietly in Brighton with his wife and three children and didn't have much to do with the Craft anymore. But Bill sent the letter off anyway. We phoned John a couple of days later and he agreed to see us.

That was the first of several visits to Brighton that we were to make over the course of many years. John took us up to the old meeting site that Cochrane had used. On the old oak that stood at the Northern Quarter, he found a sprig of Mistletoe growing — rare on oak trees. He took that as an omen and agreed to teach us, among other things, the proper way to do the "Approach to the Altar." He called it Grinding the Mill and it was the basic ritual used in Cochrane's tradition.

In our attempt at reconstruction, we had made this ritual entirely too complicated. In actuality, it is simplicity itself. One simply paces slowly around a small fire or lighted candle, eyes fixated on the light, and chants a version of the vowel chant that is, curiously enough, given in full in one of Cochrane's articles. The one thing we didn't think of, due in part to our quasi-Gardnerian training, is that one grinds the mill widdershins — counterclockwise, not clockwise. The counterclockwise motion (also called "Moonwise") churns the energy against the Earth's axis, producing friction and, therefore, energy for manifestations, or whatever. Deosil was used for worship rituals or for festivals. If one wanted to raise power, one went widdershins.

Grinding the Mill served to be the missing piece of the puzzle. It constitutes the means by which Cochrane and his group traveled between this world and the world of the Gods - a process which forms the cornerstone of any shamanic tradition. This method of trance induction, while simple on the surface, requires practice to do properly. However, once the technique is mastered, the energy it generates is tremendous and produces a variety of psychic and even physical manifestations. One is, quite literally, calling down fire from heaven and much preparation and commitment from all the members is required so that nobody gets singed.

Evan John Jones

With this bit of information in hand, we were instructed to return to the States and try it out, reporting to John what results we got. We discovered that, in our absence, most of the original people had drifted away to other endeavors. We were left with only a core group of a half a dozen people who were willing to begin implementing what we were learning from John. For the next several years, we experimented with this ritual. At the quarter and cross-quarter festivals, these six people met and experimented with whatever John suggested we do. After the ritual was over, we would write down what happened and report to John, who would then send us more rituals and suggestions.

Many practices that are now an integral part of the Roebuck were developed during this time. The rituals from John did not replace the Roebuck rituals, only enhanced them, giving them a grounding in tradition that they didn't have before. We decided to keep several ritual practices that we developed in the years before going to England, such as invocations to the quarter deities, even though the original group didn't do them. However, our circle casting ritual, cakes and ale consecration, group structure and so on were gradually brought into line with what we were learning from John.

Our work with John resulted in several revelations about our approach to ritual: 1) we were on the right track as far as simplifying our rituals and 2) we had not nearly gone far enough. The circle casting ritual that we learned in England ended up being far more minimal than anything we had previously suspected. We had eliminated all the "right" bits, but had kept some of the unnecessary ones, because we simply did not know any better. So, when we returned to the States, we revamped the entire Roebuck ritual system to reflect the original more accurately.

A prime example of this is all of the invocations - of the circle, the quarters, Goda, Tubal and sometimes Black Goddess - that are used in Roebuck circles. In the original form of the ritual, the circle is cast in silence. This, of course, is the ultimate answer to "why do we call upon the Gods when they are already there?" We do so as an aid to our concentration and to help us focus on the energy of the Gods when we enter the circle. In the original ritual, the Gods *were* acknowledged to be already there. And, since the people working the ritual had years of experience behind them, they didn't have to expend time or energy in formal invocations.

Still another example of such additions to Roebuck circles is the "group hug" at the end of the ritual. In its original form, the circle is cast before the people are brought in and cut only once before they are let out. When we began doing large training circles, we decided to cast the circle with everyone inside so they could see how it was done. When the ritual was over, the circle was "uncast" rather than merely cut for that same reason. It became necessary for the large numbers of people in training circles to hunker together in the center so that the guy with the sword could get around behind them to uncast the circle. Everyone liked the affectionate hugs at the end of the ritual so much that we continued to do it even in initiate circles. But, everyone needed to know that this was not done traditionally and that it might be eliminated if the situation called for it.

So, what parts of the Roebuck ritual actually come from the original English version? First, the circle is cast deosil, by the Magister, Summoner or Master of the Rites (a term for the presiding Priest) who wields the coven sword. The circle is cast, beginning in the north. Then, the Summoner, or someone acting in his behalf, lines everybody up and leads them into the circle. Second, the cup is consecrated with the Priestess holding the cup and the Priest wielding the blade. Cakes can also be consecrated by the Priestess before being sent round the circle, but this is not always part of the ritual. Finally, a coin is handed to the Magister (or the Master of the Rites) by the Summoner who tosses it over his shoulder after everyone is out of the circle. This is a custom called "paying for the site" which was an offering made to the ancient Gods by the man who represented the Sacred King. If the only thing asked of him was a coin or two, he was considered fortunate indeed!

We decided to keep many of our original practices, because we found them useful in orienting newcomers to the images and symbols that we learned in our delving into our ancient roots. We are not our ancestors. The cultural tradition on which the Craft is based, is not taught to us from childhood as it was in former times. We must learn it after we are adults – and then, only after several years of peeling away not only the current rational materialism in which our present culture is saturated, but often repressive Christian attitudes that underlie it. Elaborate rituals can serve as psychic training wheels to help people learn to 'ride' a tradition. We, in this country, require the training wheels to remain on the bicycle longer than our ancestors did.

We were not actually adopted into the Clan of Tubal Cain during our first trip. John performed a ritual with us that consisted of sending me on a kind of "vision quest" in which I was supposed to bring back a series of "key" visions which would determine whether or not we had been accepted by the Ancient Ones. As it happened, I did receive some of those keys and John proceeded to give us as much background material on the Clan and the way Cochrane used to work as we could absorb. However, he knew that we had our own group so the subject of bringing us formally into the Clan of Tubal Cain was never brought up. John just assumed that we would use the material with the Roebuck and, for a time, that is what we did.

However, in one of my letters to him, I had expressed a concern about whether or not the material we had (and, incidentally, the truth about Cochrane's death) would be accepted as valid in the States. We had, after all, been duped before. In his return letter, John suggested that we actually join the Clan of Tubal Cain. By this time, it was already May of 1983. We accepted and he sent us a copy of the adoption ritual, empowering Dave to act in his stead to adopt the entire Roebuck into the Clan, provisionally, while we served a year-long apprenticeship. He suggested that Dave and I give each other the oath first, then, a few weeks later, give it to the entire Roebuck.

Our apprenticeship was an intense one, even given the distance. In frequent letters, John would suggest a ritual, we would perform it and report back to him in detail what happened and who got what. Then, he would write a critique and suggest something else. There were also phone calls in which we discussed a variety of issues. John was insistent from the very first that we were to be an independent group and not slavishly copy the practices of the original clan. He was especially adamant that we not repeat any of Cochrane's mistakes.

By all accounts, Cochrane was a very colorful and charismatic leader and people would flock to the group because of him. We obviously could not duplicate that, nor could we work the way his original group did. Not only were we Americans and from a different generation, we had advantages that Cochrane's old group didn't have — an equal compliment of women, for one thing. But we did decide to keep to the core practices and philosophy of the Clan as much as we were able to, even when they ran counter to American ways of thinking.

In May, 1986, we took a second trip to England. On Beltaine, in the old calendar, John formally adopted me into the Clan in person and I, in turn, adopted David. The ritual, held on the hill above Brighton, was simple and impromptu, but would prove to have a profound effect on the future of the Roebuck. For some inexplicable reason, it was vital to have that in-person, hands-on confirmation of what we had done through the mail three years previously. Something clicked into place that night on both the material and non-material planes, something that would give us the power to solve the problems that we would face in the years ahead.

There are many Craft people that scoff at the tradition of the laying on of hands, a ritual from the Catholic church by which the Bishop confers power onto a new Priest. And, indeed, this is one of the sources of the accusations of elitism and snobbery that have been leveled at us since then. But all the members of the Roebuck knew what had happened when we returned. And, although they are no less valid and binding, the initiations and Clan adoptions that we performed after that trip had a different quality than the ones we had performed beforehand.

Eventually, the Clan ritual became the core of the Roebuck and the Clan dedicated to preserving the original ritual, and the lore surrounding it, in the form in which we originally learned it. This ritual constitutes the plug into the wall socket which carries the power of the Otherworld to the entire Roebuck, and those who are oath-bound to guard it do not take their task lightly.

The Spiral Staircase

All the while this reorganization was going on, we began to take on students. Eventually, the pre-England Roebuck experiments and techniques were distilled down into what is now known as the Roebuck training cycle. The purpose of this training was not to teach people "Witchcraft," "Paganism," or even "magic," per se. The original purpose of the training was to orient people from other magical systems or Craft traditions to Roebuck ritual methods.

What a student learns during the year of formal apprenticeship is a compilation of nearly seven years of Roebuck experimentation with god forms and techniques, codified, refined and presented in a coherent fashion. By mastering these techniques and becoming familiar with the guardians, the student essentially reaches the level that we did in 1982 when we first came into contact with the Clan and has the necessary background to do the advanced experimental work that the Roebuck still does.

From 1979 and 1986, I had been working towards a graduate degree in Experimental Psychology. During the course of my studies, I picked up a number of techniques from several different schools of traditional psychology and began experimenting with them to see if any of them could be used magically. A number of them could, with great success. While taking a certification in Hypnotherapy, I learned a number of additional hypnotic techniques. The most powerful of these was the physiological triggers (for example, the hyperventilation caused by taking three deep breaths in rapid succession) which could be used to induce trance in a group situation with far more effectiveness. My hypnotic training came from a teacher who was not a clinical psychologist, as Joe's teacher had been, but a former stage hypnotist. Therefore, the techniques I picked up in my studies were of a more theatrical nature and worked best with a group of people at one time rather than a one-on-one with a client.

From Neurolinguistic Programming (NLP) and Ericksonian hypnosis came the techniques for wording suggestions in guided journeys. The choice of words, for example, was not dictated by proper grammar, but by effectiveness in reaching the unconscious mind (present tense, run-on sentences, simplistic word order, etc.). The use of sensory modalities made invocations more effective and provided a means by which psychic phenomena could be reliably perceived.

Gestalt therapy was the source for some of our early scrying techniques and visualizations, particularly the so-called "empty chair" technique in which the participant is asked to visualize a person sitting in an empty chair. Make that person in the chair a god or Goddess rather than a dead relative and you've made the transition from psychology to religion. The only thing different, was that these techniques were put to a group purpose rather than a personal purpose.

A student, or trainee, was first introduced to all the quarter deities by means of a scripted, guided meditation called a "pathworking" from a similar technique used by ceremonial magicians to acquaint a student with the symbolism associated with the path from one sephira to another on the tree of life. These guided meditations were specially written in accordance with psychological principles so as to maximize their effectiveness. In the first place, they were read from a script in order to ensure consistency from one student to the next. The imagery surrounding the various Gods and Goddesses was carefully chosen in order to provide the student with a 'signature set' of images by which that deity is known within the group. Since many of our guardians are invoked by other groups, it becomes important to clue the student in on how, say, Bride or Cerridwen appear to us as opposed to how they appear to other groups.

The core of each pathworking is the three-minute pause in the middle in which the reader falls silent and each student is left alone to commune with the deity individually. The student is not told what to experience at this point, unlike the rest of the journey. This is the point at which the student 'meets' the god or Goddess 'up close and personal' and gets some kind of individual message or connection. Three minutes is rather arbitrary. It could be four or five minutes. We chose three minutes because we originally employed a three-minute hourglass-type egg timer so that the passage of time could be measured without having a clock in the circle. Three minutes seemed to be time enough to get whatever message the student was going to get, but not enough time for the student to become physically uncomfortable or go off onto another personal journey.

In doing the pathworkings, the student gradually learned the process of autohypnosis, or the ability to put himself or herself into trance at will in order to receive visions, messages, oracles and other contacts with the "Other Side". This step was crucial. The purpose was to produce students trained in the art of assuming a trance state whenever such was needed, whether it was in circle with the group or alone doing their own rituals. With everyone being essentially their own hypnotist, nobody needed anyone else to put them 'under.'

Also, these hypnotic procedures insured that the resulting trance was deep enough to be effective, but also safe enough so that aftereffects were minimal. While in a hypnotic trance, a person could walk, talk, respond to what others were saying and generally function in a circle. The only difference was that their psychic awareness was heightened, so that they could perceive things that they might not in ordinary consciousness. And, if properly trained, the person could 'shut down,' return to ordinary waking consciousness and be able to safely drive home and attend to their mundane activities afterwards.

The student was then required to put together a ritual, plan it and execute it from start to finish. Since the Roebuck had few standard rituals for festivals, moons and the like, there were many opportunities for creativity. The only ground rules were that the ritual had to have a purpose and that nothing unsafe was done. The ritual was not even required to "work" and very often didn't. But, if nothing else, they gave the student an appreciation of all the hard work that goes into putting together a ritual.

Finally, the student was required to demonstrate that he or she could serve as an oracle or "channel" for the energy and/or presence of a particular God or Goddess. This is often called "aspecting" in many Wicca circles. But we decided to separate this into two distinct processes: 1) a contact, in which the person served as an oracle, giving messages and answers to questions from a particular deity, but retaining ones own personal identity throughout the process and 2) a possession, another ceremonial technique called "Assumption of Godform" in which the person becomes, for the duration of the ritual, the physical manifestation of the god or Goddess in question. While in theory, these two processes are actually two distinct points on a continuum of communion with a particular deity, in practice, they serve two separate functions and will demonstrate to the student how this communion with deity can be controlled and modulated for maximum effectiveness.

After each contact or possession, the student had to undergo a debriefing session in which the more experienced members of the circle would evaluate what had just occurred. Did the messages that were given make sense? Were questions answered to the satisfaction of the querent? Did anyone see or hear anything unusual either physically or psychically? Was a god or Goddess really present, or was the channel playacting or "stained glassing", that is, filtering the messages of the Gods through his or her own personal point of view?

Senior initiates who have sat through numerous contacts and possessions as well as personal visitations are able to 'recognize' the various circle guardians by certain patterns of speech, personality characteristics ('That was Tautates all right; talkative as usual' or 'Bride always says that' or 'That was the Old Man; I'd recognize that laugh anywhere') and other clues, no matter who is channeling them. A student with only a few months experience simply can't 'fake' the presence of the guardians well enough to fool an initiate who has known them for years.

Some students, particularly those with experience in other groups, bristle at the thought that anyone would question the validity of their "aspecting." But, the sad fact is that everyone is prone to the temptation of cloaking one's own opinions, advice and pronouncements under the guise of a god or Goddess "aspect." A trance state, even when a deity isn't present, can unleash all kinds of unconscious revelations, often without the person's conscious mind being aware of it. These people aren't deliberately faking their "divine" messages, but that doesn't mean a God or Goddess is actually speaking, either.

Psychic work of any kind is a tricky thing to evaluate critically, and many people think it's sacrilegious to even try. But over the years, we have seen a great deal of emotional and even physical havoc wrought by people acting uncritically upon advice and instructions given during someone's "aspect." An emotionally troubled person could very well demand in the name of some god or other that a harmful action be taken against someone, possibly in the name of "protection" from some imagined attack. Since a person's deep seated paranoid delusions often go unrecognized even by the other members of their circle, such "oracles" can prove to be dangerous indeed.

This is why corroboration of an aspect is so very important. The other people in the circle must be especially on guard for anything that doesn't look or feel right. Even though one person was performing the actual "aspect," did anyone else see the entity in question, hear a voice, and sense a presence? Often, clairvoyant people will see the oracle's face change, clairaudient people will hear changes in the oracle's voice, will notice alterations in speech patterns, timbre and pitch, word choices, etc. Even people not normally psychically sensitive will feel a change in the energy level in the circle, or that odd mixture of panic and euphoria that announce the presence of Otherworld beings. If none of these manifestations are evident to anyone else in the circle, it is quite possible that only the oracle's unconscious mind is delivering the pronouncements.

Untrained and unsophisticated students often are impressed and even convinced that a person who is panting for breath, writhing and convulsing with their eyes rolled back is in the throes of a tremendously powerful aspect. But if what actually comes out doesn't make sense, doesn't answer the question of the person posing it, doesn't come true or, in the worst of cases, demands harmful or unethical actions, then it isn't a real god or Goddess possession. The ancient dictum from the Emerald Tablet "as above, so below" holds true today as it did 1800 years ago. If it's true in the circle, it will remain true outside the circle. If not, then not, no matter how much the oracle twitches and moans. And it takes a great deal of courage to be able to stand up and say to an oracle whose just gotten through writhing on the floor, "Sorry. No dice."

As with all Roebuck rituals, the contact and possession must have a purpose over and above just allowing students to commune with their deities of choice. We consider the ability to perform these techniques, particularly a possession, to be a sacred trust, with religious rather than purely magical purposes. By doing a possession, a candidate is literally giving the deity his or her own body and mind to use as a vehicle for manifestation for the purpose of interacting, often physically, with the rest of the people in the circle. Traditionally, this was one of the most effective ways for Gods and mortals to interact. Therefore it is not done for the purpose of the student's own entertainment, edification, satisfying of curiosity and so on.

This is why we do not allow students to be possessed by a deity of the opposite sex. Our Gods and Goddesses are traditionally very strongly polarized as male and female. We feel very strongly that if we wish to have one of our Goddesses, for example, manifest in the circle in all Her glory, we owe it to Her to provide a female body for her to inhabit. None of them would find a male body to be a very good fit. For us, the purpose of these rituals is to provide a vehicle of manifestation for the Gods to interact with the other people in the circle. This has always been, and continues to be, a Priesthood function, rather than purely a magician function. The purpose of bringing divinity into the circle is to help everybody else, not just oneself. Even if the possession were genuine for the candidate, it would inhibit the reaction of the people to a Goddess, for example, if they had to try to relate to Her manifesting in a male form, and the Priestly function of the ritual would be seriously compromised.

Finally, the possession served as a test of acceptance that the Gods had accepted the student, and, more important, the student had accepted the Gods. That being demonstrated, the student had one more hurdle to overcome. They had to pass muster with the Roebuck Group Mind. This was accomplished by a ritual officially called a speiring, but unofficially known as the Roebuck Inquisition. In this ritual, the candidate was brought before all active initiates sitting in assembly. He or she consents to answer to the best of his or her ability all questions from the assembled initiates, with the proviso that he or she could ask any initiate or all initiates, questions when the time came and be assured of the same level of honesty and candor.

This is probably the least understood of all Roebuck rituals, even by initiates. The purpose of the Inquisition is not to see whether the candidate has done all the required reading or not (often that is obvious). It is also not done to see whether the candidate is "worthy" or not. The purpose is to see whether the candidate trusts the Roebuck Group Mind enough to bare his or her soul before it, with all the problems, emotional baggage, past difficulties, previous training and so forth with no secrets, equivocation, excuses, or other avoidance techniques. The Group Mind expects nothing more of its members than ability to be bluntly honest with themselves and each other.

The Roebuck Group Mind is an entity in and of itself. In her book, Applied Magic, British occultist Dion Fortune defines the Group Mind as an Artificial Elemental "... which with the passage of time develops an individuality of its own, and ceases to be dependent for its existence upon the attention and emotion of the crowd that gave it birth." A group mind is built up automatically when a number of people gather together for a common purpose, but rapidly disintegrates when that common purpose no longer exists.

In a magical group, the Group Mind is constructed deliberately, with everyone in the group participating willingly in its construction and maintenance. This is why everyone is asked by the Summoner whether or not we are "of a mind" before we go into the circle for a ritual. We must all be reminded that we are participating in something that goes beyond our own personal purposes. Our energies are being directed to serve the group purpose, whatever it might be for that evening, and all those energies feed, maintain and build up the Group Mind.

While it is made up of the energies, personalities, problems and shared experiences of all Roebuck members, both past and present (and, I suspect, future), it survives independently of any of them. It is felt the most strongly in the temple itself, but it is certainly not confined to there. Indeed, whenever two or more Roebuck members gather together for any purpose, even if it has nothing to do with Craft or circle, the Group Mind hovers over them and sensitive people can perceive it. And, if the person in question is not aware of what is going on, his or her first encounter with the Group Mind can be terrifying.

The Group Mind, like the minds of the humans that participate in it, has inner vision, memory, emotions and dream states. It knows, senses and feels things that its human participants don't necessarily know, sense or feel. It is possible to offend or placate the Group Mind without necessarily offending or placating the people currently participating in it. This is a source of a great deal of confusion for those who have tried to manipulate the Group Mind by manipulating a few of the people in it. But the Group Mind is also a great source of power and can be very helpful and beneficial to those who make it up. It knows when its members are in trouble and will literally summon its human participants to assemble and do something about it. It will also go to great lengths to forgive and accept past mistakes if they are faced with courage and resolved with sincerity.

The Inquisition ritual has a way of stripping away pretense, personae, masks and other ways that people hide their true selves from themselves and the people around them. You stand with a naked soul (which is so much more revealing than merely a naked body) before the scrutiny of the entire group, and it is amazing how few people can hold up to it. It is truly a trial by fire and its intensity has been criticized by many former members who considered it to be needlessly critical and intrusive. However, we feel that it is necessary.

Roebuck rituals can be very soul-stripping in themselves. Initiates put themselves out on emotional and psychic limbs, and they have a right to know if their new brother or sister has the fortitude to hang in there and not run screaming hysterically when the going gets rocky. It also helps to know the weaknesses of everyone else in the circle, not to criticize or to judge, but to be able to know who can handle certain energies in the circle and who has problems with it. None of us are perfect, but we owe it to each other to reveal our weaknesses so as not to endanger a working out of pride or shame.

So, after all that, the candidate is initiated in a ceremony in which he or she is 'reborn' as a circle brother or sister. However, the Group Mind does not accept people into itself automatically just because an initiation ceremony has taken place. Participation in the Group Mind is a deliberate and voluntary process. Each initiate, as he or she is introduced into the Group Mind at Initiation, must choose to what extent he or she will "plug in," depending upon how comfortable he or she is with the Mind itself.

The first way is, of course, to attend circles frequently, particularly initiate and student circles. In these circles occur the shared experiences that contribute to the Group Memory. If the initiate misses these experiences, then they will be like someone who stands around confused while others chuckle at an inside joke. An initiate can, if desired, "tune in" to the Group

Mind and retrieve the memory without missing out on much. It depends entirely on why the initiate chose not to attend that particular circle in the first place.

Another way of participating in the Group Mind is to continue to study the tradition in more depth than was offered during training. Many students read the required books grudgingly, protesting all the way, demanding the reasons why such dry and obscure books are mandatory. The answer is this: The required reading familiarizes the student with the images by which they can communicate with the Group Mind.

The *White Goddess* in particular constitutes a dictionary by which the Group Mind can be talked to and understood. This was the book that provided much of the symbolism that functioned as a blueprint for the construction of the Group Mind in the first place. Without this dictionary, the Group Mind is obscure. If the student has no idea what the group did in the past, he or she can have little clue as to where it should go in the future.

However, the *White Goddess* and *Celtic Myth and Legend* (Charles Squire) are only the beginning. The more books the new initiate reads and the more questions that are asked of more experienced initiates, the more the new initiate can understand and contribute to the knowledge contained in the Group Mind. Books on history, mythology and other Pagan and Craft traditions will reveal the historical context in which the Roebuck fits. Chats with other initiates will give other perspectives on various topics, personal reminiscences and experiences that happened before the newcomer arrived and so on. All of these constitute the memory of the Group Mind and it is the responsibility of the newcomer to seek out these memories and opinions in order to better understand the Group Mind as a separate entity.

Another way of participating in the Group Mind is to socialize with other initiates outside of circle nights. While this is not required, it seems to lead to a much fuller participation in the Group Mind. Whenever two or more initiates gather, the Group Mind follows. Attending a social function or outing with initiates often enables the student to gain valuable information, opinions and perspectives on a number of circle-related issues. This can be particularly enlightening in non-circle situations when the initiates have their guard down and are speaking candidly. These discussions can give more information in, say, an afternoon than in several months of more controlled training.

The downside of this is that student or new initiate becomes involved in the various interpersonal squabbles and rivalries that arise between initiates. They also find themselves drawn into the personal problems that various initiates have. They witness arguments, temper tantrums, whining and complaining about a variety of issues, bad-mouthing of other initiates, and so on.

While this can be distressing, the newcomer must realize that this is what constitutes the Shadow side of the Group Mind. Every personal experience contributes to the Mind, and that includes personal problems, unresolved issues, rivalries and so on. In short, one has to take the good with the bad. The Group Mind has its own unresolved issues, anger and hurt feelings. The newcomer must accept these and strive, along with everyone else, to resolve these problems even though he or she might not personally share them.

Sometimes, a new initiate will balk at plugging into the Group Mind. There seem to be a number of reasons for this reluctance. The most common appears to be that the newcomer expects this process to happen instantaneously, without effort and is daunted and annoyed when it does not. This expectation is what lies at the root of the "now what?" syndrome that new initiates often exhibit during the first few months after initiation.

As students, newcomers tend to be taken by the hand and led through the variety of new experiences. At initiation, they are plunked down in front the Group Mind, as it were, and told "Okay, you're on your own." Some new initiates go forward eagerly, finding within the Group Mind the home and family they have sought for a long time. Others need a shove, especially if they find the Group Mind intimidating rather than welcoming.

This feeling of intimidation usually occurs when the new initiate comes into the group either with ulterior motives, or unwillingness to face certain personal problems. This process of coming to terms with the Group Mind has been dubbed the 'Maiden Year Blues' by initiates who have struggled through it. New initiates very often are unaware that the Group Mind senses things that the individual members do not and find, to their chagrin, that the Group Mind knows that they are being dishonest, either with themselves or with the rest of the group. They find that their usual excuses, evasions, denials and previous ways of coping with problems don't work anymore. An unseen force has stepped in to compel them to begin walking the walk rather than just talking the talk.

Occasionally, a new initiate will find the Group Mind so unsympathetic that he or she will actually leave the group altogether rather than sort themselves out. This seems terribly cold and heartless and often the other initiates will attempt to mitigate the process out of sympathy and concern. But it must be understood that the Group Mind, although composed of human energy, is elemental rather than human in its character. Therefore, it often appears to be distinctively lacking in social niceties such as tact and politeness. It calls a spade a spade and will kick out those that try to manipulate it without so much as a "by-your-leave" or an "excuse-me." And it seems totally indifferent to what those thus rejected may think of it, leaving its human participants to bear the brunt of the angry lies and accusations that the rejected members may put out to the community at large.

Although distressing to many initiates, this is the process by which the Group Mind protects the group as a whole from those who would seriously harm it while allowing those experiences that will teach its members what they need to learn. Roebuck members are basically nice people. Taught to be polite and considerate by our modern society, they sincerely desire to be liked and accepted by others in the Pagan community. This often leaves them vulnerable to manipulation and abuse by those who seek either control over others or validation of their own dysfunctional behaviors. But the Group Mind isn't fooled by excuses and rationalizations. Like a protective parent, it will put up with only so much and no more and the violator will find himself or herself suddenly booted out without warning once that limit has been reached.

It must be stated here that it is not necessarily the action itself that affects the Group Mind but the motivation behind the action. Many initiates will be absent from circle, often for extended periods, for a variety of different reasons. Sometimes, initiates may need a breather from the intense emotional involvement of magical work. Some initiates live far enough away that they can't attend circle regularly. Yet, they remain an integral part of the Group Mind because they have chosen to do so by communicating frequently with the rest of the initiates, continuing to study and contribute to the tradition, helping with problems when they arise and so on. It is their sincere effort and involvement which matters, not their physical presence.

In contrast is the initiate who attends circle fairly regularly, but contributes nothing in the way of feedback, encouragement, emotional or physical effort to the proceedings. Such a person will be overly critical, distant, demanding of other initiates' time and attention but will withhold all sympathy, understanding, compassion and consideration for others when called upon to do so. The Group Mind senses that such a person is there only to take, rather than share, sucking in a parasitic fashion off of the bountiful emotional energies of the group. If this persists over a long period of time, the Group Mind will begin to react, giving off feelings of annoyance, resentment and anger. Finally, if the situation remains unresolved, it will make the decision to eject the parasitic member.

First, it will discourage them from attending circle, giving them feelings of being unwelcome. They will feel uneasy as though they are somehow on their guard and can't open up to the group either in circle or out. The other members of the group may avoid them or look upon them with suspicion or indifference. Whispered discussions between other initiates will cease as soon as they walk into a room. They will not be informed about social events or non-circle gatherings, often as a result of quite accidental oversight. They may be hard pressed to put their finger on any overt actions which might give this impression. Often all other initiates will be polite, nice and possibly even friendly. But the longer such people persist in remaining the more unwelcome they will feel.

Thus discouraged, they will begin finding excuses to avoid attending circle. Chronic illness, personal troubles and other social commitments are the most common reasons for begging off coming to circle. The longer this goes on, the more estranged they become from the Group Mind. Once they make the decision to leave, the pressure is off. If they persist on remaining out of pride or stubbornness, the pressure will increase until there is a crisis. Then, they will find something to be angry about and leave in a huff, spouting lies to justify their action. This leaves the Group Mind angry and frustrated, which affects the emotions of those who had nothing to do with the upheaval in the first place.

Since there are no degrees in the Roebuck, every initiate is a full fledged member of the group entitled to all rights and responsibilities thereto up to and including the right to go off, form his or her own circle and initiate students. The training manual and other ancillary material is given to the initiate and he or she can choose to stay or go. Most choose to stay and work within the group as Priests and Priestesses, running festivals, helping with the training and so on, but it is by no means required.

If they stay long enough, they may be considered for Clan. This process was less arbitrary and more intuitive than the process by which a candidate was considered for Roebuck initiation. It wasn't just a matter of a person fulfilling certain specific requirements. It was a feeling, a sense that the person was plugged into the group mind on a deeper level. We watched to see if the new initiate would see or hear things not specified in the standard training such as darker aspects of the Gods that weren't described in the pathworkings, or certain Otherworld beings that often turn up in workings that students aren't told about.

We also watched to see if the new initiate showed any curiosity about the tradition other than the standard party line. We waited to see if they would ask questions about things they had read regarding the history of the tradition, whether they wanted to know the background of certain ritual practices or policies. Also, we waited to see if they reported any significant dreams or visionary experiences that would lead us to believe that they were being contacted on a deeper level by those on the Other Side that also guard the tradition.

We felt that now we could initiate someone into the Roebuck and watch them for a year. They would either plug into the root tradition, in which case they would be considered for Clan, or they would take their training and go off to do their own thing as Roebuck members had done in the past. The year between Roebuck initiation and Clan adoption would function as the same kind of apprenticeship that we had served under John.

The decision was then made to split the Clan off from the Roebuck and have separate Clan workings that Roebuck initiates were unable to attend. The main reason for this decision was caution. We were beginning to raise a great deal of power in Clan circles as our own contacts began to be established, and we felt that, for the time being, it would be best to keep the Roebuck as a separate group so that people would not feel pressured into committing to, what we were beginning to discover, was a powerful and potentially dangerous system.

The main difference between Clan and Roebuck structure involves the Clan Oath. In the Roebuck initiation ritual, there are no oaths asked for, no measure taken, no promises given, nothing to tie an initiate to the group by bonds of obligation. Initiates obey the will of the Magister only so long as they are in the circle. Should they choose to leave, they can do whatever they please. And there are many who have chafed under the discipline of the circle, and have gone off to form their own group. And some have even returned after a year or two with a renewed appreciation for what we do.

Members of the Clan, who are oath-bound, remain under the will of the Magister no matter what they do. They must also keep to the original tradition and not vary it in any way. Indeed, that is what they have taken the oath for - to carry on and guard that tradition. In a sense, they have given up their spiritual autonomy and now "belong" to the Clan in the way that a medieval knight "belonged" to his liege lord.

As we continued doing our research, this idea made more and more sense. Most of the families that practiced the old ways were from the West Country or the North Country, places in England where the Celtic influence is still strong. Celtic Clans were (and in many cases still are) not only families but fighting units as well. If you were battling a rival clan, the only people you could really depend on were your kinfolk, bound to you either by blood or by some kind of binding oath, such as marriage. Back in the days when practicing the Old Ways was a hanging offense, such loyalties were vital to preserving the well being of a clan which still practiced the old ways in secret.

Some Roebuck initiates recoil in horror from the very thought of taking such an oath. And so, from them, no oaths are asked. They remain in the Roebuck as long as they wish as Priests and Priestesses, teachers, performers of festival rituals and so on with no obligation whatsoever. However, they will not be adopted into Clan, no matter how many years they remain in the group.

Another difference is that the Clan works the original ritual with little if any variation. There is little of the experimentation that goes on in the Roebuck. Again, the purpose of the Clan is to preserve that ritual and provide a traditional foundation for the Roebuck experimentation. If one looks upon the Roebuck as a tree with many branches, then the Clan is the root.

The Magical Mystery Tour

Once we figured out how to invoke our various Gods and Goddesses, we had to figure out what to do with them. That meant the Roebuck had to come up with a corpus of rituals and ritual techniques that matched its developing mythos. It became clear, very soon, that different rituals were needed for different purposes. We needed festival rituals to celebrate the seasons of the year, full moon rituals and dark moon rituals. Festival rituals had to commemorate the specific time of year and nearly always involved a significant number of visitors, some new to not only our circle but often to the Craft and Paganism in general. Rituals involving serious magic (pathworking, channeling, etc.) did not work well in this environment.

Full Moon rituals were more restricted in who could attend, but more open in what could be done. "Traditionally," (at least according to the Gardnerian tradition), full moons, or esbats, was the time in which spells were cast as opposed to the festivals where a scripted mystery play would be performed. Initially, we tried keeping to this tradition and performed a variety of spells at the full moon just like good little Witches were supposed to do. However, Roebuck members being what they were (and are), quickly became bored with the standard spell-casting fare and wanted to do something else.

Spell casting in the traditional sense often has an unfortunate tendency to degenerate into a 'laundry list' of requests - jobs, money, partners, etc. - are supposedly conjured up for the person requesting it. We quickly learned that this was undesirable in a large group. While we tried to avoid the Ceremonial Magic distinction between High Magic (where Gods or angels are summoned and asked for advice on spiritual matters) and Low Magic (where spells are cast for mundane things such as jobs or lovers), we discovered a few practical reasons for discouraging this practice. Not only do people become dependent upon the group rather than themselves for their personal magical workings, but you tend to attract to the group people who only want spells done for them rather than more spiritual aspirations.

We managed to avoid this problem by requiring that every person in the group do his or her own spells on his or her own time. Spells work, after all, by affecting the aura or mindset of the requestor. Another person, even one well meaning and sympathetic, cannot do a spell for anyone else. All one can really do is plant the suggestion, in the mind of the requestor, that a magical ritual has been performed on his or her behalf and that the desired result will soon follow.

Far better to have the requestor light his own candle, write out his own request to be burned in the cauldron/tossed into the water/buried in the earth/ blown away in the wind or whatever technique he or she might choose. We had numerous books on spell casting available for consultation and other members could offer advice and/or feedback, or even agree to be present in the circle when the spell was performed. But, we did our best to make it clear to everyone that personal magic was not to be done on group time - with one exception.

Healings. The group took on certain healing rituals when they agreed that a group effort was necessary, such as in the case of serious or life-threatening illnesses or injuries to either members or their close families. Certain conditions had to be met, however. We had to have the expressed consent of the person for whom the healing was to be done, if at all possible. Better still was the actual participation of the recipient, if not physical at least "in spirit" with the assurance of the recipients cooperation with the healing and the follow-up afterwards, such as any diet or lifestyle changes, following doctor's instructions, etc.

The ethics of healing is a murky topic that has plagued occult circles for a long time. Briefly, what concerned us was the possibility of coercion, interfering with someone else's karma or healing someone for the convenience of the requestor, rather than the health and well being of the recipient. As Pagans, we acknowledged that death is a natural transition from one phase of existence to another. Keeping a person trapped inside a diseased and pain-wracked body just because a selfish relative doesn't want to let them go is cruel.

Another issue is that of the recipient or requestor expecting the ritual to serve as a 'magic bullet' which would heal their illness without any responsibility or effort on their part. Chronic illnesses, except in the case of congenital causes (and there might well be karmic issues involved there as well) are usually the result of unhealthy habits over many years. A patient with lung cancer who won't stop smoking, the heart patient who won't exercise and the diabetic who won't control his diet are not likely to benefit much from healing efforts in the long run.

Roebuck healing circles employ a particular technique that has proven to be most effective. The problem is described in as much clinical detail as possible, including x-rays or consultation with Gray's Anatomy. This is done so that each member can visualize the problem in his or her mind. Then, a course of treatment is decided upon. Should a tumor be shrunk or blasted away altogether? Or should it just be altered in shape so that surgery would be possible? Then, a visualization is constructed, with everyone in the circle concentrating on the same images - a bone knitting together, a tumor shrinking, a limb growing well and strong, the recipient running, laughing, looking healthy and happy. A Cone of Power was raised and the energy released with the appropriate images invoked.

Occasionally, a situation presented itself which was too ambiguous to formulate a specific treatment. In such circumstances, energy was raised and sent to the person to aid them in solving their own problem and we left it at that. Whatever we ended up doing, the healing was always conducted with the assumption that the appropriate medical care was also being employed. We worked in conjunction with medical care, not as a substitute for it. If all we could do was make a hip replacement more successful, that was what we did. We did not presume to heal the already badly diseased hip bone.

The technique we use to raise energy isn't fundamentally different that the one we were taught by Ed, but we added a few refinements. Although, we move around the circle when we can, more often than not (especially in a crowded temple) we raise the Cone with everyone standing in place. The key is the guided imagery and controlled visualization where all participants see and feel the same things while raising the energy, thus being 'of a mind.'

The group is arranged in a circle (or oval) with everyone holding hands. One person functions as leader, keeping up a constant patter of sensory suggestions as well as physical instructions in order to keep the energy flowing and consistent. After the energy is flowing well, the participants are told to intensify it and see it build, usually with everyone raising their clasped hands slowly until they are extended above head level. This is kept up for as long as the leader deems necessary and depending on just how much energy is needed for a particular purpose. Then, the energy is released all at once with a sharp command, at which all members will drop hands and visualize the energy going to the predetermined target, person or situation.

When the energy is dissipated, the members are free to 'ground' by whatever means suits them. Some will shake their hands, others will kneel and touch the ground, and still others will touch their own bodies to take the remaining energy within, in order to combat the fatigue that often comes from intense healing rituals. And, last but not least, those members who are in a sexual relationship can go home and ground the energy in a far more enjoyable way. In any case, if the energy is not grounded properly, a group will have a tendency to 'bounce off the walls' and suffer irritability, nervousness and other problems.

An interesting variation on this energy raising technique proved to be extremely effective in an outdoor public ritual where there were a number of enthusiastic but untrained people participating. An outer circle was formed containing the majority of the participants. These people were given a chant to sing and instructed to hold hands if possible and pace the circle clockwise or deosil.

A smaller inner circle was also formed with people who either had previous magical training or were familiar with the process of raising energy. These people were set to pacing the circle counterclockwise and either given the same chant, a different one or merely pacing in silence concentrating on raising the energy. This technique has the advantage of being able to raise a great deal of energy in a short period of time due to the friction between the deosil circle and the widdershins circle.

Dark moons were chosen as the time when purely experimental rituals would be performed. These were usually restricted to Initiates, since only initiates would have demonstrated the kinds of magical skills that were needed to not only put together often an uncertain experimental ritual, but to evaluate the results afterward. Pretty much everything was fair game for being experimented with, including energy raising techniques, contacts and possessions with Gods or Goddesses not in our pantheon (provided they were Anglo-Celtic and not, say, Egyptian), trance induction techniques, pathworkings to a variety of interesting places and alternate ritual forms. The only stipulation was that the ritual could not involve anything physically dangerous (like having people ingest dubious mind altering substances, light fires in inappropriate places or otherwise inflict bodily harm on someone).

Some notable rituals developed during dark moons were:

Silent ritual. In this odd ritual, no words were permitted, only gestures. All quarter god and Goddess invocations were done silently. Members were instructed to visualize as clearly and intensely as they could the deity in question and use their emotions to call them into the circle. A group contact was performed, also silently, then the circle was taken down. The only rule was that if anyone forgot what they were doing and uttered a word, then the ritual would end right then and there. The ritual could only proceed to its conclusion so long as everyone refrained from speaking.

Shape-shifting. This was a ritual in which members were given suggestions to turn themselves into ravens - body part by body part from the head down to the feet. This technique involves as much sensory detail as possible using as many sensory modalities as we could think of. One variation of this ritual included all members becoming ravens, going out and returning with a raven's-eye view of the world. Another variation involved one member, chosen by lot, turning into a raven and going out to find information in answer to a specific question or task.

Animal pathworkings. This was another series of rituals in which each member found or was found by his or her personal power animal. One of the ways in which we discovered that this ritual actually worked, was the unexpected nature of the animals people came up with. There were the usual wolves, tigers, cats, bears and ravens. But there were also snakes, armadillos, moles, hares, bees and a variety of other singularly unromantic but still useful creatures, often from parts of the world foreign to the person receiving them.

Double quarter calling. This was a circle casting technique by which the entire eight point circle is invoked with a pair at each quarter in which a woman calls the Lady and a man calls the Lord. This technique was used as a circle set-up for other rituals and produced a particularly high level of polarized energy. Similarly, cross invocations where the woman calls the Lord and the man the Lady of each quarter, as well as the center, also produced a great deal of energy. Other circle-casting techniques included having the women call quarters for a male mystery such as Hunters Moon and the men call quarters for a female mystery such as Imbolc.

The most important part of all these ritual experiments was the debriefing or critique session afterwards. Whatever occurred during the special Otherworld atmosphere of the circle had to stand up to the cold, clear light of critical evaluation or it didn't pass muster. Each member in turn would relate whatever psychic impressions, feelings or emotions that the ritual evoked, along with any problems and suggestions for improvement. The ritual was either added to the Corpus, or sent back to the drawing board for further development.

Other opportunities for magical experimentation presented themselves during festivals. Since there were no scripts, whoever had volunteered to run the circle could take whatever seasonal elements they wished and weave them into a ritual. Some rituals emerged that were so popular and seemed so "right" that they continued to be done year after year, finally taking on the dubious mantle of 'tradition.'

Rekindling the Yule Fire was one of these. The first time we performed this ritual, we were in our living room with three other people in attendance. Dave, as Master of the Rites, prepared a cauldron with kindling and magnesium in order to produce the desired effect. As we all bent down over the cauldron to watch, Dave ignited the spark with flint and steel. The resulting flash nearly singed everyone's eyebrows. But there was no doubt in anyone's mind that the sun had indeed returned with a vengeance. Similarly, for Imbolc, the youngest woman in the group would rekindle the need fire in honor of Bride. This was performed either in a cauldron or brazier, or in a fireplace if one was handy.

The Sacrifice of the Year King at summer solstice was another practice that evolved into 'tradition.' This ritual was first performed around 1985 when Dave as Oak King was to be ritually slain by the Holly King, the first available man next in line in order of initiation. A plastic knife was chosen as the prop for the slaying. However, at the last moment, the man acting the role of Holly King decided to substitute his Damascus steel athame. As the powerful archetype took hold of him, he actually took a swipe at Dave's bared chest with the razor sharp blade. The tip of the blade caught in the heavy chain that Dave wore around his neck which held his deer tag (Roebuck initiates wear a military-style dog tag with the Roebuck logo printed or engraved on it). Consequently, the worst of the blow was deflected, still the tip of the blade caused a small scratch from which oozed a drop of blood. One drop. But the blood of the Oak King still fell upon the land and the spirit of the ritual was accomplished.

Despite the near tragedy, this ritual continued to be performed year after year, with the man next in line of initiation battling with and ritually slaying the king of the previous year. Of course, we made certain modifications in the interests of safety. We made very sure the two men in question knew ahead of time what to expect from each other in terms of weaponry and so on in order to avoid any more unpleasant surprises. Each pair of men worked out a ritual unique to them. Sometimes it was a ritual slaying, other times it was a duel, sometimes with swords or with quarter staves all with appropriate face, hand and body protection to avoid injury. But despite the safety precautions, it was always understood that in order for this ritual to work, both men would have to channel the energies of their respective year king aspects and that the combat had to involve real weapons with an element of a real duel, or else it was religious drama rather than ritual

The second part of this ritual involved the women of the circle claiming the body of the slain king, covering it with red roses and keening. Again, the women were expected to actually mourn rather than just playact, and actual tears flowed on more than one occasion. All the women were expected to keen, not just sing or hum. We had learned the fine art of keening from historical recreationists who worked the various renaissance faires. It consists of an odd combination of a wail and a groan, with a cadence that rises and falls in pitch. If done properly, the sound can raise the hair on your arms.

Hunters Moon and Running the Stag. This ritual was first performed at the full moon closest to Samhain, the so-called Hunter's Moon. It was based on a fragment of a ritual we learned on one of our England trips in which the candles at the quarters are extinguished by four women who call the Old One out of the darkness. A man dressed in an antlered headdress appears and presides as the Lord of the Hunt in one of his many guises, depending upon whichever man is channeling him.

The variations we have made in this ritual over the years are myriad. We have used a full deer's head, stylized brass antlers on a fillet and a complete deer skull over a black hood. In one variation, the man will pass around an arrow for everyone to charge, then fit it into a bow and shoot it, either into a tree or out into the brush. Then, a plate of cooked venison cut into small pieces is passed around, with everyone in the circle partaking of the deer which is the gift to the tribe from the Hunter.

Another variation, the Running of the Stag, could only be done outdoors. This practice involved the choosing by lot of one of a group of people who were willing to play the role of the stag. The chosen one would be dressed in deer's antlers, and was instructed to take off running as fast as possible and hide. The other people in the circle played the role of the hounds and gave chase after the stag, howling and baying and generally raising a ruckus. When the hounds caught the stag, they divested the person of antlers and hide and brought them back to the Hunter. The former stag would then discreetly rejoin the circle while the venison was passed around. A cup of Stag's Blood (Bushmill's Irish Whisky with red food coloring) was also discreetly passed around to those wishing to partake.

Still another variation, also to be performed outdoors, involved the Hunter choosing by lot a dozen or so 'hounds' from the assembled company. The rest of the people in the circle were the souls of the dead who needed to be rounded up and chased into the otherworld. Those wishing to participate were sent running out of the circle. After a couple of minutes, the 'hounds' were sent to chase them down and herd them back into the circle where the Hunter gathered them up for their sojourn across the veil.

Some of these experimental rituals worked and some didn't. Others worked too well, bringing through powers that we had trouble controlling. All the while we were painfully aware that we tread upon the razor's edge between having the ritual be effective and have it destroy us in the process. The power that often came through carried with it the potential of causing a great amount of physical, real-world harm. It was a chance we all took.

The worst risk was that people with mental or emotional instabilities would "flip out" and go ballistic under the pressure of magical ritual. This is a risk with any magical ritual that has any power at all. When people confine their activities to the mundane world, their emotional and mental problems can be controlled and masked through medications and other anesthetics, or channeled into fantasies, entertainment or other relatively harmless pastimes. But magic can cause previously unknown or unacknowledged weaknesses to surface, which in extreme cases can result in threats of suicide, violence, paranoid delusions, obsessions and other pathologies. Such people might lose jobs and/or relationships, get into trouble with the law or, in the worst-case scenario land in a mental hospital.

In these cases, professional help tended to be useless. Other than drugging the patient into oblivion, modern psychology and psychiatry in this country is for the most part unable to deal with magically induced pathologies. Except in rare instances, just the act of doing magic at all is looked up on by the mainstream psychological community as a pathology in and of itself. The technical term for it is "magical ideation" and it refers to the mental pathology of believing that one can influence the outside world by means of magical ritual. Consequently, members who flipped out as a result of magical rituals had to pull out of it on their own - if they could.

Other potentially disastrous results of powerful ritual were simply caused by the hard-driving, technological, economically demanding world we lived in. Simply driving home after a particularly intense ritual was dangerous. As anyone who has driven Los Angeles freeways will attest, driving anywhere in this city isn't just a matter of pointing the car in the right direction and stepping on the gas pedal. One must be alert and aware to avoid clobbering or being clobbered by road-enraged drivers going eighty miles per hour. Driving in such an environment with one's mind half in and half out of the Otherworld was potentially fatal - that is, if the Highway Patrol didn't pull you over first for a possible DUI.

Staying at the covenstead or bunking down with a covener who lived close by was an option often taken. But here again, demands of an economically driven society intruded. There was no night that we could meet where some member didn't have to get up early and go to work the next day. Many members held highly technical jobs in which working evenings, nights and weekends was common in order to earn enough money to survive. If we had waited for the luxury of having several days to shake the effects of a ritual before returning to the mundane world of work, we would have never done magic at all.

The Wolf Pack

As the years went by, we began to collect a veritable Rogues Gallery of temperamental, strong minded and eccentric people who simply did not fit in with more autocratic groups or who had, like us, run afoul of the abusive or ineffectual ones. Gradually, we discovered the humbling truth that many of these groups serve as kind of a testing ground to determine the mettle of a prospective student.

Most people come into the craft naive, starry-eyed and innocent. Many come from a background of Christianity or Judaism, where there are strict codes of ethics which everybody subscribes to, even if they break them regularly. These are folks who are used to following those in authority and are simply not prepared for the self-serving chicanery that they often find. They believe everything they are told, because it never occurs to them that there are people who will try to exploit them in the name of religion. They fall in love with the Goddess and it often hurts - a lot - when they realize that not everyone who claims to worship Her is either genuine or scrupulous. The cry always is, 'but they seemed like such nice people. How could they do this to me?'

Even when there is no deliberate abuse, newcomers will often be disillusioned with their chosen guru. Many people come into the occult in general looking for a mythical Great White Brotherhood of all wise, all knowing adepts who will take them in, love them, protect them and teach them the secrets of the universe. These folks will fall in with a group of ordinary, well-meaning but fallible people and discover that even experienced and ethical leaders are not Perfect Masters, but real live people who suffer from all of the problems that real live people suffer from. They may become ill and be unable to run circles, they may become tired and irritable and lose their tempers, they may suffer from unemployment and money problems, go through relationship breakups and marital discords or legal problems.

The sad part is that it doesn't take an unscrupulous or unethical leader to disillusion a student. Sometimes, just being an ordinary human being will do it. And even the leader who is trying his or her level best to treat people fairly, ethically and sensibly, open his or her home to rituals and workshops and, inevitably, assume the lion's share of the expenses for running the group, will disillusion a student if he or she turns out to be anything less than perfect.

This is nobody's fault. It constitutes part of a student's curriculum and serves as a kind of entrance exam. The student who can't accept that his teacher is a human being isn't going to go very far in any kind of group. If the teacher is honestly trying to do his or her best, then it is the student who has the problem and, quite frankly, it is a waste of time for anyone else to step in and take that student in. Now, if the student, by maturing a little, can accept that whatever his or her vision of the Craft may be, the reality, even at best, is not going to live up to that vision, then progress can be made.

Most students will gravitate to the kind of group that he or she wants to be a part of (unfortunately, even the abusive ones), stay a few years, and then want to move on. This is normal and to be expected. The problems occur when the teacher looks upon this process as a betrayal and a desertion. This happens when the teacher is inexperienced and insecure. The resulting hurt feelings often result in emotional confrontations that are painful for everybody. But if the student has been drawn to a close and nurturing group because he or she wants to belong, then he or she must accept the consequences of wanting to leave.

Students sometimes choose to leave the craft altogether at this point. If their devotion was to an individual teacher, or group, rather than to the Craft itself, then disillusion with the group will cause them to be disillusioned with the craft as a whole. These are also people that it is a waste of time to try to teach, as they will form a personal attachment to the group and/or leader and will not look upon the teaching as a means of their own development.

Another kind of student, rare but still existent, is the experienced street-wise student who has been 'around the block' a few times. They land in the first group they find and proceed to ask troubling and inconvenient questions about the group leaders, their qualifications and antecedents. They try and test the leaders, noting inconsistencies, laughing at foibles and pricking pretensions. These are the 'black-sheep' that inexperienced group leaders dislike for several very good reasons.

One, such students tend to be extremely well read and have experience in other occult groups other than the craft. They may not know much about the craft, but they know when they're being told something that doesn't make sense or isn't true, and they question all unsubstantiated claims. Two, such students, for all their annoyance factor, are extremely dedicated to the search for truth. They come to the craft in the first place because their former faith/tradition/group fell short and they resent being fed a snow job or having their lack of information taken advantage of by a group leader. They want training, not games and do not suffer fools - especially group leaders with pretentious titles that they discover to be all show and little substance.

Handling this kind of student is an art in itself. It takes absolutely scrupulous and blunt honesty in answering questions, the ability to present all sides of an issue not just the group's 'party line,' the humility to admit that one doesn't know the answer, the resources to challenge the student to go find the answer him or herself, the self confidence to allow him or her present it to the rest of the group - and the self control to refrain from saying 'I told you so' when it doesn't work they way it's supposed to.

Such a student, when confronted by this kind of approach, finds the tables turned. The group leaders, confident in who and what they are, challenge the student to 'put up or shut up.' If the student is a genuine seeker and not just a troublemaker, he or she will be forced to prove him or herself before a leader and company of people just as ornery and iconoclastic as he is. Thus, a bond of genuine respect is formed between leader and student in which the strengths and weaknesses of both are accepted.

This approach leads to a kind of "wolf-pack" mentality in which every member has to prove his or her merit and when such merit is proven, the rest of the group has to either put up with their eccentricities or idiosyncratic behavior or leave. If someone wanted to be with us badly enough, they would put up with our annoying quirks - a kind of "I'll put up with you if you'll put up with me" bargain. If not, they were free to leave. As heartless as that sounds, it served to demonstrate that the people who remained with us really wanted to be there and were willing to learn the lesson of tolerance in order to do so.

From this came the rumors of Roebuck snobbery. We, as a group, simply would not put up with pretense, fabrications about one's background or unsubstantiated claims about ones abilities. People who claimed anything special were put to the test to see if they really had what they claimed or whether they were just pitching a yarn. The magical community fosters a wide variety of Great Magi, Witch Queens, Adepts and Avatars of various Gods that go about bragging about their abilities and trying to impress everyone with their magical prowess. For the vast majority of these, it was only talk. When put to the test, either physically or magically, these claims ended up being spurious.

For a few, it was a case of they simply didn't know any better. They thought they had magical ability and training because they had been told a self-serving line by someone wanting to impress them and they had believed it. It was a painful revelation for them when they had problems in one of our circles and had to be gently told that their visions didn't hold up to scrutiny or verification, their information was inaccurate or incomplete and their touted ability was really very rudimentary and met only the most basic requirements for functioning in the circle.

For others, there was not even a basis in fact for their claims of magical prowess. Their experiences came from dreams, mystical experiences or chance encounters, with no training or validation at all from anyone who might possibly know what they were doing. These people, termed by a noted science fiction writer "Cosmic Muffins" were usually young, spent all their free time reading science fiction and fantasy books and/or playing various role playing games. Ours was the task to inform them - with the subtlety of a bucket of cold water - that all they were demonstrating was a vivid imagination. And while such an imagination can be a useful magical tool, it takes years of intense study, training and practice to turn it into genuine magical ability.

There were also people who came into the group with initiations and degrees from other groups and were sometimes quite put out when we refused to accept those initiations or degrees at face value. As a result of our experience with other groups, we were never sure just what the initiation and/or degree actually meant in terms of training or knowledge. A third degree initiation after many years of study is quite different than a third degree initiation given over the course of a weekend ritual marathon. We eventually had to insist that whatever the degree or rank the person held in another group or tradition, they would have to demonstrate their abilities in our circle before being initiated into our system.

Finally, for a few, it was a case of deliberate deception. These were the predators who prowled the community looking for innocent people to recruit as students by offering them elaborate and entertaining fantasies of power and visionary experiences and using them for sexual or financial or ego gratification instead. They came to us in the early days, looking to impress us and either gain our stamp of approval or pull a few of our students into their fold. After a few of them got caught out, they began to not only avoid us but do their best to discredit us before we could expose them. This absolute refusal to accept anyone's claims at face value earned us the respect of many and the absolute hatred of some who didn't like the fact that they had to 1) prove their ability in circle rather than just be able to talk about it or 2) get their lies and fabrications caught out and exposed in public.

Because we only had one initiation, you were either one of us or you were not. What level you assumed within the group was settled after you were initiated, with the exception of those who held offices, the only real "rank" was seniority. Anything else was a kind of pecking order that everyone coming in to the group had to find their place in - sometimes with conflict. Part of the test of the Maiden Year for new initiates consisted of seeing whether they could find their place in the group by proving their merit and earning the honest respect of the other members, or whether they would leave with their tails between their legs. The people who survived their first year tended to be with us for many, many years.

Some didn't make it. There were a few people that, despite all the preparations and warnings, still cracked mentally and emotionally under the intense pressure of their maiden year. The signs of impending problems were always the same. First, the member would start to avoid coming to circle, often with a variety of excuses. Soon, there would be no more excuses; they simply would not come to circle. Then, the accusations would begin, usually of mistreatment by another member. When questioned closely, what mostly emerged was that the offending member either exhibited the same behavior problems that the troubled member himself or herself had or in some cases, refused in some way to "put up with" or enable the troubled member's problem. The troubled member would then come to us and demand that we "do something" about the offending member. Usually, the offending member would have no idea what caused the situation and any attempts at reconciliation would engender more accusations against us of conspiracy or favoritism.

Finally, the troubled member would flee the circle amid totally unfounded accusations of retaliation. All consequent troubles and difficulties would be blamed on Roebuck members individually or the Roebuck as a whole and lurid tales would be spread to everybody who would listen about how they were the innocent victims of Roebuck cruelty and torture. One such member called me, hysterically accusing us of doing rituals to try to influence her and demanding that we stop. Of course, nobody was doing any such rituals, for the simple reason that, by that time, everybody was so tired of her manipulation games that they wanted as little to do with her as possible.

These untrue accusations were rendered all the more painful by the fact that this person had once been a beloved brother or sister and that we had done all we could to try to resolve the situation in a fair and equitable manner. Perhaps we had not succeeded. We were, after all, human. Few of us had any kind of professional training to deal with this kind of problem. We were angry and deeply hurt, particularly when we were accused of doing things that we not only hadn't done, but had, in some cases, bent over backwards to avoid doing. Maybe we weren't perfect, but we had never offered perfection to anyone at initiation. It was bad enough when someone we loved left the circle blaming us for their problems but to have a such a person resort to deliberate lies in a desperate attempt to justify their actions made a bad situation worse.

The group mind would bleed for a time after every one of these incidents. Watching one of your own go off the deep end is made even more tragic by the fact that it could have so easily been you and every time it happened we were all sobered by how close to the edge of the abyss each one of us were. Little problems would be blown out of proportion. We began to watch each other closely for signs, wondering who would be next. Every complaint or angry word caused a ripple of panic through the group. Is this person just venting their anger or frustration or are they going to run off and accuse us of killing their cat? However, after the pain wore off and nobody else broke, the group would go through a period of reaffirmation, reassuring each other in a variety of ways that we all were still dedicated to the path of wisdom and that nobody else was going to betray the others and we emerged stronger and more bonded than before.

As time went on, new initiates found it more and more difficult to find their place in the group. Every new candidate was examined like a bug on a plate. Small inconsistencies or peccadilloes were questioned closely. Did they mean that this person was going to crack, go away and spread more lies, or did this person really have what it takes to face their problems and work through them? And if we went ahead and initiated them anyway, which we nearly always did, we watched them guardedly for the next few years to see if they could stand up to the increasing pressure.

Some new initiates complained bitterly about the "ruling clique" which seemed to be passing judgment on them. They felt, and often justifiably so, that they had to try even harder to earn the trust of the more senior members of the group after they were initiated than previous members had. This was unfortunately true. The more senior the member, the more betrayals he or she had endured and the more suspicious of newcomers he or she had become. The "ruling clique," if such there was, consisted of the dozen or so people who had proven themselves to each other over many years as being willing to stay with the program rather than 'wimping' out. There was trust that had built up between them and, despite the frequent squabbles, a respect for each other that came with watching each other stick with it despite some very strong temptations to do otherwise.

However, it was also true that the newcomers who complained the most about the "ruling clique" were the ones who had come into the group expecting to be able to assume some measure of power and influence within the group and were miffed when it wasn't handed to them along with their deer tag. Many of these people had degrees or rank in other groups and were understandably annoyed when that rank was only not acknowledged but often scoffed at as inconsequential. They learned the hard way that in a single initiatory system, rank is earned by hard work and ability, not conferred by a ceremony.

All of the members of the Roebuck, past and present, have been very strong minded and opinionated people with very definite and passionately held ideas about what should and should not be done. And all were capable of the desire to impose their own particular viewpoint or agenda upon the others. It was only when the others would gang up on him or her, that such ego trips would be squelched. If someone who has earned your trust and respect over years in the magical trenches tells you that you're out of line, you tend to accept it more easily than you would if some untried newcomer (who more than likely has an agenda of his or her own) tells you the same thing - even if they're right.

Eventually, the Roebuck began to attract another kind of member - the power seekers. With our circles whomping up tremendous energy, our rituals producing results, and our numbers growing, there were those who sought to harness that power for their own purposes. There were several over about a seven year period. Some were more obvious than others. But all of them had the same modus operandi. They were all highly intelligent, talented people. They came into the Roebuck proclaiming it to be what they had been seeking all their lives, the pot of gold at the end of the rainbow. We were the ones who really had the power, the rest of the community were all wimps and wannabes. We were it, we were the chosen ones of the Gods.

However, as soon as they were initiated, their enthusiasm turned into harsh criticism of the way people were doing things. Everything was being done wrong and if we would only listen to them, everything would be all right. It didn't take long to see what was happening. Each of these people had a hidden agenda, some way in which they wanted to influence the world. And instead of doing the difficult work to do it themselves, they sought to harness the power of the Roebuck into doing it for them. We would do all the work and they would tell us what to do and what to do it for.

Needless to say, this wasn't tolerated by the group for very long, so these folks would eventually leave as well. But when they did, the lies that were spread about us were different in tone. Instead of claiming to be helpless victims of our horridness, they spread the lies about illegal and dangerous practices. We have been accused over the years of 1) supplying guns to people involved in civil disobedience, 2) ritually killing someone's cat and leaving it in the owners garage with a paper facsimile of our logo around its neck, 3) sacrificing animals and burying them in our backyard, 4) breaking and entering someone's house as well as personal assault and 5) using guns in our rituals.

Not only were we dreadful to them, we were dangerous people in general and must be eliminated for the good of the community. In short, if we refused to listen to them and let them tell us the "right" way to do things, we were a danger and must be destroyed. And the lies, some of which approached legal slander, justified the fact that they wanted to get rid of us because we wouldn't serve their purposes.

The bitter irony of these situations was that these people tended to blend in with us very easily, at least at first. They were, like us, strong-minded, opinionated, psychic, talented, temperamental people who were bored and fed up with the airy-fairy, sweetness and light groups in the community and wanted magic with a little more tooth to it - gosh, our kind of folks. Welcome, brother/sister. You've come home.

As difficult as it was for us to admit, these people served a very important purpose. They presented to the group mind a personification of its Shadow. They came into the group not to devote themselves to the Black Goddess of Wisdom but with the express purpose of promoting their own agenda – often with the very best of intentions. They sincerely wanted to use the power for what they considered 'good.' However, their definition of 'good' tended to be what pleased them, rather than what helped anybody else.

One classic example of this was a woman who entered the group with many years of magical experience to the point of having even run her own group in the past. She took initiation during a time of severe drought in Southern California when the hillsides were tinder-dry and the authorities were rationing water. Not being a California native, she was concerned about this state of affairs and proposed doing a series of rituals for the purpose of making it rain.

After a couple of these rituals, the rain stubbornly refused to arrive. She demanded that we 'let out all the stops' and do a complicated outdoor ritual demanding that the rain fall. We refused, saying that we had made our polite request to the ancient powers and if they chose not to grant it, there must be a reason.

We also pointed out to her that this was Southern California, not New England. The climate was semi-arid desert, subject to a natural cycle of droughts and floods. The native plants that grew here were adapted to the climate and knew how to survive through the dry periods. If the people who came here from other places wanted green lawns in August, they were just out of luck. We figured that Mother Nature had things well in hand and didn't need us to tell Her what to do.

The woman threw a fit. Calling us heartless and cruel, she stormed out of the house and never returned. Obviously, she had wanted us to support her plans for saving Southern California from the drought without stopping to think just who needed saving and why. She was distressed at the sight of dead and brown vegetation and wanted us to do something about it even if it meant messing with the delicate balance of nature.

Our refusal to support such a plan was bad enough. But our presumption at questioning of whether or not that cause really existed or was just a manifestation of her own personal insecurities or guilt, was intolerable. After all, magical power was a gift from the Gods. It should be used to do good for people. To withhold that power - which could do so much good if 'properly' used - was selfish beyond belief. It never seemed to occur to her that using that power to "fix" something that didn't suit her personal sensibilities was equally selfish.

The Two-Edged Sword

In any discussion of magic and ritual, the topic of "black magic" and "cursing" always comes up. To many Wiccans, any powerful ritual is assumed to be *de facto* a baneful one, particularly if it involves the darker aspects of the god and/or Goddess or employs swords, daggers or other weaponry of some kind. After all, magic is for healing, loving, nurturing and making things grow. Why would one invoke a fierce Goddess such as the Morrigan, mark the circle widdershins or use a dagger to draw one's own blood in a ritual unless one was up to no good?

Why, indeed? There are many reasons, legitimate and unselfish ones, for invoking the darker aspects of both the god and Goddess. Knowledge is one. After all, nature herself isn't always as she is depicted in a Disney cartoon. Hungry predators abound, just looking for an opportunity to attack. The unwary fawn who munches pretty flowers and dances in a meadow while the lion prowls nearby becomes lunch. But a stalwart buck standing guard at the edge of the meadow with a dozen sharp tines on his antlers can impale a careless lion and hurl it several feet into the brush.

The sad fact is there are predators in the human realm too, who would like nothing better than to feed on the unwary in a variety of destructive ways. Knowing how to defend oneself, both physically and psychically, against those who wish one harm is a legitimate reason to invoke dark powers. There is no virtue in being a victim. And wearing psychic rose colored glasses and living in constant denial that there are truly bad things and people out there is a real good way to become one.

So, when is it justifiable to defend oneself magically? When all other physical attempts at defense fail, is one instance. In our early days, we performed a binding ritual on a young man who had preyed upon women in the science fiction community for some years. His modus operandi was always the same. He would play upon a woman's maternal instincts by presenting himself as a sad, lonely, needy man. Once she took him in, he would wheedle money from her. Then, he would coerce her into having sex with him. Eventually, he would bleed her dry and find himself another victim until he had exhausted the available supply. Then, he would move on to another city and do the same thing.

He had made the mistake of choosing as victim, one of our members. All of our advice to her to get rid of him before it was too late fell upon deaf ears. Her roommate, also a member, decided to take matters in her own hands and show the fellow out the door. He resorted to violence, beating her up with a strength one would have hardly given him credit for. She tried to call the police, and was told it was a domestic dispute and since the victim herself wouldn't take action there was nothing they could do. She filed for a restraining order, but he ignored it and visited his victim when the roommate wasn't there. Finally there seemed to be no way she could free her friend from this Shadow or stop him from preying on others.

On the night of a dark moon, she made a doll or poppet in his image and brought it to us. We named it with this fellow's name and bound it tightly, hands, feet and loins, with a silken cord. We declared that his power over women was broken. He wouldn't be able to attract any more victims. As long as he behaved himself, he would remain unharmed. But if he tried to seduce another woman he would be seen through, caught out and punished. We buried the poppet in a remote place and awaited developments.

They weren't long in coming. Our member, who was his present victim, suddenly woke up and refused to see him anymore. From all reports, he went back to the science fiction club and tried to get another victim but everybody seemed wise to him and nobody, male or female, would have anything to do with him. Months went by. Eventually, he was caught pilfering something from the club's archives. Charges were filed and he left town in a very big hurry, to go we know not where. But that poppet is still buried where we left it.

From this experience, we learned a very serious lesson. No ritual of this type, even if justifiable from an ethical and moral perspective, is performed free from karmic repercussions. We paid dearly for doing it. Not only were we all exhausted afterwards for some days running, we also lost both the members involved soon after that under very painful circumstances. We had accomplished our purpose, but we were hardly rewarded for our pains. A price must be paid for every ritual one does. One must consider whether the result is worth the price demanded. In this case, it was. It isn't always that way.

Another need for protection came nearly fifteen years later. Someone who had nursed a vendetta against us for political reasons had begun to post messages on the Internet and various bulletin boards, falsely accusing us of, among other things, supplying weapons to people involved in civil disturbances. Since this occurred a couple of years after the 1992 Los Angeles riots, this charge was particularly nasty. Anonymous letters were also being sent to various members of the Pagan community, some containing falsified documents attributed to us, warning them of our violent proclivities. It was clear that his intention was to arouse the interest of the authorities and get us investigated for a survivalist, gun-crazed cult.

There was nothing legally we could do. We knew who the person was. The sysop of one of the bulletin boards he posted on was a student of ours and looked up his pseudonym in the files. But even armed with that, we couldn't do much. The posts were worded so as to make it seem as though the writer was only reporting rumor, not fact, therefore making the posts not subject to libel laws. And there was no way of tracing the anonymous letters and falsified documents to the same person.

Still, the danger of being investigated by the police was very real indeed. And since we were innocent of all the accusations, we felt we were justified in performing a protection circle in order to ward off any further anonymous attacks. Still, all we had was one man's word as to the identity of the attacker. Was that enough to warrant a counter attack? And was the person acting alone? Were there others we didn't know about? Would we disable one attacker only to be broadsided by another?

We decided on a two-fold course of action. The first was a protection ritual which was designed to deflect any other attacks from any person, known or unknown. Everyone in the group got themselves a small hand-mirror and we convened in the temple. We declared our intentions and called upon our circle guardians for aid. Finally, we huddled together as a herd does when under attack by a predator and, at a prearranged signal, turned around facing the walls with our backs to each other and held up the mirrors. We visualized anything being sent to us of a harmful nature being reflected back to the sender, just as the light was reflected by the silvered surface of the mirrors.

The next step was more complex. Somehow, we had to find out the identity of the other person or persons involved. Again, there would be nothing we could have done legally or physically, but just knowing who else was responsible would be useful as a defense. For this, we employed a powerful ritual that John had taught us in which the Otherworld Hounds are summoned and sent to flush out the person, just as a pack of dogs will flush out a deer, flock of birds or other game. This was done. Every member of the circle reported seeing their huge, white, red-eared forms and/or hearing their terrible baying.

However, the price we paid for that knowledge was dear, indeed. The immediate cost in terms of human exhaustion was bad enough. One member had to be carried half conscious from the circle. The rest of the members suffered from lack of energy, nightmares, and other physical symptoms of various kinds. And, when the hounds began to return with their quarry, the cost was even greater. There were several people responsible for the attacks. Not only that, one of our very own members had been supplying all of them with stories, incidents, documents and other inside information to be used against us as retaliation for not expelling another member against whom he had a personal grudge.

The ways in which these people were revealed is worth noting, however. The information came to us by physical, rather than psychic means. We received a number of letters, phone calls and, in one case, a personal visit from people who had been sent the questionable documents, who came right out and said "so-and-so sent us this material. Are you responsible for it?" From this, we were able to determine where the documents were coming from, diffuse much of the damage done by pointing out where the documents had been falsified and accusing the perpetrators in public. While this didn't lessen the pain of knowing that one of our own betrayed us, it did allow us to guard against further incidents. Eventually, the attacks ceased and we were bothered no further.

Many Witches say that there is no such thing as white magic or black magic. There is only gray magic, or magic that can be either white or black depending on how it's being used. This is true as far as it goes. The problem lies in the assumption that there is a different kind of magic for every intention – one for 'black,' another for 'white' and still another for 'grey.' We mustn't do 'black' magic. We mustn't try to coerce anyone against their will or wish harm to them, no matter what they might have done or might be planning on doing to us. If we do magic at all, it must be the 'white' variety which works for love, harmony and healing or at the very least the 'gray' variety in which the intent is often intentionally vague.

Many well-meaning practitioners attach something called the Karmic clause to a spell or magical working. After they declare their intent, they add: "this or something better for the highest good of all concerned." The argument for this dubious addendum is that we mustn't limit the power of the universe to give us what we really need. If we think we require a hundred dollars to get us out of a temporary financial mess, we might do a spell for a hundred dollars and get a hundred dollars. No more, no less.

Every Witch I know has done this kind of spell at least once and it's truly amazing how exact the amount we receive turns out to be. I once did a spell for money to pay an overdue telephone bill so that we wouldn't get our phone shut off. Two days later, the money arrived in the form of an unexpected rebate check in the amount, almost to the penny, of the bill. We cashed the check, paid the phone bill and had about enough left over to pay for the stamp.

However, as the argument goes, if the universe is endless, why should we limit ourselves to a hundred dollars? Maybe the Great Banker in the Sky has a thousand dollars he'd like to give us, or ten thousand, or a million. But since we only asked for a hundred, that's all he's going to send us. So, we tell him to send us as much as he is willing to send us. In fact, we don't really know what we need so we say "send us what you think we need without taking it away from anybody else. On second thought, just send everybody involved everything they need and disregard the original request."

This sounds good, but is actually a moral cop-out. If we do a spell for a specific thing, we want that particular thing, not 'something better for the highest good of all concerned.' If we don't, why bother doing the spell? And if what we want isn't for the highest good of all concerned, should the Gods deny us our request like cosmic parents or should they just let us have it - along with the unpleasant karmic consequences – to teach us a lesson?

Another statement of magical ethics asserts that whatever magical energy a practitioner sends out returns to him or her threefold. There is far more to this concept than just 'what goes around, comes around.' A magical practitioner, who presumably has more knowledge and skill than the average person, should be held more accountable for his or her actions. And a magical action, performed with intent, carries far more of a punch than an ordinary action performed in the heat of the moment. However, this statement also can encourage us to think that if we only do 'white' magic for a 'good' purpose, then only good energy will return to us threefold.

This attitude underscores a prevailing ambiguity about magic. We want our spells to work so that we get what ask for, but we don't want any unpleasant consequences resulting from them. This ambiguity is best expressed by the popular interpretation of something called the Witches Rede. The Rede consists of a long poem, written in <u>faux</u> medieval language, which presumes to outline Witch ethics in excruciating detail. However, most modern Craft people know it by its shortened form 'An it harm none, do what ye wilt.'

This statement is actually a paraphrase of Aleister Crowley who wrote in the Book of the Law: 'Do what thou wilt shall be the whole of the law.' A number of well meaning Gardnerians in the fifties and sixties decided that particular sentiment wasn't very nice. After all, one mustn't do what one wants if it could hurt somebody else. 'Real' Witches (not those described in Christian propaganda) do 'white' magic for healing and prosperity, not 'black' magic for cursing and blasting. After all, the Charge of the Goddess states: "all acts of love and pleasure are my rituals." So, the Goddess says that it's okay to do whatever we want to so long as it doesn't hurt anybody. Hence the 'an it harm none,' clause tacked in front of Crowley's dictum.

Justifiable arguments aside as to what constitutes 'harm,' the Rede is often trotted out to the press and the public to indicate that 'real' Witches are harmless and therefore shouldn't be persecuted by the authorities. However, if Witches are harmless, then they are also powerless. In the real world, magical power is a natural force, like electricity or nuclear energy - neither good nor bad in and of itself, but capable of both, often at the same time.

The power to do good is always the exact same power as the power to do evil. A sharp scalpel in the hand of a skilled surgeon is capable of either excising a life-threatening cancer, or slicing an artery and killing the patient. A dull scalpel will do no harm but neither will it do any good. A medicine that isn't capable of poisoning the patient in the wrong dosage is also not capable of alleviating the painful symptoms of disease in the proper dose. In both cases, knowledge, skill, and intent are what determines whether the outcome is good or bad - not the agent employed. And, sadly, just because someone is a trained physician doesn't mean that he or she will automatically use that knowledge and skill to cure rather than kill.

There is no way around this dilemma. If we employ magical power to get something we want, we must face the consequences of that choice. Even if we are convinced that our magic will serve a benevolent purpose, there is no free lunch. We will have to pay some kind of price for our action. If we don't want to pay that price, we can do a nice ritual to ask the Gods to give us whatever it is they think we need. We can even tack on the Karmic Clause if it makes us feel better. However, that's not a spell, that's a prayer – and now we are in the realm of religion rather than magic.

Religion nearly always assumes that the Gods (whatever their names) are more powerful than we and are capable of giving us things we can't get for ourselves – or withholding them from us if we don't behave ourselves. Magic, by contrast, is the process of employing the aid of natural forces to make changes in our world according to our will. The aid of the Gods is helpful and often vital to give us information and inspiration to keep our will on track. However, ultimately we are the ones who decide what needs to be done, we do it and we take the responsibility for whatever happens.

Very few Witches set about to do evil with their power. In fact, more damage is done by Witches thinking they are doing 'good' magic than by those who deliberately do bad 'black' magic. The problem lies in our interpretation of what good magic consists of. Too often, it means 'what is comfortable for me' rather than what may actually be beneficial to anyone else in the long run. Many practitioners think they're doing good for others when the real intent - often unknown even to themselves - is to make themselves feel as though they've done good magic and are therefore guaranteed of having good karma return to them threefold.

Consequently, there is no such thing as black magic, white magic or even gray magic. There is magic. Period. There are harmless Witches who perform entertaining rituals. This is fine if 'all acts of love and pleasure' are the only rituals you're interested in. But if you want rituals with more tooth to it, you have to shoulder the responsibility of doing it according to your will, taking the consequences whatever they are, and not foisting the karmic rap off onto the Gods. If we wish to have power to do good in this world, we must also grapple with the temptation to use it for evil. We must take responsibility not only for the power we have, but for our own tendency to want to use it for our own ends, rather than those of the Gods.

Robert Cochrane also had a 'Rede' of magical ethics. "Do not do what you want," he wrote to Joe. "Do what is necessary." This no-nonsense dictum views the world not as a nursery school administered by all-powerful but benevolent Gods but as a jungle – a place where doing 'what thou wilt' may mean the difference between surviving and perishing. In the natural world, animals must often fight for what they need to survive and flourish as individuals and as a group. It isn't much different in the unnatural world of humans. Sometimes we also must fight to survive – on both physical and psychic levels. And if that means giving a predator a harmful kick in the astral, then so be it.

Death, Transformation and Rebirth

It is the nature of living things to grow, spawn and die, and the Roebuck was no exception. As a living thing that took on a life of its own, the group matured to the point where a stable core group of about a dozen people kept the center together while new blood came and went, leaving their mark before they vanished entirely.

As the group mind grew in strength, however, so did the Shadow. It eventually drew into its darkness, several people at one time, rather than just one random person, forming a sort of negative group mind of its own. Eventually, instead of one person seeking to turn the power of the group to serve an individual power agenda, several people, each with their own individual agendas, worked together to destroy that which they could not control.

It must be made very clear at this point that this process of working together was not a conscious conspiracy of people meeting in secret to plot and scheme in a coordinated fashion. The fact is that the people under discussion didn't much care for each other, and had nothing good to say about each other at least within earshot of the rest of the group.

They all were, in effect, rivals as well as allies in their desire to control the group and splinter it apart when their attempts failed. But their methods of doing so, as well as their individual motives, were identical in each case. And so, each contributed his or her part to the function of the shadow mind and so worked in cooperation with it.

The modus operandi has been described in detail in a previous section. Briefly, each of these people came into the group as savvy students. All had initiations and degrees in other magical groups. All were well read and experienced and, most significantly, all came into the Roebuck declaring that they had found their spiritual home.

It wasn't long, however, before the complaints to us began, primarily about the actions of certain senior members of the group. This was a departure from the previous pattern. It wasn't just the other rank-and-file members that were the subject of their criticism, but those members who had official titles and functions, such as the Summoner, the councilor or the Man-in-Black. Also, the nature of the criticism wasn't of a personal nature (he/she was mean to me, I don't like him/her) but a complaint that such people had certain personal problems that rendered them, in the complainant's opinion, incapable of doing their job properly. The insinuation was blatant in some cases and more subtle in others: 'remove this person from the position of authority and substitute me. I am more worthy than they are. I will do a better job.'

When these complaints failed to obtain the desired results, the problems began. One person continued to level stronger and stronger accusations. When challenged to confront the accused member in open council, he left rather than do so. Another person went one step further. When we refused to remove the offending party from his position, she went to every senior couple in the group to get them to hive off and begin their own group with her as their guiding light. The arguments she gave each couple were identical in all cases. In essence, it was: Dave and Ann don't have 'it' anymore, they have fallen from the grace of the Gods because they put up with incompetent people like X. But you have what it takes to be the great and powerful group that the Roebuck could be but isn't. All you have to do is do it my way.'

So blatant was this ploy, this person actually came to us to inform us that one particular couple wanted to hive off but didn't want to hurt our feelings. We went to the couple in question to offer our support, our continued good will and any further training or information that might be useful in their endeavors. We were greeted with incredulous looks. Gradually, the machinations came to light as couple after couple refused the person's offer. Eventually, she herself left the group in a huff.

Retaliation soon followed. Several documents (diaries, memoirs and private correspondence) written by high ranking members of the group intended for use only within the Roebuck suddenly appeared in public forums - anonymously mass mailed to members of the community and posted on various computer bulletin boards. The documents in question were not only expressly chosen to provide as much negative exposure as possible, but in two separate cases were actually altered in order to provoke possible lawsuits.

A great deal of self-restraint on everyone's part was needed to quell the firestorm that resulted. It took a staunch refusal to comment on the documents save in private correspondence, the willingness to provide copies of the genuine documents with apologies and retractions for inaccuracies to those people with legitimate cause for grievance, and the firm threat of legal action against those who continued to distribute the altered documents and/or commentary thereon, in public.

This course of action, difficult as it was, proved to be the correct one. It wasn't long before certain other coincidences occurred that resulted in the exposure of those people responsible for the distribution of the documents along with their self-serving motives. Those people who didn't like us and were determined to discredit us were silenced, we were, for the most part, vindicated in the eyes of those who didn't know us and who were wondering what the flap was all about. Eventually, the entire mess blew over with none of the threatened legal actions materializing.

Several things resulted from this brief, but intense situation. On the positive side, the entire Roebuck, even those not responsible for producing the problem documents, stood together against the outside forces bent on the group's destruction. Those who could only keep silent did so. Those who could obtain information, or offer written support also did so. Others engaged in damage control, serving as emissaries and go-betweens in order to mend the fences that could be mended. All members realized that the attack was against the group as a whole, not just the individuals who wrote the objectionable material and many interpersonal rivalries that had plagued the group were set aside or got resolved altogether.

On the negative side, however, the group assumed a kind of siege mentality with an us-against-the-world kind of cohesion that only contributed to the notorious Roebuck snobbishness and arrogance. We became extremely insular, suspicious and critical of outsiders, and protective of our traditions and secrets. We began working on a more intense level and were even more critical and demanding of our students.

But our numbers swelled all the same. Prospective students lined up with classes numbering as many as fifteen at a time. Of course, most of these dropped out. But that only seemed to increase the determination of the survivors to continue with the training. The more secretive the group became, the more prestigious it was to obtain initiation from it. Everybody wanted to count themselves among the few, the proud, the Roebuck.

It wasn't long before we outgrew the temple. Inquisitions and initiations were packed. Even our outdoor sites proved to be too small to fit everyone in. We made serious attempts to find larger places for circle, but failed for the most part. Halls were expensive to rent and didn't provide the convenience, security, privacy and atmosphere (both psychic and aesthetic) to be able to perform the kinds of high-powered rituals that all the initiates wanted.

As we approached thirty people, the group began to show signs of fragmentation. Newer initiates resented more senior members who considered them upstarts. Slumbering interpersonal rivalries and squabbles erupted again. Other ones formed when new initiates tried to find their place in an increasingly crowded pecking order. Being 'of a mind' was becoming more and more difficult to achieve with the increasing number of minds to bring into alignment. The Roebuck had reached its limits of growth.

The Roebuck had reached a decision point in its history. We could either remain one huge group and assume a more lodge-like structure, or we could break apart into several pieces, with enough experienced initiates within each piece to allow them to continue to function. A lodge structure would have been undesirable for a variety of reasons. For one thing, the numbers of people would have necessitated an increase in centralized authority, discipline and structure. People would have to toe the line more closely in order to prevent chaos. Procedures would have to be codified and adhered to more closely, rituals would have had to be more rigid and we would have to become far more autocratic than was comfortable.

We opted instead to encourage the Roebuck to break apart into daughter groups. Due to intense financial and health pressures, Dave and I were unable to continue to hold Roebuck rituals at the house. Unless someone could come up with another reliable venue, pay for it and perform all the necessary administrative tasks that go with it, the Roebuck full moons, dark moons and training circles would cease. If members wanted to be able to attend a Roebuck full moon, they would have to host it themselves. If they had students they wanted trained, they would have to do it themselves. If they had a dark moon experiment they wanted to do, they would have to perform it themselves.

Some initiates enthusiastically stepped up to the plate and formed their own groups. Others were unsure. In giving our initiates the opportunity to run their own circles, we enabled them to discover just how much hard work it was. Not only did they have to host a circle, they had to clean up before and after the ritual, keep track of a schedule, see to it that all the equipment was in order and deal with any squabbles or disagreements between members - not to mention holding the ritual on the appointed day whether or not they felt like it or had something else they wanted to do that evening. Consequently, as long as they were treated fairly and equitably with a say in how the group was run and were able to do their own thing on the side when they wanted to, the vast majority of the Roebuck initiates simply didn't want to leave the mother group.

In seeking to avoid the abuses that had plagued us in our early days, Dave and I might possibly have done the job a little too well. We had noticed that the vast majority of groups split off from the parent group by the unpleasant process of schism. A rift would develop within a group, usually between the leaders and another equally qualified member of the group, usually over an autocratic attitude, or policies and practices which the problem member thought intolerable. The instigating member would then leave, taking a number of experienced people with him or her, and the group would split into two.

When the Roebuck was founded, we decided that this was an extremely unsatisfactory way of increasing the number of working covens. In the first place, the conflict between the leaders and the disaffected members usually began months or years before the actual split, making circle work unpleasant and counterproductive. When the split actually happened, it caused considerable emotional trauma for the individual members who are often expected to choose sides in the squabble. Even after the split happens, the parties involved continue to harbor animosities and carry on feuds, thus negating the benefits from having a "sister" or "daughter" coven which carry on a particular tradition.

Consequently, it had always been Roebuck policy to foster as many independent circles within the group as possible. Initiates are not only trained but required to run circles on their own. If an initiate or group of initiates wish to do a circle that doesn't involve the rest of the group, they are encouraged to do so. Hiving off is not seen as a betrayal or desertion but an expected result of years of training and practice. If an individual or small group of initiates wished to hive off and form their own group, they were given a charter, all the training material they needed and our blessing to go forth and do.

Human nature being what it is, this policy sometimes backfired. Disgruntled members who threatened to leave the group if they didn't get their way were extremely put out when we offered them a charter and showed them the door, rather than comply with their wishes and beg them to stay. Furthermore, even if the disgruntled member left the group, he or she could not get anyone to go with them - becoming, essentially, a schism coven of one.

However, despite our efforts to make it as easy as possible, this fragmentation process proved to be painful. As much as the initiates wanted to do their own thing, they still wanted to be able to circle together and enjoy the kind of intimacy they enjoyed when they were all one group. They also felt unsure of themselves, particularly in the face of increasing responsibility and hard work of training and initiating students. For the first time, they found themselves in the position of being forced to be the 'bad guy' in their own groups and face the heat for it. But instead of coming back to the mother group when things didn't work out, they bravely chose to continue to work through it themselves - a growth process as painful as it was inevitable.

Dave and I found ourselves having to completely redefine our role and determine how we were going to interact with the daughter covens. We knew, for example, that none of the daughter groups would function as Roebuck clones. But, how far could a group deviate from the mother group and still be considered part of the tradition? We decided that if a daughter group kept Goda and Tubal Cain in the center, kept the Roebuck quarter attributes, and adhered to the basic group structure, they could experiment all they pleased with making their group their own.

We were also painfully aware that the daughter groups could possibly include practices and rituals that we didn't approve of. Many of the initiates, even the old timers, considered us stuffy and conservative. They wanted to experiment with some of the more sensational practices they had learned in other groups and simply couldn't understand why we refused to allow such practices in the Roebuck. We realized that these initiates, for the most part, had not suffered through the abuses from other groups that we had in the early days. They did not believe us when we warned them that these practices won't produce the desired results, and indeed, were counterproductive. So, sadly, we made the painful decision to stand back and allow daughter groups to experiment with these practices and refrain from saying 'I told you so' when the inevitable blow-up occurred. Only in cases of illegal or dangerous practices would we intervene.

Another decision we made was to respect each daughter group's coven autonomy. We would attend their rituals only when invited, and not presume to sit in on their training, inquisitions or initiations unless specifically asked. Some daughter groups wanted us to be present during their major rituals and some did not. However, if they did not want us at a particular working, no matter the reason, we would respect their wishes. They could train and initiate whomever they wanted to, without our interference, with the stipulation that they be fully responsible for cleaning up their mess if they made a mistake.

The mother coven, however, went underground, like a creek in the summertime, invisible on the surface but still keeping to its same channel. If the Roebuck was a tree, with Clan at the root and the daughter covens as the branches, it was important for the trunk of the tree to continue to survive to convey the power contained in the root to the branches. Unknown to many of the members, the Roebuck continued to serve that function. Rituals were infrequent, specialized and involved only a few initiates who had made the decision to continue to serve the mother group exclusively rather than strike out on their own.

As the preparation period drew to an end, the Roebuck, complete with root, trunk and branches, remained standing strong and proud. Many individual members dropped away. Some were missed, others were not. All were tested to see if they truly served the Gods or only themselves and all were required to 'put up or shut up.' This testing manifested itself in the most real of real worlds - financial and personal. Many members, Dave and me included, had to undergo job loss and the restructuring of finances. Other initiates had to come to terms with marital problems, financial problems and other real world issues. The test was to see if each initiate could apply what they had learned in circle to their mundane affairs.

Those who could would be around to fulfill the Roebuck's ultimate destiny. Those who could not do so would fall away.

Then, after nearly twelve years, our apprenticeship with John came to an end. When we first began working with John, he had spent the fifteen years after Cochrane's death in retirement, working and raising his family. After the publication of his first book, Witchcraft: A Tradition Renewed, John formed his own group which took a different direction from that in which we found ourselves headed. Our letters had been more and more infrequent as our magical paths diverged.

Finally, after the publication of Sacred Masks, Sacred Dance, it became clear that we had evolved in two completely different branches of the root tradition and we mutually agreed that we were better off separate - magically as well as physically. Although we still remained a part of the Clan of Tubal Cain, it was very clear that, for better or worse, it was up to us determine the fate of the Roebuck and our branch of the Clan with no more reliance from anyone on this plane. It was frightening, but inevitable. We were on our own.

"To describe the Faith is like teaching," Robert Cochrane wrote to Joe Wilson back in 1966. "But if you teach then eventually the pupil must turn on the teacher, since wisdom is only found in freedom, and teacher and pupil alike are not truly free, since the teacher is bound by dogma in order to explain - and therefore forgoes inspiration ... The pupil has to follow the dogma in order to understand the teacher. Wisdom is not dogmatic - and when the pupil becomes Wise, he must necessarily break from the teacher and interpret dogma and the promptings of his own soul as he sees fit. Therefore I explain to you what I know - but I am not teaching you, you are taking from it what you require - and transmuting these ideas to your own needs."

At twenty-one years since it's founding, the Roebuck had finally come of age.

Ten years later, the Roebuck is still active: teaching, working and initiating students. We are still learning and our tradition continues to grow and develop. We have been in touch with former members of John's group and have acquired additional information that, in some cases, validates our tradition and in other cases, challenges it. Additional books on traditional Craft continue to be published and we have been gratified to learn that we weren't as 'far out' in our reconstruction as we had thought we were.

The Craft community has also changed considerably from what it was when the group began, and we have found much to our surprise that we have become mainstream rather than mavericks. We are also happy to see that many of the abuses that we observed in the early days are no longer quite so prevalent. With the increase in the availability of books as well as the profusion of material on the Internet, there is less of a dependence on authority and Holy Writ and more of a spirit of inquiry and experimentation.

As we have matured, so has our group. The people we have attracted over the past few years are older and have careers and families that serve to ground them firmly in the mundane world. This has caused our emphasis to shift from elaborately costumed rituals to quieter, more practical workings. And although we don't have the physical energy we once had to perform the more rigorous rituals, hopefully we have acquired an equal amount of psychic energy needed to perform equally rigorous rituals on the inner planes.

As we become elders, we have grown to appreciate more fully all the help, support and advice of the elders who mentored us in our early days. We know now what kind of effort it took for them to teach us, counsel us and put up with all our youthful impudence and know-it-all attitude. However, the most important thing they taught us is that you don't have to be perfect to run a successful group. We learned that being human is an asset, not a liability. And our early teachers taught us just as much with their faults and foibles as they did with their wisdom and knowledge.

Back when we were first studying with Ed, we would often drive to his house right after work to avoid being late for circle. Often, we would arrive as much as an hour early. There was one time, Ed had gotten home late from work and we ended up sitting uncomfortably on the couch with our feet up while Ed frantically vacuumed his carpet.

Fast-forward twenty years. We also had a couple of students who would show up an hour early for circle so as not to be late. One evening, they arrived while I was frantically vacuuming the carpet. As they sat on the couch with their feet up, I suddenly remembered the incident at Ed's house all those years ago. I also realized how tolerant and kind Ed had been. He didn't chase us out the front door with the nozzle of the vacuum cleaner and tell us to come back later, which is what I ended up doing.

And the circle turns. Students eventually become teachers and teach other students. The Craft itself develops and grows as its practitioners learn, research, experiment, stumble, fall and pick themselves up and try again. This is the greatest strength of our Craft. Everyone has a contribution to make, even if it's only to provide a sterling example of what not to do. Our fondest hope is that we will have as much of an influence, both positive and negative, on our students as our mentors did on us.

And that someday they will pass on the torch to those who come after them, just as we tried to do.

Roebuck 101

    The secret of the success of the Roebuck lies in its training. Without a systemized method of introducing would-be members to its world view and making sure that they are able to perform its basic magical techniques, the group could not function as a coherent whole. Therefore, the instructor is a vital link between the working coven and those who would enter and work with it. He or she is not so much a teacher as a guide who can steer the student into areas useful to understanding the work of the group and to prevent valuable time being lost in floundering around in areas that do not pertain to the work being done in the coven.

    The training first and foremost teaches the student the mindset necessary to function in a Roebuck ritual - the images, attitudes, beliefs and assumptions on the nature of magic which every initiate must share in order to be 'of a mind' in the circle. This mindset is what makes a ritual into a Roebuck ritual, not the words and gestures that are used in casting a circle, invoking the quarters, consecrating 'cakes and ale,' performing the libation, etc. These ritual gestures can and do vary with each initiate, depending upon their personality, previous training and other factors. Some initiates prefer grand, sweeping gestures and long, poetic invocations. Others are short, sweet and to the point. But as long as all initiates share the same mindset, they will be able to function together in a circle.

Admission Criteria

Applicants should be evaluated primarily on their sincerity and their desire to work and study. Those performing the initial interview should accentuate the disadvantages and hard work of apprenticeship and, if possible, try to talk the applicant out of joining. This may be extremely difficult in the case of an applicant that everyone happens to like, but it is necessary. Obviously, if an applicant allows himself or herself to be talked out of joining the group, then they shouldn't be there in the first place. Usually the applicant will have been in several Roebuck circles and will have experienced the energy and power that often manifests. It is important to emphasize that such power doesn't come cheaply. Most newcomers don't anticipate the hard work and training that goes into producing a ritual. Thus, they cannot be expected to understand the difficulties involved in terms of energy outlay beforehand, and recovery afterwards. Consequently, this needs to be pointed out to them.

However, each applicant must be considered as an individual and there are no hard and fast rules. True intuition and divine guidance need to be employed here. The Roebuck has traditionally required each student to be self-supporting, either employed or actively seeking employment. Exceptions can be granted on an individual basis for people in school, training programs or those who work at home. But it is important for each member to be independent and able to function in the mundane world. Not only does this insure that a member will not continually drain the group of financial and emotional resources, but it also provides a means of grounding from often intense ritual activity. A mundane job provides an incentive to learn how to close down psychic faculties when necessary, but also teaches the discipline of how to do what one must, whether one finds it pleasant or not. It is extremely doubtful that any person, no matter how psychic he or she happens to be, will be able to perform the rigorous discipline of magical work if he or she is unable to manage to feed, clothe and house himself or herself.

A certain level of emotional stability is also necessary. While we all have personal problems and emotional baggage, we must maintain, in the circle at any rate, a focus on the work at hand. A Roebuck ritual, although often personally enlightening, is not group therapy and the straightening out of personal hang-ups is engaged in only so far as it makes the individual member better able to perform the work at hand. All personal squabbles, domestic arguments and other emotional scenes must be dealt with before circle begins and all participants must refrain from any remarks of a personal nature in the circle itself.

No one will be allowed into the group, even as a visitor, who uses illegal substances. This is for security reasons as well as magical reasons. Those using legal substances such as alcohol or tobacco must follow certain guidelines. No one, student or initiate, will be allowed in the circle if they are obviously intoxicated and smokers must limit their smoking to before and after the ritual. No smoking will be allowed either in the temple or in the outdoor circle.

People can apply for the training program regardless of their marital status or sexual orientation. However, single people must learn to view all the members of the circle as brothers and sisters and not look upon the group merely as a pool of potential mates or lovers. If two single members of the circle decide to form a relationship, it is entirely their business and will not be interfered with unless such a relationship involves harm or distress to another member of the circle. Homosexual applicants can be admitted provided they agree that, whatever their sexual preferences, they perform the ritual functions appropriate to their physical gender and learn to work in partnership with a member of the opposite gender when the ritual calls for it.

The most difficult guideline to follow is to avoid evaluating an applicant on the basis of likeability. Many applicants enter surly and suspicious and blossom after a few months of training. Still other applicants enter cheerful and pleasant and leave in a rage months later. Members have no way of knowing what is going on within the soul of the applicant. Training has a way of bringing out repressed feelings both positive and negative. Granted, there will be occasions when an applicant has a personality so abrasive that working with him or her presents a problem. However, a coven is not a social club and one of the special disciplines of the group is being forced to accommodate differing personality types. Putting personality conflicts aside in order to perform a work higher than oneself is the true meaning of 'perfect love and perfect trust'. Those who are unable to do this and are unwilling to learn do not belong in the circle.

Training is normally accomplished in two phases. Phase One consists of a series of pathworkings and orientation rituals designed to introduce the student to the Roebuck worldview, guardians, methods of working, etc. This phase can be seen to be complete in itself. After performing the exercises presented in this first phase, the student will be able to participate in festival and full moon rituals more effectively. This phase may be presented to many students at the same time, as long as each student is given adequate opportunity to share their individual feelings, perceptions and have their questions answered.

It is in Phase Two that training for initiation is presented. A Roebuck initiate is considered a Priest or Priestess and must possess certain skills in order to function as such. In this phase, the student will learn to plan and conduct a ritual and learn how to contact and serve as oracle and channel for the circle guardians. Since this phase involves a great deal more individual attention, students must go through it one at a time. Each student must demonstrate not only proficiency in the various skills, but must also prove his or her dedication both to the group and to the tradition. Initiation is more than just a "graduation ceremony." It involves a process of psychic and emotional bonding with the other initiates. Therefore, it is up to the student to approach the initiates for aid and guidance so that his or her dedication is proven and the bonding given a chance to occur.

In the case of an applicant who has an initiation into another Craft tradition or compatible magical system, the year-long requirement need not necessarily apply. An initiate in another system who has demonstrated the required magical skills and who feels at home with the Roebuck way, might request adoption, a separate ritual in which the initiate is adopted into the Roebuck family, rather than re-initiated. The applicant should go through the first half of the training in order to become oriented into the Roebuck mindset. He or she should also perform a valid possession and go through a speiring. Other requirements can be waived at the discretion of the Initiates Council. In any case, the candidate can request the full initiation process despite any previous initiations if such is desired.

Should a student decide to drop out before the program is completed, then he or she is free to go with no hard feelings and may take whatever training they have received and put it to good use elsewhere. However, should the former student change his or her mind and wish to return, then the entire process must begin again with the interview, and the wait for the next training session. This needs to be done to encourage people to make their decision and see it through. A good rule of thumb is that if a student quits and rejoins three times, then quits again, the door is closed to them thereafter.

There are, of course, many reasons why a student may drop out of the program. People go through many changes at this time. However, if a student is unable to stick it out after the third time, then it is a good indication that he or she is really not suited to the group and that the Gods have been instrumental in ejecting the would-be student from the circle.

In the case of a student who is unable for some reason to complete the training, especially in the case of the possession ritual, some special considerations apply. If the student has shown good faith in attending the rest of the training, has conscientiously performed all the other requirements including the required reading, then he or she need not repeat the entire training before attempting the ritual again. However, he or she must wait at least a season between attempts. Such a student usually has some deep-seated emotional problem in which the conscious mind desires initiation, but the soul is not ready. There is nothing that can hurry this process. The student can either remain with the group and work through the problem or leave altogether. Which option is chosen should be determined on a case-by-case basis.

As with any human endeavor, the above guidelines can and will be changed and modified according to the growing needs of the group. However, any future guidelines must remain fair and equitable, while insuring the highest quality standards for membership. The work we do in the Roebuck is difficult and risky. We owe it to ourselves and future members to insure that our working companions maintain the highest caliber of knowledge and dedication possible.

Magical Mental Training

Magical training begins first and foremost in the mind - before a ritual tool is even picked up. Psychic 'ability' is primarily a process by which a person perceives (by any one of the five normal senses) things that are not included in everyday consensual reality. It is a perfectly normal process. Children are born being able to perceive things in the unseen realms and use vivid imaginations to construct thought forms for non-physical entities to inhabit. In short, all children are natural born magicians. However, since doing magic in our culture is not encouraged, most children give up magic in order to learn other skills more suitable to survival in their society.

Gradually, over the years, a person learns to perceive only what he is told to perceive and react only to things other people tell him are real. The magician, or shaman, knows that his brain, not his society, will tell him what is real and what is not if he will only pay attention to it. Therefore, the first magical tool a student must learn to use is his own brain, employing it for his own purposes rather than allowing it to be used by those around him for their purposes. This isn't as easy as it sounds.

The mammalian brain at its basic function (all philosophical discussion of the nature of consciousness aside) is a sensory feedback mechanism. Information about the world around us comes in from our basic five senses (sight, hearing, smell, touch and taste). This information gets processed for meaning. An instinctual emotional response is set up and action results. If the senses tell the animal there is food around, it becomes hungry and eats. If the senses reveal a willing mate, a feeling of sexual arousal is triggered and the animal has sex. If the senses indicate danger, fear is triggered and the animal flees. If the senses reveal the presence of an enemy, anger is triggered and the animal fights.

The human brain functions the same way at its basic level except for one major difference. In most people, there also occurs the response of awareness of incoming sensory stimulus. We are suddenly aware of something novel happening in our environment. We stop whatever else we're doing and pay attention to it. An internal dialog begins. We ask ourselves 'what is going on here?' We try to figure it out and choose a response. Is it food? If so, what kind? Do I like it? Have I tried it before? Was it yummy or yucky? Does it look good? Smell good? Will it have unpleasant consequences later (fattening, unhealthy, expensive)? Is eating permitted at this time? This place?

All these are learned responses. We are taught them by our parents or other authorities. Our stomachs may be growling like crazy in response to the food stimuli but we don't eat right away. We stand there and wonder if we should eat. This quality of 'should' is, as far as we know, distinctly human. It's an intermediate step between the emotional response to sensory stimulus and the action. It's popularly known as conscience or free will and it causes the vast majority of our problems on this physical realm.

This awareness of physical sensation and the emotional response it triggers causes other problems as well. If certain sensory input is lacking, we don't know what our action 'should' be. Uncertainty creeps in. Doubt. If we hear something that might indicate danger but we don't see anything, is it 'really' there? Should we act? And if we do, what if we're wrong? Will there be unpleasant consequences?

This reaction is a result of early childhood training. A child depends on his parent or caregiver to tell him how to interpret the sensations coming from the world around him. If he hears something under the bed that may be danger, he calls to his mother. Mother says there is nothing there. The child still hears something which triggers a fear response. Mother gets angry and insists there is nothing under the bed and the child must go back to sleep. The child now has a choice - deny his own sensory input and squelch the emotional response to it as best he can or risk his mother's wrath. After a few years, the child learns what he 'should' sense rather than what he actually senses. Eventually, as an adult, he comes to accept consensual reality as the model of his universe. He dare not do anything else.

It's a long slow process to reconstruct a model of the universe to include magic and the unseen realms. Most of the emotional upset that occurs when a student starts 'opening up' psychically results from beginning to sense things that he can't identify or doesn't know how he's 'supposed' to deal with. This is often the case when newcomers attend a powerful circle for the first time. Otherworld entities show up and manifest to the newcomer in some undeniable way, causing a fear reaction. Early childhood training (by this point largely unconscious) kicks in. The newcomer simply can't identify what he senses as belonging to the 'real' world. Therefore, it doesn't exist. He will insist there is nothing there even though the hair is prickling on his forearms, and his heart is pounding. So, the first thing a student must do is relearn to trust his or her own sensory input and accept a model of the world which includes things that most people deny exists.

The first thing that has to happen before the process can proceed any further is the person must give his consent to have his universe altered. This consent can be implied by the mere behavior of showing an interest in magic and attending training sessions. But after the initial novelty has worn off and a comfort threshold has been reached, a more formal consent needs to be given. A public commitment to the work needs to be made, usually in the form of a dedication or initiation ritual. By declaring his or her intention to study magic before one's peers, a student's pride, self-respect and integrity is put on the line. He can't slink out the back door and claim it was only a joke and he didn't really mean it.

After the initial consent has been given, the denizens of the unseen realms need to be introduced to the student and the appropriate behavior towards them is described. In some schools of magic, this introduction is accomplished by a description, either written or verbal, of who the various unseen entities involved with the particular tradition are – Gods, angels, elemental spirits, ancestors, master teachers or whoever. This method is rarely completely effective, since we are dealing with two different levels of the mind - the conscious awareness and the unconscious level of emotion. A description of a god or spirit may be accepted by the conscious intellect, but intellectual awareness alone does not enable the person to perceive the entity in question. The student knows what he 'should' perceive, but that knowledge remains an intellectual abstraction until the student actually perceives the entity and has an emotional reaction to it. Then, and only then, does the entity become 'real.'

What writers and lecturers often fail to take into account is that actual perception is always followed by emotion. We only react emotionally to things that are real to us, so the level of emotional response will indicate just how 'real' the perceived entity is. Often, that emotion is fear. If a student feels fear upon first perceiving an unseen entity, even when he's told the entity is benevolent, the reaction is sometimes worse than if the entity was not acknowledged at all. It's a little like a mother being embarrassed when her child cries and hides behind her skirts upon meeting a beloved relative for the first time. The child knows intellectually he's supposed to feel glad to see this person who he is told loves him, but he feels fear instead. This can only make the situation worse, since his fear is compounded by his mother's annoyance and his sibling's scorn.

It is far better to introduce a student to an unseen entity in a safe and controlled environment. This is accomplished by conducting the student on a guided meditation traditionally called a pathworking. In such a guided journey, the student is led into the entity's presence and allowed to get acquainted with that entity on his or her own, much as one might do with a physical person. If this is done gradually, along with others going through the same experience, much of the initial fear response can be reduced or eliminated altogether, giving the student a far more positive outlook in the process.

Pathworking is a term used by ceremonial magicians for a guided meditation that introduces a student to the various imagery associated with the paths linking the Sephira on the Cabalistic tree of life. This technique works on the principle that the human brain makes little distinction between input coming into the senses from the outside world and sensory input generated from the brain's own cognitive functioning when deciding what to respond to. The images evoked by a properly worded pathworking can produce the same physiological changes as the same experiences would, if experienced in the physical body. Consequently, if during a pathworking you were to be chased by a hungry lion, your heart rate would rise, your breathing increase, your muscles tense, just as if you were being physically chased by the lion, minus of course, the actual danger of being eaten. As far as the brain is concerned, the experience is actually happening.

The simulated experience of a pathworking can be just as emotionally intense as a physical one, provided all the sensory input that would accompany a physical interaction are included. If certain sensory elements are not included, the brain will not code the experience as 'real' and the emotional retraining will not occur as fast and as complete. Consequently, such a guided journey must include sensory cues from all five senses. Whenever we have experienced a physical sensation, the memory is carefully stored away for future reference, even if we are not conscious of it. We have all tasted salt spray, smelled a rose, heard a flute or a harp, or felt an animal's fur. These sensory memories can be called into awareness with the use of the appropriate suggestion. Thus, all the senses can be stimulated by calling up memories from the memory banks and the experience can seem so real that it will be reacted to by the emotions as though it were. This, of course, makes it real for all practical purposes.

If a student is introduced to a Goddess in a pathworking and not only sees her but hears, smells, tastes and feels her, then emotional familiarity will be established. The subject will "know" her as well as he would if he were introduced to a physical person. The experience will be such that the subject will also know how to react to her when next he meets her in a vision or other psychic experience. She will become part of his universe. The fact that she is not a physical person will not matter in the slightest.

So, in this fashion, all the Gods, Goddesses and unseen entities normally worked with in a circle can be introduced to the student, who will then know how to react to them. This not only derails a fear/anger reaction to the unknown, but will also add the possibility of unseen, but no less real, entities and experiences to the student's model of the 'real' world. When the student accepts one unseen element, it is far easier to accept others. Soon, his universe will include all manner of things that are 'real' but not 'physical' and he will be on his way to being able to do actual magical workings.

Invocation Techniques

The cornerstone of both magic and religion is the ability to call upon a variety of non-physical beings (God, Gods, angels, spirits or what have you), have them appear in some perceivable form and give some kind of advice or aid to the querant in answer to a request. This is where many 'cookbook' spells given in popular new-age books fall short. They prescribe a variety of ritual actions to be performed: candles to be burnt, jingles to be recited and so on in order to achieve a variety of personal desires. Many of these are valid, that is, they have been carefully researched as to color correspondences, and so forth. In fact, any action performed with intent constitutes a valid ritual. And the ritual actions might very well work, in the sense that they give the person doing them increased confidence and self assurance, along with positive suggestions that something "magical" is being done about the problem.

The difference between these 'cookbook' rituals and those rituals done within a magical circle is akin to the difference between a flashlight and a floor lamp. The flashlight works on batteries and the finite amount of energy they contain. They work very well until the battery is dead. The floor lamp, however, is plugged into the wall socket. It will continue to work until the bulb breaks. Another bulb can be installed and it will continue to work (unless the connection to the power plant breaks, which is yet another part of the metaphor). In other words, a group ritual within the confines of a magical circle will continue to raise energy after the individuals involved run out of 'juice.'

This plugging into the 'wall socket' of the group mind, rather than just running on individual batteries, involves the invocation of some kind of guardian spirits or deities who provide energy and focus for the group as a whole, rather than the individuals within it. Every magical group has them (even if they aren't specifically named) and they serve as guardians of the group mind. The more vivid they are, the more power the group mind has, since the group mind gives them their form. When they are invoked and brought into the ritual, the operation ceases to be personal and serves the purpose of the group, not the individual within in (although the group may be working on behalf of an individual)

During the process of training, all students are expected from the very first session to invoke the Gods and Goddesses at the quarters and in the center. This is done even before they experience the pathworkings to all of the guardians. There are no hard and fast rules for how this is done. The student faces the quarter, raises arms or athame in salute and calls upon the guardians of that quarter to come and join the circle. The words said are entirely up to the student, and the invocation can be as short, long, poetic or informal as the student wishes.

At the beginning of each Roebuck ritual, the quarter guardians are invoked to witness and lend their aid to whatever the purpose of the ritual may be. Some students wonder why the quarter guardians need to be invoked at all. After all, if the circle is the world between worlds, presumably the Gods are already there. Why do we have to call them into the circle? Well, we don't. Sensitive students might even perceive some divine foot-tapping during long-winded invocations as if to say "aren't you done yet?" We're here, already." And, so they are. But, we call them anyway for the benefit of everyone in the circle. Not only do we announce and acknowledge the fact that they are there but we remind everyone in the circle whether they think they need it or not, just who these beings are and why they are being called. The act of invoking reinforces the presence of the guardians for the student himself. Every time a student or initiate invokes a particular deity, the stronger that deity becomes in the Group Mind and the more the student participates in that Mind.

So, what are these Gods of ours, anyway? There are forces working through the Collective Unconscious that have been called Gods and Goddesses in the past by a variety of different cultures. Jung termed these forces 'archetypes' which appear in the pantheons and mythologies of people all over the world and throughout history. The Warrior, The King, The Great Mother, The Madonna and Child, The Wizard, the Harlot and a host of others, called by a variety of names and wearing a variety of forms. The big problem with the term archetype is that most people look upon that just they do with the term Collective Unconscious. An archetype is seen as just a figment of the imagination, therefore not real and certainly not a being with a mind of its own that can say "no" to the imaginer. In essence, the Gods are forms the CU gives to certain natural forces. But these natural forces have intelligence and will and are no more subject to being ordered about than the rain and the wind.

Jung himself taught that these great archetypical forces exist in nature and can be seen to function within species other than humans. Indeed, there is evidence that these archetypical patterns of behavior are "hard-wired" into the human brain as parts of powerful instincts such as self-preservation and procreation. Different cultures at different eras have given these archetypes their various forms and names (Mother Goddesses for example, named Hera, Juno, Astarte, Danu, Mary, etc.) But the force remains distinct from the form, and to confuse the two is asking for trouble. These forces, in whatever form we call upon them, guard certain portions of the collective unconscious. They don't automatically do what we want them to do. If they do, they will demand a price, and they always retain the right to refuse us altogether.

Frederick Nietzsche once wrote that man makes god in his own image. And this is true as far as it goes. Humanity does indeed fashion its Gods using itself as a template - male and female, related to each other in families and clans, beings who can love, lust, hate, make war, make love, make lots of other things, in short, beings with superhuman powers, but always with human attributes. These are the images in which we make our Gods. We give them a human form so that we can relate to them on a human, therefore, emotional and unconscious level. We can have a familial relationship with them, since that is the most primal of human relationships.

So, how do we give them form? We invoke them, we call on them, we talk to them, and we describe them with as much detail as possible so that they live in our imaginations. Over the centuries, certain cultural groups have painted such a vivid three dimensional picture of certain deities that everyone in that group mind automatically picks up a remarkably similar picture of each one simply by being in that group. We've done this with the Roebuck for only thirty years. Think of how vivid a deity would be after many centuries?

So, again we come to the chicken/egg question. Do we invent the Gods or did they exist before we came on the scene? Nobody knows, but the answer is probably yes to both. We invent the Gods' forms, each culture painting essentially the same picture (e.g. mother Goddess) in different ways. If the picture we create is accurate, that is, if it accurately reflects the force in the collective unconscious, that force will "animate" the form and make it come to life. Many myths detail this and we can see this in popular culture. Certain fictional characters take on a life of their own, sometimes years after their creator has died and function in ways their creator never envisioned, and in some cases, actively tried to stop.

This takes care of the form. What about the familial relationships and attributes? That's where stories and myths come in. Every culture has its myths and stories passed down from generation to generation, detailing who the Gods are. The Greek myths are classics of this, but every culture has them. Most of this was done orally originally, but when it was committed to writing, it could become more widespread and more reliable. They also became more codified. In a sense, the Druids were right. Once the myths were written down there emerged Holy Writ: Bibles, Torahs, and Korans, each with adherents who insisted that there was only one "right" version of the myth and the others were heresy.

Did the Gods themselves conform to the Holy Writ? Hardly. The stories told about the Virgin Mary throughout the Middle Ages were very different than how she was portrayed in the New Testament. These were stories in the old tradition, oral, whispered around a circle, related around the peasant hearths and noble great halls, told by the old to the young, changed and enlarged upon in the process, generation after generation. That was how the Jewish handmaiden in the Bible, whose only claim to fame was giving birth to a child, became The Holy Virgin, The Mother Of God, and, eventually, Our Lady Queen of the Angels.

So, did the Roebuck invent our Gods or did we actually inherit them? Probably a little of both. We chose them or they chose us or a combination of both. Or, we could have been brought into a much older group mind that still exited on the astral but had almost faded on the physical. We picked up the pieces, reassembled them the best we could and the patterns sprang to life again. It was probably a combination of all these things. In any case, the reality of these forces can be attested to by every Roebuck initiate.

At first however, especially before the pathworkings are completed, the student is not entirely convinced that the Gods are 'real' and not just psychological abstractions or characters in a mythological saga. A good part of the reluctance of students to call quarters is the embarrassment they feel at talking to someone or something that they aren't convinced is really there. Some students feel a sense of offended dignity, like an adult being coerced into participating in a child's tea party and being expected to 'pretend' to drink tea and make small talk with the teddy bear.

That is precisely the reason a student must learn to call quarters from the very first training session. Calling the guardians to come and join the circle, 'as if' they really exist, will add to the demanding characteristics of the circle experience. The student finds himself in another consensual reality – one radically different from the one he has left behind – where the Gods and Goddess are real people. They are talked about by the other members of the circle as if they are real and they are called upon as if they are real. By the act of calling quarters the student gets used to this 'as if' behavior so that when he is introduced to the guardians during the pathworkings, they are somehow more familiar. In this way, the student sets himself up emotionally and psychologically to accept the reality of the guardians before the pathworking, so the emotional impact of meeting them during the pathworking is enhanced.

Invocation by definition is a way of bringing something unseen into manifestation. Some being from another plane is called into being upon this plane so that everyone can experience him or her on some level. To some people, this means that something is expected to appear in physical form which can be perceived by the physical senses. Occasionally, this actually happens and physical phenomena are seen, heard and felt by everyone in the circle. This process can by accentuated by employing such media as black mirrors, crystal balls, incense smoke and people dressed in elaborate robes and masks. However, most of the time, the entity thus invoked will manifest in non-physical but still very tangible ways.

The biggest problem students have with the manifestation of non-physical entities is the issue of 'how do I know it's 'really' there?' This is again a problem with consensual reality. People tend to look to those around them to validate their own sensory input and decide that if someone else senses it, too, it's really there and not 'just in their head.' Again, this is behavior learned in childhood. When a child senses something scary lurking under the bed, he looks to his parents to see if they sense it, too. If they don't, then it must not 'really' be there. Adults unconsciously continue this process, constantly looking to see if other people perceive the same thing they perceive.

The problem with this is that other people's perceptions aren't always right either. Recent research on eye-witness accounts indicates that out of a group of people watching an event, particularly a highly emotionally charged event like a crime, no two people will be able to agree exactly on what occurred. People who have stood side by side during an event will relate such divergent reports that they make an observer wonder if they both saw the same event after all. Therefore, all the information one has about the event in question is X's perception, Y's and Z's. What 'really' happened during the event becomes moot.

It's difficult enough to get validation from other people about sensory input coming from purely physical sources. It's worse when that input comes from non-physical sources. However, it is possible to get everyone in the circle to perceive the invoked entities in some way or another and produce the required validation and consensus that an entity has, in fact, manifested.

We can accomplish this by means of employing sensory modalities in all invocations. A sensory modality, according to NLP theory, is the sensory system that provides a person with their primary referent to how he or she relates to the world. Even though everyone perceives with all five senses, there will always be one or two that are the most important to the individual in determining internal and external reality. Most people in our culture are visual. If they can see something, it is real for them. Their speech is filled with sight-related metaphors such as 'I can see that …,' 'It appears that you …,' 'I don't see why …'" and so on.

Other people are auditory. If they can hear something, it's real for them. They say things like 'I hear you …,' and 'It sounds to me like …' Still others are kinesthetic. They feel reality as physical sensations in their bodies. 'I feel that you …' or describe something as 'rough' or 'heavy.' They are most likely to have 'gut reactions' to things. Less numerous are people who use taste or smell as their primary sensory modality although phrases like 'that leaves a bad taste in my mouth' or 'that stinks' can give a clue. These modalities are still powerful since the sense of smell is located in a more primitive part of the brain than the other senses.

When dealing with internal realities, it is important to realize that different people in a circle will have emotional reactions to different sensory perceptions. Therefore, when we cast the circle, we do it by means of hypnotic suggestion employing the use of sensory modalities. That is, we describe the deities in terms of how they would appear according to each of the senses. When we have described a deity in terms of all five senses, we can make him or her real to everyone in the circle. Then everyone in the circle will be able to recognize their presence.

The five sensory modalities are:

Sight: This is the most common one because our culture is so visual. What does a deity look like: hair color, age, clothing, accouterments? Where are they? What is the setting in which they are to be found: indoors, outdoors, grove, castle, river, ocean, spring? What are they doing? Are they performing some kind of action or are they just standing there?

Sound: Also a common modality in our culture. Are they talking? What are they saying and how are they saying it: choice of words, sound and timbre of voice, talkative or taciturn, matter-of-fact or flowery and effusive. Also, what other sounds are around? Animal or bird noises, music, wind, waves, rumblings, roaring, whisperings, rustlings?

Smell: Less common but very emotionally powerful since the sense of smell is located in a more primitive part of the brain than the other senses. What odors are present? Elemental odors, like burning, smells of the forest, smells of the sea, the smell of rain and wind, of rot, mildew decay and death? Scents of plants and flowers? Food, perfume and incense? Animal smells? Human smells such as sweat?

Taste: There are tastes associated with the quarters as well. Sweet: water, fruit, wine, a kiss? Salty: brine, blood, broth? Bitter: ale, herbs?

Touch: This sense can be both tactile and kinesthetic. Do you feel a hand or fingers touching your body or hair, lips kissing you, bodily closeness? Soft: fur, feathers, silk? Rough: stone, tree bark, metal? Painful: claws or teeth, blades? Or perhaps just an increase of energy or tension, a tingling feeling, sensations of hot, cold, wet or dry?

As an exercise, the instructor can go around the room and have each student practice invoking a particular guardian by the use of only one modality, e.g. invoke the Morrigan only by the sense of smell, or Lugh by the sense of sight. This helps the student learn to think in terms of all the sensory modalities, not just the ones with which he is most comfortable. This, in turn, will make his invocations all the more powerful for the rest of the group.

These sensory modalities also constitute the source of what people "get" in circle, either during a pathworking or other ritual. The term "extrasensory perception" is a good one for this phenomenon. The impressions that are perceived are not physical, but they are registered in the brain as being from one of the sensory modalities that are hard wired into our bodies. The brain will consider these perceptions, even though they are not physical, as being real, thereby evoking an emotional reaction in the person. The person will then think, feel and behave as though the deity were real. At that moment, the deity has, for all intents and purposes, manifested in the circle and will produce some kind physical action from those present. The fact that the deity did not appear in physical form is totally irrelevant.

Most people will naturally gravitate towards one or two dominant modalities in their extrasensory perception. This is purely an individual preference and is not dictated by - and indeed often runs counter to - prevailing cultural notions. Not everyone will "see" even though our culture is primarily visual. Some people will 'hear' voices, 'feel' presences or even 'smell' aromas. A student who is expecting one modality and doesn't achieve it can be reassured that no modality is any better than another. Just because one doesn't see visions doesn't mean one doesn't perceive a presence. The best thing for the student to do is relax and pay attention to what other senses are coming into play.

One or more will soon stand out and produce the kind of reaction in which the person 'knows' on an emotional level that something is there, even if he or she can't see or hear it. When the person learns to experience these sensations through whichever sensory modalities they favor, the invocation of the deity has gone beyond the conscious mind into the unconscious. Then, from that sensory experience, an emotional reaction is elicited – love, fear, awe. When this happens, the deity has become real, not just a figment of the imagination, and a relationship can finally be achieved with him or her. All the rest of the ritual is a means to that end, for it is in achieving a working relationship with the otherworld beings of whatever kind that the shaman is born and magic is achieved.

Casting the Castle

One of the cornerstones of magic involves the creation of a personal astral temple or sacred space on the inner planes which can function as a place of meditation and refuge. In many shamanic traditions, the apprentice is instructed to find such a place and use it as a kind of 'base camp' for his or her forays into the otherworld or as a meeting place in which he or she can commune with Gods, ancestors, power animals and the like.

The following is a ritual adapted from one written by Mara Schaeffer in 1976. In it, Caer Sidi, or the Spiral Castle, (as described in Graves' *White Goddess*) is magically created by means of the four elements. Since the Roebuck Tradition sees the circle as a reflection of Caer Sidi, then the student will also be learning how to visualize the circle as well.

This ritual needs to be performed in a place, preferably outdoors, that is large enough to move around freely. The instructor should make sure that certain pieces of equipment are available. This includes the following:

1. Sword or athame
2. Four small white votive candles in votive jars

3. Large red candle, also in a glass jar
4. Covered container of rock salt, or even soil or gravel
5. Silver colored bowl and a container of water
6. Joss stick or small incense burner that can be carried
7. Cakes and wine (optional)

A typed copy of this ritual should be distributed to all students at least a week prior to the time the ritual will be performed. Each student should be assigned an element or (possibly two, if there are less than four students in the group). If there is a large group, the students may double up with a man and a woman both doing a quarter with one speaking and the other performing the ritual action. If desired, all the students can be instructed to memorize the parts for all the elements and on the night of the ritual, assign each student or pair of students to a quarter, possibly by lot. This will ensure that all students have mastered all the elemental parts. Each student must memorize the lines and be able to perform the ritual without prompting. The student can ad lib, but the imagery of the lines must not be altered. While performing the ritual, the student should visualize the castle being created in enough detail to be able to recall it later.

Other work may be done after the castle has been cast. If it is desired, the Trance Induction workshop can be performed at this time. Also, consecrating cakes and wine, dedicating talismans, healing or guided meditation can be done if desired. This is to be seen as a magical place in which all kinds of meditations and rituals may be performed safely and effectively. The castle can also be used as a place of protection against any form of psychic disturbance. The student needs to be reassured that these disturbances are a normal part of development and most of these are harmless. However, the fear and emotional upset are very real and the student can use this ritual to establish a safe haven.

Draw the circle and light the votive candles at the quarters. Have the red candle at the eastern quarter, salt or gravel at the southern quarter, the bowl of water at the western quarter and the incense at the northern quarter.

Begin at the east. The member at the eastern quarter invokes: IN THE NAMES OF LUGH AND BRIGIT, LET THE FIRE OF THE TORCHES OF CAER SIDI BE LIT TO ILLUMINE OUR WAY. Member takes the candle, lights it and goes around the circle once with it. Visualize torches burning at every quarter driving back the darkness.

Member at the southern quarter invokes: IN THE NAMES OF CERNUNNOS AND NIAMH, LET THE GRANITE WALLS OF CAER SIDI BE RAISED STRONG AND HIGH. Member takes the salt or gravel and sprinkles it around the circle once. Members should visualize walls of granite blocks or stones reaching high as can be seen but still open to the sky.

Next member at the western quarter invokes: IN THE NAMES OF NODENS AND CERRIDWEN, LET THE MOAT FLOW AROUND CAER SIDI TO PROTECT AND INSPIRE US. Member takes the bowl of water and sprinkles it around the circle once. Visualize the temple surrounded by an enormous lake, stretching as far as the eye can see.

Next member stands at the northern quarter and invokes: IN THE NAMES OF TAUTES AND THE MORRIGAN, LET THE PORTALS OF AIR BE OPENED TO CAER SIDI SO THAT THE HIGH GODS MAY JOIN US IN OUR RITES. Member lights the incense and marks each quarter all the way around, drawing large rectangle-shaped windows. Visualize openings in the granite walls with iron gates that can be opened or closed.

Invoke the guardians of the circle. At each quarter, raise your arms until they are over your head. This opens the drawbridge at each quarter so the god and Goddess may enter.

When bidding the Gods farewell, lower the arms from a raised position. This closes the drawbridge of the castle. After the drawbridges are all closed, cut the circle at the northeast and exit, keeping the castle intact.

Pathworking Techniques

Because pathworkings are easy to do and require no props, special settings or training, many people do them thinking that they are easy and foolproof. However, with a few simple guidelines, they can be done even more effectively.

1. Introduce a trance state. Pathworkings are not nearly as effective in a state of normal waking consciousness as they are in an altered state of awareness. Many people expect to have their students just close their eyes and instantly start imaging. Of course, most people cannot. A more satisfying experience will result if a relaxed state is achieved first. This is easier said than done. Many people still have a fear of 'hypnosis' and will resist the suggestion of a hypnotic state. If this attitude is a problem, simply having people take a few deep breaths with suggestions of relaxation and calm is better than nothing.

2. Read a script. Many practitioners make the mistake of 'winging it' and this produces a sense of insecurity in the subject since the leader will stammer, pause, repeat himself or herself and generally meander. Having the script memorized does not

always help, either. The leader of a pathworking tends to enter a trance state as well and the memorized script goes fuzzy and drags. Imaging takes much less time than words and your subjects will have to wait for you to keep up with them if you get too verbose. If you want to do the pathworking too, have someone read it to you, or tape it. For best results, write it down, read it aloud and pay attention to what you're doing.

3. Make it short. Many people attempt to pack a lot of imagery into on pathworking, but the subject will forget some of the images if there are too many of them. Even though they are relaxed, people tend to tire during a long pathworking. Their concentrations may wander and they may drift off to sleep. Or else they may grow stiff if they are kept motionless in one position for too long. A better way to deal with many images is to write a number of short pathworkings and have breaks in between them for discussion and leg stretching.

4. Keep positive. The subconscious does not understand the word 'don't.' If you say 'do not enter the gate' the subject will enter the gate anyway, before he realizes what he is doing. 'Avoid the gate' would be a better way of phrasing the suggestion. The subconscious interprets anything it hears literally. It must visualize what it is not supposed to do in order to understand the suggestion. Consequently, the suggestion: 'You do not feel afraid' will produce feelings of fear as the subconscious struggles to understand what it is not supposed to feel. Better: 'You feel calm and secure.'

5. Use all the senses. Include touch, hearing and smell, and taste as well as sight. This enhances the experience. Have people feel hot or cold, hear a voice, smell a flower or taste a salt breeze or sweet wine. The sensations are just as real as if they were physical, and have the capability of producing profound emotional reactions. Many senses, smell for example, have centers in parts of the brain that are more primitive than the thinking areas, such as the cerebral cortex. This means that these sensations will further bypass the consciousness and affect the more primal feelings and emotions of the subject.

6. Use contact points. These are pauses in the narrative where a subject will gather a personal message from an entity, read words written somewhere, or look at some meaningful scene. You

can't tell a person what to experience here. You must leave them alone to experience on their own. Pause long enough for them to have the experience but not long enough to grow restless. Don't trust your own judgment, on this. Sitting in silence in a darkened room affects everyone's sense of elapsed time. You could count the seconds, or wait for a certain number of heartbeats, using your pulse as an indicator. Better still, use an egg timer, and not one that rings or buzzes. A 3-minute hourglass is ideal. Three minutes is long enough to experience and not long enough to grow restless, and the hourglass is silent and easy to use in a circle.

7. Bring people out of trance. Don't assume that, just because you tell people that they're 'back in their bodies' they are completely awake. People tend to like relaxed states and want to remain in them. Count people back to normal consciousness, e.g. '1,2,3, more and more awake, 4,5, open your eyes and stretch.' Do not, repeat, *do not* use loud, sudden noises like shouts or claps to bring people around. The startle reaction can cause heart palpitations which are uncomfortable at best and fatal at worst. If someone lingers in trance, count them out again in a firm tone and have them stretch their arms and legs. Then, have them stand and eat or drink something. They'll soon be back to normal.

The vast majority of pathworking experiences are meaningful and enjoyable. The worst that usually happens is that 'nothing happens' and a subject will not experience the imagery. There is usually a good reason for this. Some people are simply not visual. They respond more to touch or sound. Others may be so tense that they have trouble relaxing. Many modern people are so locked into logical and critical modes of thinking that they have trouble switching into imagery mode, no matter how much they may want to and trying harder only makes matters worse. A taped pathworking, preferably one with a long relaxation suggestion beforehand that a subject can listen to over and over at home often helps. And finally some people are just frightened of the unknown and will subconsciously block the experience. As much as they may resent it, these people are best left alone. Forcing the issue may open a psychological can of worms that requires professional help to straighten out.

What then of the occasional subject who has a bad experience in a pathworking? This happens mostly in instances where a subject is led to confront a past life or relive a death experience. If this was filled with terror and pain, a subject might become emotional, cry, scream and show signs of fear. *Avoid panic!* Stop the pathworking and suggest calmly to the subject that he distance himself from the experience, possibly by seeing it on a screen, or in a mirror. The subject will usually follow a suggestion of that nature without hesitation. Then, when the subject is calm again, either continue with the pathworking, or bring everyone out of trance and end the ritual. Above all, do not make a big deal of it. Your subject will be embarrassed enough.

A guided meditation has several features that make it different from ordinary narrative. These features consequently make them rather difficult to write at first, since the usual rules of what is considered good composition must often be suspended in order to achieve the desired effect. The purpose of a pathworking script is not to entertain, but to reach directly into the intuitive unconscious mind, which is not a literary critic and is less concerned with grammar and syntax than it is with powerful, evocative words. Consequently, a few simple modifications to one's writing style will prove useful.

First, use the present tense and the second person viewpoint: 'You are doing this or walking there or seeing the other thing.' This adds immediacy. Your purpose is to give the subject an experience that is occurring in the here and now, rather than telling them a story that happened in the past. Use short sentences with minimal description and concentrate on descriptive nouns and verbs rather than relying on adjectives and adverbs. e.g. 'trotting down the path' rather than 'walking quickly.' 'Temple' or 'Castle' rather than 'stone building.'

When you must use an adjective, always put it before the noun, rather than after, no matter how stilted it sounds. 'You see a stone archway,' rather than 'you see an archway made of stone.' The reason for this is that by the time you have said the word 'archway,' the subject will have already begun to visualize the archway. If it isn't made of stone, then the suggestion that it, in fact, is will jar the subject's concentration by forcing him to reconstruct his image according to your instructions. Using the adjective before the noun will enable the subject to use your instructions in constructing his initial image and will make the pathworking flow better.

Use lots of transitional words such as 'and,' 'as,' 'then,' 'while,' etc. These words facilitate further the flow of imagery and are particularly useful in reaching the unconscious by giving a feeling of continuity, especially if they link some sort of sensory experience with an attention point. e.g. 'As you feel the salt spray sting your face, the crashing of the waves give you a message meant for your ears alone. (Pause).'

Your voice, too, can enhance the experience as you read the pathworking. Some people have naturally hypnotic voices. But anyone can learn to read a pathworking effectively. The first thing to do, of course, is to slow down. Most people talk too fast. This is not a problem during normal waking consciousness, but in a trance state, words become difficult to follow if they are spoken too quickly. Read slowly enough so that you notice it. If you feel as if you are dragging, then your speed is probably just about right. A sing-song tone, although useful for inductions, is not necessary for the entire pathworking. However, be sure to enunciate your words. Pronounce every syllable. Take a breath between phrases. Practice by reading the pathworking into a tape, then playing it back, preferably in a relaxed state. If you constantly do this, adjusting speed and voice inflection until you are happy with the results, it is very likely that your listeners will be happy as well.

Although it is really not necessary, optimal results are produced from pathworkings if they are done in a ritual setting, such as a temple or a circle. The ritual act of casting a circle or opening a temple along with the setting of a sacred place will very often enhance the experience for the student and make it more intense than the same pathworking would be if worked in a living room setting. If a living room must be used for some reason, it helps to do a ritual cleansing of the place and a simple invocation to an angel or deity who will bless and watch over the proceedings. Although they are enjoyable, entertaining and enlightening, pathworkings are not a parlor game. They deal with very real and, often very disturbing, emotional and psychic issues. They delve into sacred realms, using images and themes drawn from the very beginnings of humankind. Treat them like you would the most ancient of rituals, for indeed, that is what they are.

Trance State Induction

For a guided meditation to be optimally effective, an altered state of consciousness needs to be induced. The student needs to be isolated physically and psychologically from the demands of the mundane, everyday world – not only those demands coming from the outside but from the demands coming from inside his or her own consciousness. The mind of the student must be stilled from random and unrelated thoughts and the attention focused on the magical work at hand.

Some eastern traditions teach the art of meditation, and this can be a useful skill for the student to acquire. But meditation is, by definition, a solitary act in which the mind is focused on an internal stimulus, such as a mantra or symbol. In the case of a pathworking, the mind must focus on the words spoken by the leader of the circle and no extraneous thoughts, particularly those of a critical or analytical nature, must be allowed to intrude. In order for the pathworking to be effective, the student must allow himself to have the experience suggested to him by the leader's words in its full sensory detail, without stopping to question whether the experience is 'really' happening or not. A well-written pathworking will help. But a formal induction of an altered state of trance is useful as well, at least in the beginning stages of a student's training.

Teaching someone how to achieve a trance state is both easy and difficult - easy because inducing it in yourself or another actually requires very little in the way of time, effort and equipment; hard because it involves a spectrum of psychological variables that vary from person to person. These variables will be responsible for the success or failure of this exercise. The instructor needs to be aware that this step is critical in the magical development of the student, since the ability to achieve trance state easily, comfortably and reliably is vital to achieving the steps that follow.

Most of the problems that both the instructor and the student will face in achieving this step will involve misconceptions about what the trace state is and how it is achieved. The instructor might remember the following:

1. The achievement of trance state in the Roebuck involves hypnosis. This term might be frightening to some people since it implies control over another's will. The student needs to be assured, even if it does not appear necessary, that what is being taught is a process of self-hypnosis. The student is actually learning to put himself or herself into trance. The suggestions given by the instructor or by the Priest or Priestess of the circle are merely aids in helping the student achieve this process. An appropriate analogy is the training wheels of the bicycle. The training wheels help the student learn to balance while still being able to ride. When the student is able to balance unaided, the training wheels are taken away, and the student is left to achieve trance alone. When the student has accomplished this effectively, the suggestions will no longer be necessary and will not be used.

2. Hypnosis produces a trance state that is deep enough to achieve magical development and perform magical work in the circle. Some students might feel that the effects of the trance are not as intense as that produced by other means, either chemical or natural. The student needs to be reassured that the purpose of the training is to achieve maximum benefit with the minimum of risk and that the bells and whistles are not necessary. When the student learns to control the process, then the experience will increase in intensity. This ensures that, although the process might take a little longer,

no damage is done. The student needs to be reminded gently that the purpose of these exercises is not excitement, but learning and that often dull work needs to be done before results are apparent. One must learn the scales before one can play the concerto.

3. Some students will make progress faster than others. The majority will achieve very good control in just a couple of sessions. However, there may be an occasional student who will have no end of trouble relaxing, experiencing the images in the pathworkings, and will generally complain that he or she will 'get nothing' from the sessions. These are people with severe emotional blocks. Achieving a trance state necessitates withdrawing into oneself and this can open up a psychological can of worms that may require competent professional help.

The instructor needs to realize that such people are not being stubborn and uncooperative. The inability to achieve a trance state is a defense mechanism against dealing with severe problems and may well be a valid way of protecting the integrity of the personality. These people are often heartbroken that they cannot share the experience and may blame the instructor. There is a choice for such students. They can blame the group and find an excuse to leave, or they can admit that they have a problem, decide to stick it out and ask for special assistance. People can be 'blown open' psychically by certain hypnotic procedures, but this should NEVER be done without the express and repeated desire of the student and then ALWAYS by a competent and trained person *with a supplemental therapy program*. If the student has the courage to undergo that upheaval, then all the coven can do is offer support and encouragement while it is happening. There is the possibility that it can cause permanent damage. The members of the group must be prepared, then, to assume partial responsibility for whatever happens.

The following pathworking has two purposes. The first purpose is to induce a trance state easily and quickly by establishing a breathing trigger that can be used by the individual, or the coven, in subsequent trance state exercises. Such a trigger is easily used. It is quick and powerful, since it involves a physiological change that can be felt by anyone. Associating the entrance into the trace state with the disorientation caused by slight hyperventilation will be easy for the student to achieve, both with the group and alone. Also included are visual and kinesthetic cues for dissociation of the body and mind. These are useful in achieving astral travel. Repeated suggestions that these abilities are comfortable, easy to achieve, and useful for the student are used.

The other purpose of this pathworking is to obtain a kind of 'permission' to leave the mortal world behind and explore inner realms. This permission to cross the barrier between normal consciousness and the world of dreams is given by the Guardian of the Threshold, traditionally the keeper of the gate between these two modes of thought. When the Guardian gives his consent, then the student can be assured that his or her soul is indeed ready to break its mortal bonds and begin the ascent to the Temple of Wisdom. If the conscious desire is there but the soul is not ready, this inner consent will not be given and further examination of motives is indicated.

A circle is cast and the guardians are called. The student is seated before a dark mirror carefully lit by candles to achieve maximum visibility. This pathworking can be done by several students at once, all seated comfortably so that they can see the mirror to full advantage. The instructor is best seated off to the side so that the small candle used for reading the script will not cast a glare on the mirror. The students' faces should be in view, in order that reactions can be watched. The instructor should talk in a soft, clear tone, speaking slowly and enunciating words as clearly as possible. The pause indicated in the script is sustained for three minutes. A sand-type three minute egg timer is ideal, since the passage of time can be clearly seen and there is no sound to distract or startle the students.

FIRST, TAKE THREE DEEP BREATHS - ONE: IN, IN, IN AND OUT, BLOWING OUT ALL THE CARES OF THE DAY. TWO: IN, IN, FILLING YOUR LUNGS WITH PURE AIR, AND OUT, BREATHING OUT ALL THE IMPURITIES AND IMBALANCES. FINALLY, THREE: IN, IN, IN AND OUT, LEAVING YOUR BODY PURE AND REFRESHED. AND NOW YOUR BODY IS BEGINNING TO FEEL VERY VERY CALM AND RELAXED. AS I COUNT FROM 10 TO 1, YOU ARE FEELING MORE AND MORE RELAXED. TEN, NINE, MORE AND MORE RELAXED, EVERY MUSCLE AND EVERY NERVE JUST LETTING GO. EIGHT, WITH EVERY EASY BREATH THAT YOU TAKE, WITH EVERY BEAT OF YOUR HEART, GOING DEEPER AND DEEPER INTO A RELAXED STATE. SEVEN, EVERY MUSCLE BECOMING LIMP AND LOOSE,

LIKE LOOSE, LIMP RUBBER BANDS. SIX, FIVE, DEEPER AND DEEPER, RELAXED AND CALM, FOUR, THREE, EVERY PART OF YOUR BODY BECOMING HEAVIER AND HEAVIER. TWO, ONE, VERY VERY RELAXED, VERY VERY HEAVY. YOUR BODY IS FEELING VERY HEAVY, VERY INERT, LIKE A LUMP OF CLAY OR A LUMP OF WAX. SO HEAVY AND SO INERT THAT YOU COULDN'T MOVE EVEN IF YOU WANTED TO.

AND AS YOUR BODY BECOMES MORE AND MORE HEAVY, MORE AND MORE INERT, YOUR CONSCIOUSNESS, YOUR AWARENESS, THAT PART THAT IS TRULY YOU, YOUR BODY OF LIGHT, IS BECOMING MORE AND MORE ALERT, MORE AND MORE ENERGETIC, MORE AND MORE LOOSENED FROM YOUR PHYSICAL FORM. AND AS IT BECOMES MORE AND MORE LOOSENED FROM YOUR PHYSICAL FORM, YOU FIND THAT YOU CAN DETACH YOURSELF FROM THE PHYSICAL BODY. FIRST, YOU RISE ABOVE YOUR BODY, UP, UP, UP, JUST A FEW INCHES, AND SLOWLY SETTLE BACK DOWN INTO YOUR PHYSICAL FORM ONCE AGAIN, FEELING CONFIDENT THAT THIS IS EASY FOR YOU TO DO. NOW, YOU SINK INTO THE EARTH BELOW YOUR PHYSICAL FORM, DOWN, DOWN, DOWN, JUST A FEW INCHES. NOW, RISE BACK UP INTO YOUR PHYSICAL FORM AGAIN, CONFIDENT THAT THIS IS AN EASY AND COMFORTABLE THING FOR YOU TO DO. NOW, BACK UP OUT OF YOUR PHYSICAL BODY, BACK, BACK, BACK, JUST A FEW INCHES, JUST ENOUGH SO THAT YOU CAN SEE THE BACK OF THE HEAD OF YOUR PHYSICAL FORM. NOW, MOVE FORWARD AGAIN BACK INTO YOUR PHYSICAL BODY, CONFIDENT THAT THIS IS AN EASY AND COMFORTABLE THING FOR YOU TO DO, AND THAT YOU ARE ABLE TO MOVE IN AND OUT OF YOUR BODY WHENEVER YOU DESIRE.

NOW, EASILY AND GENTLY, MOVE FORWARD OUT OF YOUR PHYSICAL FORM, BUT THIS TIME CONTINUE MOVING FORWARD, LEAVING YOUR PHYSICAL FORM BEHIND, SAFE AND SECURE IN THE CIRCLE. AND AS YOU MOVE FORWARD OUT OF YOUR PHYSICAL FORM, THE MIRROR BEFORE YOU BEGINS TO GROW LARGER AND LARGER, THE EDGES GROWING LESS AND LESS DISTINCT UNTIL THE MIRROR GROWS LARGE ENOUGH TO BE A DOORWAY, A DOORWAY

INTO ANOTHER WORLD. NOW STEP THROUGH THE DOORWAY, STEP THROUGH THE MIRROR,

IT IS NIGHT. THE FULL MOON SHINES ABOVE YOU. YOU FIND YOURSELF STANDING IN A MEADOW WITH ROLLING HILLS AROUND YOU WITH CLUSTERS OF OAK TREES ON THE HILLSIDES. AT YOUR FEET IS A PATH. YOU WALK ALONG THE PATH TOWARDS THE CREST OF THE HILL BEFORE YOU. YOU CAN HEAR THE TRILL OF NIGHT BIRDS AND THE WHISPER OF THE BREEZE THROUGH THE BRANCHES OF THE TREES. THE BREEZE CARRIES WITH IT THE SCENT OF SAGE AND HONEYSUCKLE. YOU'D LOVE TO STAY WHERE YOU ARE, BUT THE MOON BECKONS YOU ONWARD.

THE PATH BEGINS TO GET STEEP AND ROCKY. YOU FIND YOURSELF CLIMBING UP OVER ROCKS AND AROUND BUSHES, BACK AND FORTH ALONG SWITCHBACKS SO THAT YOU CAN'T SEE WHERE YOU'RE GOING AND YOU CAN'T SEE WHERE YOU'VE BEEN. THE PATH IS MUCH STEEPER NOW AND YOU FIND YOURSELF HAVING TO CLUTCH AT THE ROCKS AND BUSHES WITH YOUR HANDS IN ORDER TO CONTINUE TO FOLLOW THE PATH.

SUDDENLY, YOU REACH THE TOP OF THE HILL. YOU LOOK UP AT THE SKY. THE MOON HAS NOW WANED UNTIL IT IS NO MORE THAN A SLIVER IN THE STAR STUDDED SKY. YOU CONTINUE A FEW STEPS UNTIL YOU COME TO A SINGLE DOLMEN ARCHWAY, MADE OF TWO STANDING STONES WITH A STONE ACROSS THEM. AS YOU APPROACH THE ARCHWAY, YOU SEE THAT EACH OF THE STANDING STONES HAS A NICHE CUT OUT OF IT. IN EACH NICHE IS A SKULL. BOTH SKULLS NOTICE YOUR PRESENCE. THEY ASK YOU WHAT YOU SEEK. YOU ANSWER AS HONESTLY AS YOU CAN. (SLIGHT PAUSE). THEN, YOU STEP THROUGH THE ARCHWAY.

(Three minute pause)

IT IS NOW TIME TO RETURN TO THE MORTAL REALM. YOU EXIT THROUGH THE DOLMAN ARCHWAY AND MAKE YOUR WAY DOWN THE PATH. THE WAY SEEMS SHORTER THIS TIME. SOON, YOU ARRIVE AT THE MIRROR DOORWAY LEADING BACK INTO THE CIRCLE, AND STEP THROUGH BACK

INTO THE CIRCLE. THE DOORWAY SHRINKS BEHIND YOU BACK TO ITS ORIGINAL SIZE AND YOU FIND YOUR PHYSICAL FORM SAFE WHERE YOU LEFT IT. NOW, SLOWLY, EASILY AND GENTLY MERGE BACK WITH YOUR PHYSICAL FORM, FEELING IT RETURN TO LIFE AGAIN. AND AS I COUNT FROM ONE TO FIVE, FINDING YOUR PHYSICAL FORM REGAINING ALL OF YOUR VITALITY AND ENERGY. ONE, TWO, MORE AND MORE AWAKE, MORE AND MORE ENERGETIC, THREE, FEELING WONDERFUL AND CONFIDENT, FOUR, EYES OPENING AND FIVE, TAKE A DEEP BREATH AND STRETCH.

The instructor should observe each student to see that all have regained normal consciousness. If in fact one student remains in trance, the instructor should repeat the awakening paragraph, and gently call the student by name until some signs of life are visible. Then the student should be helped to his or her feet and told to move around. A useful addition to the circle would be cakes and wine. The act of consecration and the ingestion of food help awaken reluctant students. A reluctance to return to normal awareness happens occasionally. It occurs mostly in people who don't relax easily and who may so enjoy the experience that her or she does not want to leave it. It is not a danger, but is an annoyance and should be discouraged. The instructor needs to be gentle but firm in insisting that the student awaken properly, but the instructor should never nor allow others to shake the student, yell or otherwise awaken the student in a rough manner.

Quarter Pathworkings

The Roebuck quarter pathworkings are a compilation of nearly nine years of study and experimentation, in the attempt to discover the inner plane guardians of our circle. They include symbolism that was felt to best represent the forces that we contact. In order to insure consistency, they should be read as is. Any changes should only be made after consultation with the rest of the group.

All pathworkings should be performed in a cast circle. A dark mirror should be placed in the appropriate quarter with candles lighting it such that there is no glare. In the case of Goda and Tubal, a crystal ball should be placed in the center of the circle. Have students assume a relaxed position, either sitting upright or lying down. They should be facing the mirror, at least initially. The instructor needs to have at hand a small candle to light the script and a three minute hourglass.

The following induction is suggested for all the pathworkings. The instructor may elaborate upon it or eliminate parts of it depending on how long it is taking for the students to enter the trance state. A longer induction will generally be required for the first one or two, with the induction decreasing with the later ones. The instructor needs to gage this carefully, so that students don't get restless or get left behind.

>   FIRST, TAKE A DEEP BREATH - IN, IN, IN, AND OUT, BLOWING OUT ALL THE ILL HUMOURS, ALL THE IMPURITIES AND CARES OF THE DAY. NOW, ANOTHER DEEP BREATH - IN, IN, BREATHING IN THE ENERGY OF THE GODS, AND OUT, GETTING RID OF ALL THE MUNDANE DROSS. AND A THIRD - IN, IN, IN AND OUT, CLEANSING AND PURIFYING EVERY CELL IN YOUR BODY. NOW, WITH EVERY BREATH THAT YOU TAKE, WITH EVERY EASY BEAT OF YOUR HEART, YOU FEEL YOUR BODY BECOMING MORE AND MORE LIMP, MORE AND MORE RELAXED. AND AS YOUR BODY GROWS MORE AND MORE LIMP, MORE AND MORE RELAXED, IT GROWS MORE AND MORE HEAVY, MORE AND MORE INERT, WAZEN, JUST LIKE A LUMP OF CLAY.
>   AND AS YOUR PHYSICAL BODY BECOMES MORE AND MORE WAXEN, MORE AND MORE HEAVY, YOUR ASTRAL BODY BECOMES LIGHTER AND LIGHTER, MORE AND MORE SEPARATED FROM YOUR PHYSICAL FORM. NOW, IT EMERGES, FLOWING OUT EASILY AND GENTLY, LEAVING BEHIND YOUR BODY, HEAVY AND INERT, SAFE AND SECURE IN THE CIRCLE.

Insert pathworking here. At the pause point in the script, remain still for a period of about three minutes measured by the hourglass. Then continue until the end. (Pathworking scripts are given in Appendix I)

>   NOW, AS YOUR ASTRAL BODY RETURNS TO THE CIRCLE, IT SLOWLY, EASILY AND GENTLY MERGES AGAIN WITH YOUR PHYSICAL FORM, ENERGIZING IT, FILLING IT WITH LIFE AND ENERGY ONCE MORE. NOW, OPEN YOUR EYES, TAKE A DEEP BREATH AND STRETCH.

As before, the instructor should observe each student in order to make sure that each has returned to normal consciousness. If someone has not, the instructor can use the methods given previously. If the reluctance to return to normal awareness after a pathworking persists over more than one or two of the pathworkings, then the student needs to be made aware that this is annoying to the rest of the group and may be seen as an attention-getting device. If this is the case, and if all attempts to rectify the situation fail, then the student can simply be left alone in the circle while the rest of the group leave. The behavior will probably not persist after that.

Occasionally, the instructor will encounter a student who seems unable or unwilling to follow the script and experience what the rest of the group is experiencing. Such a student may resent having to 'stay with the tour group' and want to strike out alone to have his or her own experiences. The instructor needs to point out firmly that these guided journeys serve the purpose of orienting the student to the system as quickly and efficiently as possible. Everyone had to undergo the same journeys. They are necessary to tie the group together. The student can be assured that there will be ample opportunities in the future to have personal experiences with the Gods and that nothing is preventing him or her from doing other guided meditations at other times.

The Path To Initiation

Ritual Planning

    Each student during the course of his or her training is required to plan and conduct a complete ritual. This exercise has two purposes. The first is to allow the student the hands-on experience of putting together a ritual, both in its psychic aspects and its physical aspects. The second is to help the student appreciate fully the efforts of others. In many groups, the Priest and Priestess conduct all the rituals. In the Roebuck, however, all initiate members take turns at planning the rituals and the student must know how this is done before taking his or her turn.

    The instructor should begin preparing the student for the ritual planning exercise several weeks in advance. A date should be set as soon as possible so that the student will have a deadline to work towards and will know what the phase of the moon is, what planets are visible, what the weather is likely to be and other pertinent information. This will also give the student time to obtain any permission necessary, if the ritual is to be done in a place other than that usually used by the group. The student needs to understand that the ritual plan must be complete at least a week ahead of time in order that any speaking parts which must be memorized by the participants can be distributed in time to be learned.

The student should first decide on the purpose of the ritual, since the purpose will determine everything else. Will it be a full moon, or a Festival? Will it be a celebration, a worship ritual or a working ritual? Will there be a healing? Will power be raised to accomplish something? Will there be a god or Goddess manifested in the circle by some means?

Once the student considers the above questions and comes up with a purpose, he or she must decide how best to accomplish this purpose. Details that need to be considered are:

1. Who will participate? Will the entire group have something to do or will there only be a few who perform the ritual actions?

2. What will the participants actually do? Are the actions to be learned ahead of time or will everyone follow a leader? This also applies to any speaking parts. Are there songs or chants that need to be learned ahead of time?

3. What equipment will be needed? Standard ritual regalia can be supplied by the group. However, anything special needs to be procured by the student himself or herself. Is such an item available? Is it practical in terms of cost and difficulty in obtaining it? Is there enough of it? Can it be used safely and practically? What can substitute for it if it is not available at the last minute?

Roebuck rituals have a loose but definite outline of elements that occur in a particular sequence in order to provide a coherent structure to the working. This outline can be varied if the need arises, but the student should keep to this outline at first until enough experience has been gained to be able to vary it without having the ritual fall apart. This outline is as follows:

> **Opening**: The circle is cast by inscribing a sacred space, the quarters are called and Goda and Tubal greeted. These are parts that need to be assigned ahead of time.
> **Core**: The work itself, whether it is a pathworking, healing, god or Goddess contact, power raising or whatever. The core should include a building up of power, a climax or peak, and then a winding down.

Consecration of Food and Drink: What the food and drink actually is doesn't matter. The purpose of this phase is to ground the power and prepare the participants to return to normal awareness.

Closing: The quarters, Goda and Tubal are thanked and bid farewell and the circle is cut. A libation of a bit of the food and drink is made by the person conducting the ritual. The closing includes the debriefing or critique afterwards.

The instructor needs to constantly be aware that all the actual work in the ritual is to be done by the student or anyone that the student designates. The instructor can guide and counsel the student during the planning phases, answer any questions, offer any advice, reference material and other help. But when the actual ritual is performed, the instructor must remain silent and uninvolved, unless asked a specific question or if he or she perceives an actual danger to all in the circle. Otherwise, the student is totally in charge. Instructions are to be followed cheerfully and all actions and parts performed as planned.

This will be difficult for the instructor, who will notice problems and oversights. But unless the oversight would result in actual harm to anyone, the student must be allowed to make mistakes and even botch the ritual. The strengths and weaknesses of the ritual can be discussed at length during the debrief session.

Within the above outline, the opportunities for creativity are endless. There is no 'one, true, right and only way' to do any ritual. The purpose of each part of the ritual remains the same in all cases. However, the method with which the purpose is carried out can and does vary with often dramatic and elegant results. Some students have introduced a variety of new and interesting ways of performing the "standard" ritual gestures. This is as it should be. Ritual is an art form as well as a magical and religious ceremony. There is no reason why any ritual has to be the same all the time.

In the Roebuck, the magic is not in the gestures or words themselves, but in the emotional response of the people in the circle to those gestures and words. If the ritual gesture or speech produces a desired response, it 'works.' If it doesn't produce the desired response (or worse, the opposite response), then it 'doesn't work' no matter how flawlessly it was executed.

Over the years, we have had students who have had a problem getting used to the way the Roebuck does its rituals. Some of the things we do in the circle are familiar and standard. Some of it is off the wall and requires considerable explanation. Depending upon their previous circle experience, newcomers have claimed that it is too minimal while others consider it overly theatrical. Analyzing the reasons behind these observations has been useful in crystallizing the Roebuck approach to ritual and why we are so different from the Gardnerians or other more strict Wicca traditions.

The most consistent reference has been to our minimalism and our lack of consistency. People with a strong Gardnerian or Ceremonial Magic background complain that Roebuck circles are never cast exactly the same way twice. These people unfortunately have been taught that there is one, true sacred formula for doing magical ritual which has been passed down through untold generations. This ritual formula must not vary or else it either will not work or the practitioner will be guilty of sacrilege.

The problem with this attitude is that it is only half right. There *is* a sacred magical formula passed down through generations. But it lies in the mind and heart of the practitioner and not in the words said, the gestures performed or the props used. People who are not secure in their own magical ability or relationship with divine powers will attach almost superstitious significance to certain magical tools or ritual forms in order to guarantee that their ritual will work because they've done it "right."

This is also the reason behind a lot of the nonsense about ritual secrets that have been promulgated over the years. If one is of the mindset that certain rituals are magical formulae passed down through untold ages, it follows that one has a sacred trust to keep them secret and not give them out to the unworthy, whoever that may be. Discretion about the contents of one's rituals can be useful, if it is used to further cement the bonds between the members of a group as in-jokes and family secrets often do. However, the secret that is being preserved is not the ritual or practice itself, but the significance of that ritual or practice to all the others in the circle.

Very often, a secret ritual or practice is actually revealed to outsiders, but the significance of that ritual or practice will be lost on them. Such outsiders will wonder what all of the fuss is about and may very well mock and make fun of things that have deep emotional meaning to the members of a group. For that reason, and that reason alone, a group is justified in keeping certain practices under wraps. But while it is not good to cast one's pearls before swine, as it were, these secret rituals eventually have to be passed down to someone or the tradition peters out. If only the ritual is passed along, and not the reason for the ritual, the result will be a group who will blindly perform some ritual action with no clue as to what they are doing and why.

The opposite criticism - that of theatricality - is also interesting. There are people who want simplicity in their magical workings and would be happy with no props, no ritual dress, no words, indeed, no ritual at all. I have been in circles where all everyone did was sit in a circle on the floor in their street clothes in the dark and visualize the entire ritual inside their minds.

This can be a powerful form of ritual provided: 1) everyone has had enough experience in ritual to know what to visualize or 2) there is a leader who will guide the visualization as is done in a pathworking. If neither experience nor leadership is present, all you get is a group of people meditating together with each person going off into his or her private experience and not interacting with everyone else. If this is the case, why get together in a group at all?

Ritual is a group experience and, especially when you have newcomers, any props, speeches, invocations or whatever that helps focus everyone's attention on the same thing is useful. Indeed, theater began as a form of religious ritual in order to get a large group of unschooled people to be able to visualize a certain set of divine symbols. In this context, the "Cu and Epona" or dog-and-pony show will be much more effective than a simple ritual in which no props are used or no words are said.

The caveat here is that such an elaborate ritual form is not necessary for the powers to manifest. It is a teaching tool, nothing more, which enables a person without years of magical training to understand the sometimes obscure and esoteric aspects of a faith. That certainly does not mean that the powers cannot manifest during the course of an elaborate ritual. Sometimes, they do. But it is not the ritual in and of itself that causes this manifestation, but the love and belief in the hearts of the people performing it.

If you have an open festival with many people who have no idea of who Lugh is, for example, it will do no good to invoke Him privately in your mind. It is far better to invoke Him out loud for everyone to hear, elaborating His attributes and appearance so that everyone will know just who He is supposed to be. And, in circles so large that words are not always heard by everyone, the best way of getting people to know Lugh is to have a Priest impersonate Him by dressing in the appropriate costume, wielding the appropriate symbolic props. Anyone with half a brain standing in the circle will know consciously that what they are seeing is an ordinary man in a Lugh costume. But the emotional impact of seeing a god-form manifest when called can be tremendous and can have results which completely bypass conscious awareness.

The Roebuck has always acknowledged that both extremes of the ritual experience are valid for the people practicing them. But we continue to stress that ritual, *any* ritual, is merely a physical tool to achieve a result on the unseen planes, whether it is the private communion with divine powers by a trained initiate or a public demonstration of those powers to an untrained audience. To use a minimalist approach in a large, untrained group is worthless. To use an elaborately theatrical approach for a small group of trained initiates is overkill.

God or Goddess Contact and Possession Rituals

From ancient times, the purpose of Priesthood was to manifest deity on the physical plane. The Oracle at Delphi performed this function when she went into a trance and answered a supplicant's questions with the words of Apollo. So does a Roman Catholic Priest when he performs the Transubstantiation of the Mass in which he turns the communion wafer and wine into the Body and Blood of Christ. Both are bringing the power of their respective deities into a form in which the ordinary person can understand.

This Priesthood function is distinct from that of a Minister who performs standard rites of passage or comforts and counsels troubled people. A Priest or Priestess may do these things as well, but they do so as ordinary mortals. They may express opinions, relay information or provide perspective on personal problems and situations. However, when an Oracle speaks, he or she isn't just offering an opinion. He or she is speaking the words of Deity – a direct transmission, not an interpreter – and is treated as such.

In our modern 'new' age, this process is called channeling. An ordinary person goes into an altered state of awareness or trance state and allows his or her body to be taken over by another entity, who in turn uses the vocal apparatus to speak to a collection of listeners. This is nothing more than an updated form of mediumship by which a person makes himself a medium through which people who have departed this earth plane can communicate messages to those still living. In the Bible, the Witch of Endor served as medium to enable Saul to communicate with the shade of the prophet Samuel. This is the same process used by modern-day Spiritualists to allow bereaved people to communicate with departed loved ones.

The opportunities for abuse are inherent in the process itself. Especially if money changes hands, the temptation to tell the recipient what he or she wants to hear, rather than relate the actual message (or lack of one) is tremendous. Spiritualist mediums, even those who don't charge money and only take donations have been grappling with this problem for centuries. New Age channelers who function as mediums for Inner Plane Masters with esoteric teachings and advice for people with personal and spiritual problems are even more hard-pressed to 'perform,' particularly if they are doing so in front of an audience of several hundred people, all of whom have paid a significant sum of money for the privilege.

When the entity being channeled is an aspect of divinity, a god or Goddess of any pantheon, the pressure to perform is even more intense. Added to the normal stage fright attendant to being the center of attention is a profound sense of unworthiness. Fevered thoughts race through the mind of the student waiting alone in the temple for a contact or possession ritual to begin. A dozen or more people have traveled often long distances to talk to this particular god or Goddess. What if he or she doesn't show up? Worse still, what if the god or Goddess finds the student to be an unworthy channel? After all, every person has problems and has done things they secretly are ashamed of. Will those things somehow disqualify the student for the awesome honor and responsibility of being a channel for divinity?

This is an awesome responsibility and one that has been shunned by Christians for two millennia. So, why do we do it? For the same reason our ancestors did. Being an oracle requires years of dedication and training as well as an innate ability in order to be able to do it effectively. The average person simply could not take the time and expend the effort to hone the skill. If a burning question arose in their lives that no other source could answer, they could consult a god through the mouth of an oracle. It was a sacred function of a devoted Priesthood then and remains so for modern-day Pagans as well.

Often students will ask by what right do we presume to do this? Who are we to speak with the voice of the Gods? The answer lies in the difference between the Pagan attitude towards divinity and the Christian one. Our Gods are not our creators but our ancestors. They speak through us, and we allow them to do so by virtue of that sacred kinship. They choose us as much as we choose them. And if they do not choose to speak through a particular oracle at a particular time, the oracle remains silent and nothing on this earth can force it to speak.

Contact and Possession Training Exercise

Mediumship is not an easy skill to master for many people. The biggest difficult appears to be where to begin. Most of us learned in childhood to put up a barrier between ourselves and the unseen. Making the first breach in that barrier and learning to control that which comes through is the purpose of the following exercise.

Set up the contact medium depending on the quarter to be called: East - Candle flame; South - Crystal ball; West - bowl of water; North - incense. Seat the student in front of the contact point.

TAKE THREE DEEP BREATHS - ONE, TWO, THREE. RELAX AND STARE AT THE (Contact Point).

Have the working partner of the student (or the Priest or Priestess) invoke the God for a man or the Goddess for a woman.

DO YOU FEEL A PRESENCE? WHEN DID YOU BEGIN TO FEEL IT - BEFORE OR AFTER THE INVOCATION WAS FINISHED? HOW DO YOU FEEL? WHAT IS HAPPENING? HOW DOES THE GOD/DESS APPEAR? IS THERE ANYTHING BEING SAID TO YOU? CAN YOU FEEL A PULL TOWARDS THE ENTITY?

If the student is 'getting nothing,' then repeat the invocation again, using stronger imagery and more sensory modalities. Wait for the student to report a presence.

GO CLOSER TO THE ENTITY. FIND THE POINT AT WHICH YOU ARE THE CLOSEST YOU CAN BE AND STILL STAY YOURSELF, WHERE THE GOD/DESS PRESENCE IS THE STRONGEST, BUT YOU ARE STILL YOU. HAVE YOU FOUND IT?

Wait until you get a 'yes' answer. The student may take a few minutes to find that point. You may observe some physical swaying to and from the contact point. When the student reports a 'yes,' continue with:

OKAY. HOW DOES THAT FEEL? WHAT IS HAPPENING TO YOU?

Student will report feelings, with promptings if necessary.

FINE. NOW HOLD THAT POINT FOR AS LONG AS YOU CAN. THIS IS YOUR POINT OF CONTACT. THIS IS THE FEELING YOU WANT.

Ask the student's working partner what the student's face looks like. Is the person still there? How has he/she changed? To student:

OKAY. NOW PULL BACK A LITTLE. RESIST THE PULL. CAN YOU DO THAT? WHAT'S HAPPENING?

Have working partner bid farewell to the deity.

PULL BACK EVEN MORE. IS THE PRESENCE GONE? WHEN DID IT GO? HAVE YOU PULLED BACK COMPLETELY? HOW DO YOU FEEL?

If the student still reports a presence, have the partner bid farewell again. Cover or have the student turn his or back on the contact medium.

Contacts

Contacting a god or Goddess is a process by which the student perceives the deity manifesting into a specific medium such as a dark mirror and is able to relate messages from that deity to the rest of the circle. This is also called 'aspecting' in some circles, although this term has also been used to refer to god or Goddess possessions. In the Roebuck, contact rituals are kept distinct from possession rituals. It is vitally important that a student learn control, not of the deities involved, but of his or her own psychic faculties. Learning to assume a trance state deep enough to contact an entity, but not so deep as to be unable to communicate with the rest of the circle is not an easy task.

There are two main methods by which the student can achieve a contact with a god or Goddess. The first involves a partner. A full circle is cast by others in the group. The student stands or sits in front of the focal point, usually one that corresponds to the element in which the student will be working, e.g. a candle flame or brazier for fire, a crystal ball for earth, a bowl of water for water and incense smoke for air. The student clears his or her mind of all extraneous thoughts. At this point, a trance state is induced by the partner. This process might take a long time, or it might consist of only a few deep breaths. The partner then invokes the deity to be contacted into the medium, making sure that the intention is for the god or Goddess to manifest WITHIN THE FOCAL MEDIUM. It is important that this is made clear, since this is vital to the maintenance of control by the receiver.

After a time, the receiver is questioned by the partner as to whether the deity is present. When this occurs, the receiver will either see an image, hear a voice or both. Occasionally, students will receive impressions from the entity in other ways, either by a certain odor, or kinesthetically, i.e. a 'feeling' from the entity. This could manifest as a tingling sensation, a vibration or a perception of increased energy within the circle. When the receiver reports that the entity is indeed present, the questioning can begin, not only by the partner but by the others in the circle. These questions can be personal, can request information about the entity, or anything else the circle members would like to know. When the questions have been answered, or the receiver reports the contact fading, the partner bids the entity farewell, removes the focal point by covering or extinguishing it, and directs the receiver back to normal awareness.

In the second method, the receiver works alone. The setup is the same as that used with a partner, but the trance state is either achieved by the receiver alone or with the aid of the Priest or Priestess of that circle. The receiver invokes the deity into the focal medium as above, until the deity manifests sufficiently to be perceived. The ritual then proceeds as above, until the deity is asked to withdraw from the focal medium by the receiver. This method is far more difficult than the first and involves a great deal more control on the part of the student. It is suggested that this method be used only by students who have some experience in psychic work, or who are initiates in other magical systems. If a student wishes, he or she can perform two contacts, one by the first method and one by the second.

Since each student is different with respect to talent, previous experience and emotional makeup, the instructor needs to be extremely vigilant as to how the ritual is progressing. Occasionally, students who are very analytical in nature will have difficulty 'letting go' enough to perceive the manifestation. If a student appears to be having trouble with this, several things can be done to make it easier. First, additional suggestions of calm and relaxation can be made to the receiver, interspersed with the invocation. Secondly, the invocation can be made more extensive, using a great deal of poetic imagery, in a sing song tone of voice. Also, the entire group can assist in the invocation by whispering the name of the deity or invoking using a 'round robin' approach by which everyone takes a turn calling the deity into manifestation. Perhaps the most important thing for the instructor to remember is that, in certain extreme cases, ANY perception of the deity by the receiver needs to be interpreted as a successful contact.

At this point, the invocations should cease and the receiver can be questioned as to the nature of his or her perceptions. If no messages are forthcoming and the perception begins to fade, the deity should be bidden to withdraw. It is important that this be done, even if the receiver reports the deity has already withdrawn: it is good practice for the receiver; the entity might not actually be completely gone; and the other members of the circle might perceive the entity as well. The opposite problem occasionally occurs with natural psychics or people who have experience in mediumship. These people are accustomed to being 'taken over' by an entity, and have a tendency to lapse into a full scale possession. While this is not dangerous per se, the point of this exercise is for the student to develop control of the situation. Thus, a possession, at this point, is to be discouraged.

This can be achieved in the following way. First, the student employs the second contact method, as described above. That is, he or she invokes the deity into the focal medium alone. This is a good way to control depth of trance, since the student must speak. It also fixes in his or her mind that the entity will manifest in the focal medium. The student, then, will see the entity within the medium, and hear the voice externally. Second, all questions from the other members of the circle should be addressed to the receiver referring to the deity in the third person, e.g. 'How does the Goddess appear to you?' or 'What does (name of deity) say about such and such?' The receiver should answer also in the third person, that is, 'He said . . . ' or 'She is showing me an image of . . . '. Under NO circumstances should the receiver be addressed as the deity.

Finally, the deity should be bidden to withdraw by the receiver, several times if necessary, and the focal medium put out of sight. Often, psychic people instinctively find their own methods of trance control. The receiver may wish to rise and walk around the circle, sometimes sitting, sometimes standing, and may look away from the focal medium from time to time. This is vital if the naturally psychic student is to develop personal control methods, and should be encouraged.

The question arises at this point as to which god or Goddess to contact. This depends on the student. Often, a student will be asked to contact a god or Goddess from the quarter or element that he or she feels least comfortable with in order to achieve elemental balance. For example, extremely intellectual people might be asked to contact south, or emotional people might be asked to do north. This will make the contact a little more difficult, but the results are very often worth it and make the successful contact all the more meaningful. Although this is not normally done, it is permitted for a student to contact a deity of the opposite sex, that is, a woman to contact a god or a man to contact a Goddess. Since identification with the contacted deity is not encouraged, there isn't the problem in this situation as there would be with a possession. It might also serve to further discourage a possession.

For the most part, students will request contact with one of the guardians of the circle. Occasionally, however, one will wish to contact a deity not in our pantheon. This is permitted provided the student has some experience with psychic work, and can provide the rest of the members of the circle with a detailed summary of the deity's characteristics before the ritual proceeds. However, this entity must be from one of Celtic pantheons and be similar to or another form of our circle guardians. Deities from other pantheons have mind-sets associated with them that may not be harmonious to the Celtic folk soul. Middle eastern deities are examples of this, especially ones that have been viewed as 'demons' in the past by rival faiths. These are not suitable for invocation by students in a training circle, although initiates have done this in regular circles for some specific purpose.

Whichever deity is invoked, it is important for the instructor to remember that the student will often be frightened of a contact, but also want it very much, in order to 'pass the test' and progress to the next step. Nobody really fails a contact ritual. Most people receive something. If the contact was less than optimal, the student can do another one, perhaps by a different method. Students can be encouraged by the experiences of others, but there is still the apprehension of plunging ahead that no one can allay. Encouragement and firm guidance on the part of the instructor is essential. The student must not be allowed to 'chicken out' or delay the contact for another time. A date is set and barring illness, work or other unavoidable situations, the ritual must proceed. Most students are eager, but occasionally avoidance behavior is seen. This should be gently but firmly confronted, and the ritual should proceed as planned. After the ritual has ended, all members should critique the ritual, praising good points and discussing weak points. This should be a learning experience for everyone, initiates and students alike.

Ritual Outline

1. Discuss the deity to be contacted. Brief participants as to attributes, etc. Answer questions from the student at this time.
2. Make sure the ritual area is set up with the focal medium in place and all necessary equipment is at hand. This can be done by the student doing the contact. It is suggested that a checklist be made up ahead of time.
3. Cast the circle as usual. Invoke quarter guardians including the one to be contacted.
4. The receiver sits or stands in front of the focal medium. If there is a partner, then the partner prepares the medium. If the receiver is alone, then he or she prepares the medium.

5. Trance is induced in the receiver, either by a partner or alone.

6. The invocation begins, either by the partner or the receiver. The members of the circle can join in as needed.

7. The receiver reports that contact is achieved. All invocations stop. The deity is greeted either by the receiver or the partner.

8. The partner or receiver requests a message from the deity to the entire group. This sometimes gets the flow of communication going.

9. The receiver calls for questions. The members can either take turns around the circle or just speak up. Wait for the complete answer before another question is asked.

10. When there are no more questions, or the receiver reports that the contact is fading, the partner or the receiver can call for a few moments of silent meditation to allow all members, but especially the receiver, to personally commune with the deity.

11. The partner or receiver requests that the deity withdraw from the focal medium, gives thanks and says farewell. Then the receiver or the partner removes the focal medium.

12. All members stand up and move around. Cakes and wine are suggested at this point since they ground the energy.

13. The guardians are bid farewell and the circle is closed.

14. The receiver is congratulated on his or her success and all members tell their experiences. Critical evaluation should be gentle and constructive, giving the receiver suggestions for improvement.

Group Contacts

Another way to do a contact is to invoke an entity into the circle and allow everyone to serve as a channel. A dark mirror, candle, statue or other focal point can be set up on the edge of the circle, arranged so that it is visible to everyone. Whoever is leading the circle invokes the presence of the entity, instructing the members of the circle to concentrate on the focal point. When the entity in question begins to manifest, anyone who perceives a presence can speak. The leader of the circle, who deliberately stays out of the trance state, can also pose particular questions that have been decided upon ahead of time.

If more than one member gets a message, they can all speak in no particular order, interrupting each other at will and using messages from the rest of the group to corroborate and augment their own. Some people will get words. Others will receive pictures. Still others will get impressions and feelings. Having everyone contribute their input in such a seemingly random fashion will eventually achieve a multifaceted message free from the individual bias that is unavoidable when one person only receives the contact.

In another variation, all the members sit in a circle and hold hands. A focal point is placed in the center of the circle, making sure that it can be viewed by everyone from any angle. A crystal ball, candle flame, bowl of water or round black mirror laid flat upon the floor will work well. Other props can be arranged aesthetically around the central point to narrow the focus of the working and small votive candles can be used for illumination if necessary.

As in the previous variation, a leader can invoke the entity or each member of the circle can take turns invoking the entity, round-robin fashion, until everyone has had a chance. As before, anyone who perceives a presence or receives a message can speak out loud in no particular order, adding to each others' messages as they wish. With all members of the circle holding hands, more energy is built up than in the previous version and the telepathic rapport between individual members is enhanced. Consequently, the contact will be a great deal stronger in this variation and the temptation to lapse into full-scale possession will be greater.

Since all participants are essentially 'on their own,' monitoring their own depth of trance and so on, this particular method of contact work is recommended for either all initiates or initiates plus senior students who have been through at least one contact if not contact and possession too. However, it has the advantage of dispensing with the need for one person to be 'on stage' and decreases any performance anxiety or temptation to stain-glass. All the members of the circle share in the energy requirement so one person is not as drained. And since no one person is serving as medium, the focus is less on the person doing the contact and more on the entity being contacted.

Possessions

God and Goddess possessions are perhaps the most complex and controversial part of Roebuck training. In this ritual, the student performs what ceremonial magicians call 'Assumption of Godform.' One of the guardian deities is called upon to take over the student's body and mind, and interact directly with the other members of the circle. The student assumes the identity of one of the deities, and brings that deity into the circle. Sometimes this is called 'being an oracle' or 'channeling,' although these terms can also be applied to contacts as well. Unfortunately, the term 'possession' despite its negative connotations, most accurately describes the process.

Ability to achieve god or Goddess possession is used as an initiation test in the Roebuck, because it requires trust and acceptance from both sides of the Veil. After nearly a year of training and working with the Roebuck, the student has learned about the guardians through pathworkings and contacts, and has grown to know and love them. In order to turn over body and mind to one of them, the student must be absolutely sure, both consciously and subconsciously, that the guardian is benevolent and will cause no harm to the student or to others in the circle. If this is not felt deeply, then certain reflexive psychic defenses come into play, and the deity will not breach them. It has been our experience that if the student is not absolutely willing and, indeed eager, that a possession take place, it will not, despite the power that the guardian has to force the issue. The Gods do not take us against our will. Consequently, despite conscious doubts and fears, if the soul is trusting, the Gods will come.

This also implies acceptance on the part of the guardians for the student to enter the Roebuck Priesthood. The Roebuck guardians have a way of ejecting those people who are unsuitable, sometimes without a reason that is discernable to the other members. However, this usually occurs well before the student has reached the level where he or she is required to do a possession. A student can be reasonably assured that if he or she has been allowed this far, then the Gods have accepted him or her. It remains on the part of the student, then, to do the lion's share of the acceptance.

Ritually, possessions are relatively simple. They are always done with a partner, either a working partner or initiate of the opposite sex from the student. This partner will be responsible for invoking the deity and seeing to the welfare of the student doing the possession and does nothing else in the circle. If the working partner of the student is also a student, the instructor needs to be at hand to coach the partner on what to do and make sure all is well. First, the student needs to meditate and prepare. This preparation might have been occurring for some days before the ritual, with the student doing personal contacts with the deity and contemplating what is about to happen. Some prior preparation is necessary, since no one can really go cold into a possession without some kind of meditation.

So, the student goes off alone while the rest of the members prepare the ritual place and cast the circle. The student doing the possession should not be expected to do any of this, but should concentrate only on the possession. It is useful, although not entirely necessary, for the members not to speak with the student before the ritual, since the student must not be distracted with trivia before the ritual. Meditating alone in the temple prior to the ritual, or out of sight and earshot in the case of an outdoor circle, usually is the best preparation. Preparing too long before the ritual can cause undue nervousness and apprehension.

When the circle is cast and all is in readiness, the student is brought to the ritual place. In the case of the temple, he or she waits quietly while the circle is cast, and the guardians invoked. The student is brought into the circle if necessary and the partner begins to call upon the deity to descend into the body of the student. The student remains quiet during this process, although he or she might well have felt the deity begin to take over well before this. A useful exercise is to imagine that one has become hollow and the energy of the deity is beginning to fill the empty vessel with light. The partner will then greet the deity and ask for a message. The ritual proceeds much like a contact, with members asking questions, or awaiting personal messages. The difference is that the student is treated like the deity incarnate, addressed as such and shown due reverence and respect.

When the questions have ended and no more messages are forthcoming, the deity is asked to leave the body of the student and bidden farewell. Then, the student is brought back to normal consciousness, held, massaged, addressed by name, fed wine and cakes, and generally revived before the circle is dismantled. This is important. It is not a good policy to leave the student half conscious, open and vulnerable when the circle is dismantled. Even though the deity in question has left, other things less benevolent may be hanging about. These might move in if the student is allowed to remain open. So, when the working partner of the student is satisfied that all is well, the circle is dismantled.

The debriefing after a possession circle is very important. The student will generally have no idea of what actually occurred. It is vital that the student be reassured that the test was passed, that the Gods have indeed accepted him or her and that the possession took place. This must be said even though the possession might not have been as strong as had been expected. Some students are better mediums than others. However, even if only a glimmer of deity came through, the possession should be counted as successful. Future possessions will only grow stronger as the student gains confidence. The instructor is responsible for making sure that the student is reassured, before the other, more experienced members critique the ritual. The critique may actually wait for another time. The student will most likely be very emotionally unstable for several days after the ritual. Waiting for a while will assure that constructive criticism will be taken in the spirit in which it is offered and not seen as an indication that something went wrong.

Possession rituals, like contact rituals, are extremely individual. They depend a great deal on the individual student's talents, emotional makeup and prior training. Consequently, there are few real hard and fast rules. However, there are a few guidelines that the instructor might keep in mind to make the possession ritual as rewarding as possible for the student and the other members.

Deity possession is rarely an all or nothing process. It usually happens on a graduated scale. The energy of the deity will fade in and fade out. Often students with dramatic abilities or communications skills will augment the possession by 'playing the part' and allowing his or her own personality to come through. This is done quite outside conscious awareness and should not be seen as an attempt to 'fake it'. Students are 'on stage' during a ritual like this and may lapse into this out of insecurity and doubt.

The more experienced members of the circle will be familiar enough with the personality of the student to be able to point out places where this occurred. They will also be able to discern when the deity was actually present. Each guardian has a certain 'feel'. Certain ways that things are said, emphasis on certain images, heightened energy levels that are tangible are indications that a certain deity is indeed present. Rarely are students able to fake this convincingly. Members will point out to the student when the deity manifested the strongest and when the student's personality intruded the most. It is up to the student to take such criticism seriously and work on increasing self confidence to the point where such augmentation is no longer necessary.

Occasionally, props can be useful in increasing the self confidence of the student. Dressing up as the deity, wearing certain things that bear the mark of the deity such as certain colored robes, crowns, swords, cauldrons, books, knives, flowers and the like can be carried or held to enable the student to 'get into it' better. However, these props are by no means necessary. Possessions can proceed very successfully without them. However, even experienced circle members might have a problem accepting a god or Goddess dressed in jeans and a T-shirt. Even if elaborate props are not used, the student should dress appropriately in a simple hooded robe or cloak out of respect for the entity who will be using the body for a time.

Needless to say, a recent bath and an empty stomach are also recommended. There are no rules for this; some students have health needs that need to be considered. However, students should be reminded that their bodies are going to be inhabited by Gods and consequently, those bodies need to be cared for as much as possible. Deliberate abuse, such as overwork, lack of sleep, certain chemicals and lack of nutrition should be avoided prior to the ritual. The Gods should not have to inhabit damaged vessels, especially when that damage could have been prevented.

As in the case of the contact ritual, the question of which deity should be called arises. There are a few rules here. One rule is that the deity chosen be one of the circle guardians. Possessions at best are risky, and the guardians of the circle will reduce the risk. We know them, we trust them and we love them. It is far better not only for the student, but for the members who must judge their performance to have a deity that is familiar. The guardians manifest easily, we recognize them when they do, and we know that they will withdraw rather than bring harm to the medium. Therefore, for a student possession ritual, invocation of one of the circle guardians is required. After the student is an initiate with more experience in these rituals, then the rule no longer applies.

Another rule is that the deity invoked be of the same sex as the student. Some groups perform cross possessions, as they are called. We shun that practice in the Roebuck for the following reason. We as Pagans believe that, unlike angels that are androgynous, our Gods manifest as male and female. If the purpose of the ritual is to have a physical manifestation of a Goddess, for example, there needs to be a Priestess to lend a female body to the rite. Calling a Goddess into a male body is pointless and, indeed, counterproductive. A man does not have the physical and psychic attributes that a Goddess will need to manifest completely. The risk of psychological repercussions that are possible when this is done does not justify the desire to experiment with this technique. Consequently, we have made the decision that this technique is not to be done in a Roebuck circle.

All students, whether they admit it or not, are fearful of this ritual. This is not a fear of harm, or even a fear of the unknown. The main fear, and this never leaves completely even after years, is the fear that one is an unworthy vessel and that the Gods will not enter. This feeling of unworthiness can be overwhelming, and if it is not handled properly, can short circuit the ritual, causing the student to be unable to relax sufficiently to enter trance. The instructor would do well to remember his or her first possession and then counsel the student that these feelings are normal, expected, and indeed, necessary. It doesn't do to be too arrogant at a time like this.

If a student exhibits overconfidence or is too cocky, it might well be a danger signal. Humility in magic work is vital and nothing inspires it quite like being reminded of how vast the Gods are and how tiny we are. Being chosen by the Gods as a vessel of manifestation is both a humbling and exhilarating experience. No words can really prepare a student for that experience. It is up to the members of the circle to reassure the student with their own experiences and attempt as much as possible to lend energy in the circle and make sure that all goes as well as possible.

Ritual Outline
1. Send the student off to meditate alone.
2. Members prepare the ritual place and cast the circle. If the possession is done in the temple, the preparations are made beforehand and the student either meditates while the circle is being cast, or is brought in. In an outdoor site, the student waits out of earshot before the circle is cast and then brought in.
3. The student is seated or stands in a designated area. The partner then invokes the deity with members helping if necessary.

4. When there is some sign that the deity has taken over the body of the student, the partner greets the deity by name and all members give a sign of greeting.

5. The deity is asked for a general message. Often, the deity will give personal messages to each member.

6. Then, the members may ask questions, waiting until one answer is complete before asking the next.

7. When there are no more questions, the partner then calls for a silent moment of communion with the deity for the student.

8. The deity is asked to leave the body of the student and is thanked and bidden farewell.

9. The student is then addressed by name, talked to, held and otherwise brought back to normal consciousness.

10. Cakes and wine are consecrated by the Priest and Priestess. They are fed to the student first.

11. The partner gives the sign that the student has returned completely and the circle is closed.

12. The student is reassured and asked about his or her experiences first. Then the members of the circle are debriefed. Criticisms may be postponed for a day or two to allow the student to fully recover.

The Magical Mindset

Magic is both an art and a science. It is an art to the extent that it involves subjective experiences and a sense of aesthetics. But it is also a science in that it follows certain laws, the violation of which renders the experience unverifiable in consensual reality. This is a pretentious way of saying that if you don't follow the rules, the ritual may be pretty and exciting, but it won't do what you want it to. This results in a form of entertainment – valid in itself as ritual theater, but results in no lasting changes in the real world.

Magic, by most definitions, is a way of making changes in the world of form by making use of powerful cosmic forces that are summoned by certain symbols. These symbols serve as access codes (to use a modern term) to unleash the forces that reside in the greater cosmos. However, these forces are only accessed through their interface with the human psyche. And since the human psyche is subject to certain natural laws, these forces are as well.

There's really nothing mysterious or mystical about this process. Nor is it supernatural. The natural laws that govern it are the same as those that govern the biophysics of our own bodies – as poorly understood as that currently is by mainstream science. No doubt, science will eventually catch up to what magicians have known for ages. However, in the meantime, we can explain the phenomenon sort of like this.

The fundamental assumptions that both magic and modern biophysics share is that human beings literally create their own reality. What we perceive as "real" is a construct – some postulate an illusion in holographic form – created by our brains by the responses of our sensory organs to energy vibrating at a variety of frequencies. An energy wave vibrating at 523 cps is perceived as the musical note of middle C while the same energy wave vibrating at 514×10^{12} cps is perceived as the color green. Energy stimulates our auditory nerve at the lower frequencies while the higher frequencies stimulate our optic nerve. The brain interprets these impulses as two distinct perceptions. However, in both cases, the energy is the same.

On the psychological level, it is also acknowledged that a person's expectations can dramatically alter the perceptions of reality. A physicist who expects light photons to appear as waves will perceive waves. One who expects particles will perceive particles. On a more mundane level, a person hiking through a desert during snake season will jump at every branch lying in the trail, taking it as a snake. These perceptions are important because they dictate behavior – and behavior is what actually makes the changes in the physical world.

How does all this translate into practical magical workings? It does so by establishing the "rules" that magic must follow in order to effect changes according to will. Say, for example, a group of people assemble with the purpose of healing a woman, we'll call Jane, from cancer. Several factors must be present for this to work. We already have one – purpose. The individual will of each of the participants is the same – to heal Jane. Therefore, we can say the group is 'of a mind' on this issue. Not everybody needs to know Jane personally. One person will be enough. But the will of everyone needs to be the same. If someone in the group wants to send the healing energy to someone else, then it creates a short circuit in the circle.

But as we have seen, there is more to being "of a mind" than just unity of purpose. Energy is accessed by the use of symbols. In a group where everyone is trained to respond to the same symbolic access codes, the energy will be stronger and flow more easily than in a group with mixed symbols or people with no symbolic training at all. And since the symbols are responded to on an emotional level rather than a rational one, the process can't be forced or faked. So, for maximum efficiency, everybody in the circle should be hooked up to the same, or similar, access codes.

Once accessed, the energy must be channeled, amplified and directed at its intended target. There are a number of time-honored techniques used by our ancestors to achieve this – dancing, chanting, drumming, sexual stimulation – in order to increase the amount of energy to be sent out. Then, as the energy reaches a climax, it is released – also in a variety of ways – and sent to the target.

Here, it gets controversial, at least from a scientific standpoint. Science still refuses to acknowledge that a person can be influenced by the thoughts and feelings of others – for obvious reasons. Nobody wants to think that their thoughts, feelings and actions can be controlled from distance by people they don't even know. However, this forms one of the fundamental assumptions of magic. The amplified healing energy of the group can influence Jane and heal or alleviate her condition without her being present among them.

How? Maybe Jane is expecting the jolt of energy and believes that since such magical and mysterious intervention will heal her where conventional medicine couldn't. This constitutes standard "faith healing" and should not be scorned. Such a belief might well motivate Jane to alter her attitude and lifestyle so that her immune system – the natural healing power of her body – can do its job better. And, if her disease hasn't progressed to the point of no return, she might well recover.

There is also the possibility that the energy sent to her by such a healing will somehow "resonate" with her own energy field – what the New Agers call the aura – and will make positive changes in it, particularly if it is repeated several times. Since all "reality" is energy vibrating at various frequencies, a blast of energy tuned to her frequency by the thoughts and feelings of a friend, she might, like a harp string that when plucked will cause other strings to vibrate according to their harmonic frequencies, Jane's aura will vibrate at the same frequency and will accept the positive and loving thoughts. This could also initiate bodily changes resulting in the remission of her cancer – maybe even without her knowledge.

This is the theory and purpose behind the Cone of Power that forms the basis of most coven rituals. The uses are myriad and the purpose really doesn't matter so long as 1) everyone agrees on it, 2) everyone accesses energy by the same or similar symbols and 3) the energy is channeled and targeted effectively.

Cone of Power

All magical rituals, when done properly, raise the energy level in the circle. This is usually an indication that the world between worlds has been achieved (in fact, rather than just in theory) and we are in the presence of the Gods. People perceive this viscerally, in an almost kinesthetic fashion, often below the level of consciousness. It feels like an electric current being channeled through ones' body, making every nerve-ending tingle. People feel tense, jumpy, feel as though they can't stand or sit still, but must move about.

This is a natural feeling, and not an inherently unpleasant one. But it makes people uncomfortable, not because it's unfamiliar (although it might be so within the context of a magical circle) but usually their experience with high-energy states has been negative, such as the energy emitted by people who are having a heated argument. Highly sensitive people, particularly when they are children, often find angry displays physically painful. The energy emitted by an angry person can feel like a physical assault. Consequently, many people will learn to associate a high energy state with anger and, therefore, pain and will go out of their way to avoid it.

This is because when the body perceives a high energy field (again, viscerally and below conscious awareness), it responds by a rise in energy level itself. The unconscious mind steps in at this point and looks around the physical environment for a reason why this is occurring. Depending upon what it finds, it will put an emotional label on the reason for the increased energy level and initiate an emotional state of mind to match it. For example, if there is an attractive person in the immediate vicinity, the increased energy level will be interpreted as sexual arousal. If the tone of someone's voice is harsh or threatening or he or she has a negative facial expression, the interpretation could be one of anger. If there are smiling people around who are expressing affection, then it will be interpreted as happiness.

This is how you get some of the bizarre reactions that newcomers (even experienced people) often get in circle. This interpretation of a rise in energy is unconscious and reflexive and the inappropriate emotional state can be full blown before the conscious mind is even aware of it. All of a sudden, a person might be angry in the circle and not know quite why. If he or she doesn't know how to control their emotions (or never learned that they should), you'll get a sudden and unexplained temper tantrum. If such a person is a 'I'm right and everybody else is wrong' sort of person, he or she will insist that his interpretation is correct and won't accept any explanation to the contrary. He or she might even stalk off in a huff - especially if the person is unconsciously looking for an excuse to leave the circle in the first place.

All of this can be prevented for the most part by the addition of strong verbal suggestions of what is going on during the circle. People in a circle are in an altered state of awareness anyway, even if it's not formally induced, and therefore are highly suggestible. People can be told (or reminded) that the high energy state they perceive is a result of the presence of the Gods and the energy they feel rising in their bodies in response is the result of a ritual to raise power. This will fulfill the mind's insistence on finding a reason for the sensation and will derail most negative and inappropriate reactions.

These suggestions should be worded using as much sensory detail as possible. Have the people in the circle feel the energy rise in their bodies using various tactile and kinesthetic cues. Include vivid imagery, perhaps of the various Gods and Goddesses who are lending their energies to the rite. In the altered reality of the circle, these suggestions will be accepted by the right brain and translated into emotional responses. These responses will arouse the energy while other suggestions provide a feedback loop in order to keep the energy flowing and building in intensity.

What is this energy that is generated when we raise a so-called 'cone of power? For one thing, it isn't really generated, it's always there. It's nothing more than the normal electromagnetic energy of the body that powers the beating of the heart, the expansion of the diaphragm, and the electrical impulses along the synapses of the nerve cells. This is the normal resting state of the body. When the body becomes aroused (no matter the reason), it literally switches gears and goes into a kind of overdrive. Energy is beefed up and channeled to the various muscles and nerves that produce whatever action the body needs to take - sexual activity, fight-or-flight response to danger, or whatever is needed at that moment to survive.

This is the same energy that is measured by the various devices such as GSRs and polygraphs. When the body is aroused, it produces changes in electrical conductance in the skin, chiefly increased moisture (sweaty palms) but other changes as well. Dry skin poses a resistance to electrical current. Moisten that skin, and the resistance decreases, more current gets conducted, and the dial goes up. Since emotional states accompany this arousal, the increase in conductivity can be correlated (however imperfectly) with the intensity of emotion - guilt about lying, for instance. The way people beat a polygraph test is by being able to avoid becoming emotionally upset, and therefore physically aroused, by the act of telling a lie - usually by convincing their unconscious mind that the lie is justified in some way.

This energy can be raised in the body by unconscious suggestion. It can also be raised in response to the energy level in the circle. Everybody responds to everybody else's increase in energy level so eventually everyone is functioning at a higher than normal level. If you hook one person up to a Galvanic Skin Response meter (GSR) with a device that will beep or light up when a circuit is closed and power flows through the machine, and have everyone hold hands in a circle, this process will be demonstrated dramatically. While the circle is broken, that is, the person standing next to the hooked up person is not holding his hand, the beeper or light will not activate. But once that final person touches the person hooked up to the device, the circuit is closed and the device will turn on.

This is what happens when a cone of power is raised. Everyone joins hands, closing the circuit of electrical power. As each person allows his own energy level to rise, everyone else's energy will rise in response. Eventually the amperage (the same electrical energy that powers a light bulb) rises to a very high level. Add a series of ongoing suggestions from a leader to let the energy rise for a specific purpose (such as a healing) and everyone will literally be "of a mind," that is, everybody will have the same rationale for feeling the increased energy level. The energy will be released for whatever the stated purpose is, and people will ground, either by touching the floor or some other surface, just like the grounding wire in a wall plug. This keeps it from short circuiting and frotzing everyone like a toaster with a loose wire.

Where does the energy go from there? That's a question which transcends physics and enters the realm of metaphysics. Science has yet to prove (or admit the possibility) that energy generated in such a fashion can influence the physical realm. This is something that might just have to be taken on faith, as it were. Some writers on magic have postulated that the electrical fields of people and things can be subtly affected by a sudden inrush of energy from an outside source. This energy can transcend distances, so that a cone of power released on the west coast can help heal someone on the east coast, or in another country altogether.

This "addressing" process can be facilitated in a number of ways. The best way, of course, would be to have everyone in the circle know the recipient and visualize him or her in their minds while releasing the energy. If this isn't possible, (and often it isn't) it works to have an experienced target person who does know the recipient gather the energy and direct it to where it should go. In this case, the energy is specifically released to the target person so that he or she can send it along. There can be more than one target person for each cone of power so long as all the target people are 'of a mind' about whom is to be sent the energy.

While the energy is being raised by the other members of the circle, the target person (or people) visualizes the recipient as vividly as possible, along with any attendant feelings for that person. For best results, the target person should visualize the recipient in action, doing the very things for which the ritual is being performed – i.e., playing, running, laughing, working, loving, or whatever. Then, at a prearranged signal, the target person gathers up the energy and sends it out of the circle towards the recipient. This should be accompanied by the visualization of the energy actually touching the recipient, being absorbed into his or her aura or whatever.

If there are no experienced target people, a photograph or other personal object can be used as a focal point. The photograph or personal object can be passed around the circle, allowing each person enough time to be able to visualize the recipient's image or get a 'feel' for the recipient from the object. When this process is accomplished, the cone of power can be raised and sent along to its proper destination more efficiently.

FIRST, CLOSE YOUR EYES AND TAKE A DEEP BREATH, CENTERING YOURSELF FIRMLY. FIX IN YOUR MIND THE INTENTION OF USING THIS ENERGY FOR (State Purpose). FEEL THE EARTH BENEATH YOUR FEET, SOLID SECURE. REACH DOWN DEEPER, DEEPER WITHIN THE EARTH, TAP INTO THE MOLTEN POWER OF TUBAL'S FORGE. NOW, BRING

THAT ENERGY UP, UP, UP THROUGH YOUR FEET INTO YOUR BODY. NOW, REACH ABOVE YOU TO THE STARRY HEAVANS, THE BRIGHT CLEAR LIGHT OF THE MOON, GODA'S SPIRAL CASTLE, SHIMMERING IN THE DARKNESS. BRING THAT ENERGY DOWN, DOWN, DOWN INTO YOUR BODY. FEEL IT SWIRLING, BLENDING, MERGING WITH THE FIREY ENERGY FROM THE FORGE, PERFECTLY IN BALANCE, PERFECTLY IN HARMONY WITHIN THE CENTER OF YOUR BEING.

NOW, SEND THAT ENERGY OUT THROUGH YOUR LEFT HAND TO THE BROTHER OR SISTER ON YOUR LEFT. RECEIVE IT THROUGH YOUR RIGHT HAND FROM THE BROTHER OR SISTER ON YOUR RIGHT. SEND IT OUT TO THE LEFT, BRING IT IN FROM THE RIGHT, AROUND AND AROUND. FEEL THE ENERGY BUILD, STRONGER AND STRONGER, MORE AND MORE INTENSE, SEE IT GLOW AND PULSE BRIGHTER AND BRIGHTER, THIS ENERGY FOR (State purpose). AROUND AND AROUND, BUILDING IN INTENSITY AND STRENGTH UNTIL YOU CAN CONTAIN IT NO LONGER, AND LET IT *GO*.

Usually at this point the people in the circle have been raising their joined hands above their heads. At the emphatic command 'GO,' all members of the circle drop hands and point towards the center of the circle.

FEEL THE ENERGY FLOW FROM YOU TO (State purpose), DOING WHAT WE WILL IT TO. VISUALIZE IT BEING DONE (Specific details can be used here, e.g. see (name) well and healthy, etc.) SO MOTE IT BE!

All answer, "So mote it be."

NOW, TAKE WITHIN YOU WHATEVER YOU NEED FOR YOURSELF, HEALTH, STRENGTH AND PROSPERITY.

Members may cross their arms across their chests to bring the excess energy into their own beings.

NOW, GROUND THE ENERGY INTO THE EARTH.

Members will usually do this in their own individual ways. Some will take deep breaths, others will kneel and press their palms to the floor, shake their hands at their sides and so on. Cakes and ale are a good idea at this point, since consuming food will ground everyone further. Allow everyone to 'unwind' with laughter, jokes etc. before the circle is cut and everyone is led out.

Caveat

Despite the effectiveness of the above training techniques, there are no guarantees. Sometimes, they simply don't work. The candidate drops out of the training, or survives long enough to become initiated, then leaves under unpleasant and emotionally traumatic circumstances. We have seen how this abreaction affects the group as a whole. But what causes it and how is it to be prevented?

Most people who enter into magical work are extremely psychic people - that is, their sensory awareness is naturally tuned into realms that are not physical. Given our materialistic culture, it's a good bet that the vast majority of these people were viciously programmed as children to not consider such non-physical things as 'real' and not react to them.

Parental and societal pressure to find purely physical causes for fear, anger and love is tremendous, and can cause much emotional and psychic trauma to children who are naturally aware of unseen realms. By the time these children grow into adults, they have not only repressed the sensory awareness of the unseen, but also the trauma. It is a very rare case indeed where the sensory awareness of the unseen returns without some fallout from the emotional trauma caused by the repression.

Reality models are a way of dealing with sensory ambiguity and a survival mechanism for living in a human society. All people in a particular society agree that certain things are 'real' (i.e., worthy of response) and other things aren't. Let's say a child expresses fear about 'something' under his bed. His mother examines the room, finds nothing fearful and sternly tells her child to go back to sleep. It's painfully obvious to the child that his mother doesn't consider his fear worthy of her protection. If the threat was 'real,' that is, physical, she would respond by reassuring the child, perhaps holding and soothing him. But since her examination of the room reveals no physical danger, she feels no need to expend time and energy responding to her child's fear.

The child learns that if his mother can't perceive whatever frightens him, the danger isn't real and his fears are 'groundless' and 'all in his head.' Consequently, he grows up with the belief that if he senses something that doesn't fit into the category of what his society claims is real, he must either deny his own sensory input or society's definition of 'reality.'

The usual adult reaction to this dilemma is to find something 'real' to be afraid of. The person will look around in his environment in order to find something that is socially acceptable to react to as a substitute for the 'unreal' fear. In the absence of anything suitable in the outside environment, the person might go so far as to make up something and convince himself of its reality. An innocent remark from an innocuous person will be perceived as a threat and that person will be attacked either verbally or physically, thereby relieving the attacker of the tension caused by the 'fight or flight' response in his body. Even when the physical arousal is gone and the person returns to 'normal' he or she may not be willing to admit that he or she has been 'wrong.' He might also continue to use the other person as a scrim for the projection of his or her own fears, especially if it is convenient to do so.

This behavior is bad enough in ordinary day-to-day living. In magical work, it is disastrous. It forms the basis of much of the 'psychic attack' hysteria one finds in occult and New Age circles. Too often, the mindset in such circles demands that all rationality, logic and common sense be dismissed as 'unenlightened' and 'non-spiritual.' Untrained and unsophisticated people involved in these groups will sense the action of unseen entities and forces in their lives, usually disrupting their neat and orderly view of the world or otherwise violating their comfort zone. The unconscious fear reflex kicks in and they feel compelled to assign a physical source to the disruption.

That source is often a rival within the same group or a member of another group that is disliked for some reason. If the accused 'attacker' is functioning under the same delusions, he or she will retaliate in kind. The result is psychic warfare in which each side slings outrageous accusations at each other and performs endless protection rituals against each other, often bringing other people willingly or unwillingly into the fray.

This doesn't mean that psychic attacks and 'Witch wars' aren't real. They are. However, they don't work exactly as they're reputed to do and are much less common than most people think. A real psychic attack is a very difficult and physically draining thing to launch. It requires cold, calculated effort and a self-disciplined concentration of force, not to mention extensive training in mental imagery and familiarity with how unseen forces function. In short, it is hard work and takes a good deal more than personal pique in order to make it worth the time and trouble.

More likely, what will happen in such a psychic skirmish is that negative vibrations of anger and fear will fly back and forth with each side feeding off it and returning it back again, over and over. Unless some other force intervenes, eventually both sides will exhaust themselves and quit the battle, call a truce or otherwise cease hostilities until the next time. And, there is always a next time since both sides are doing little except projecting their own unresolved fears onto the other rather than taking the responsibility for resolving them once and for all.

The only cure for this problem is to make the fears conscious. Often this means extensive and brutally honest self-examination, reliving childhood traumas and dissecting them to find out the real source of them. Sensing the presence of dangerous or even just unfamiliar spirits and entities might provoke a fear reaction in a psychically sensitive child. Certain other childhood experiences certainly fall into that category such as being visited by dead relatives, having invisible playmates or being taken on wonderful journeys while one's body stayed behind in bed.

Discovering that such childhood experiences are in fact shared by many people is one of the compelling reasons people join occult circles in the first place. There is nothing so therapeutic as discovering that one is not alone in experiencing certain things. In fact, one finds oneself part of a 'special' group of people who are able to perceive things that 'ordinary' people don't. This can produce the euphoric rush associated with finding one's own kind that can dispel much of the childhood trauma associated with being 'different.'

In many students, a formal introduction to a god, Goddess or elemental spirit during the course of a pathworking will produce a flash of recognition. The student will find that the disturbing or frightening entities he had perceived as a child were in actuality the same guardians who had been watching over him all along. Such a student will declare afterwards 'So THAT's who that was." The sense of kinship and 'coming home' is heightened and what happened 'back then' with one's mundane family decreases in relevance.

So, why after all the training do some students still have fears and project them onto the other members of the circle? Why is it so difficult for some people to take responsibility for their own childhood issues, rather than blaming them on somebody else? It is true that some people's childhood traumas, particularly those involving deliberate physical, emotional and sexual abuse, are more difficult to work through and require professional help. However, the Roebuck has had several people in the past who did not have such issues and were simply unable to take that one last critical step towards freedom.

Humanity, or rather, the group mind of humanity, has within it two conflicting forces – the drive for individuation and the herd instinct. Every person on the planet, no matter what culture they live in, is torn between the urge to gratify his/her own desires, whatever they may be, and the urge to be an accepted part of his/her social group. The roots of these instincts are not even human. Animal behavior researchers report the same conflicting forces operating in other primate societies such as chimpanzees and gorillas.

Biological forces favoring the survival of the fittest individual of a particular social group clash with the survival needs of group as a whole, particularly in primates, where an individual, no matter how genetically fit, doesn't live long without the group. In the case of primates, the group itself is what survives, not necessarily the individual, even though individuals compete with other members of the group to make sure only the most fit pass on their genes to the next generation.

The same two forces continue to clash in human societies. They are called by different names and take different forms depending upon the culture, however they tend to break down into the individual vs. some kind of government authority. This authority outwardly can take the form of a king, a religious leader or politician. But behind every authority figure gathers something called the Force of the Majority, which assumes a group mind of its own and dictates what rules of thought, feeling and behavior an individual must follow if he or she wishes to be accepted as a member.

Like any natural force, this Force of the Majority has the express purpose of keeping the group functioning as a cohesive whole and preventing the anarchy which would result from too many of its members demanding their own gratification at the expense of the other members in the group. Traditionally, societies in the harshest of natural environments, like the nomadic Hebrews living out in the middle of the desert, have the most stringent rules of behavior since it wouldn't take many members getting 'theirs' at the group's expense for the entire group to perish in the harsh environment.

Consequently, individuals who won't follow the rules must be thrown out of the group or incarcerated in some way to keep them from preying on the other members to satisfy their own needs. Small groups of individuals who won't follow the rules are systematically exterminated. The larger the group grows, the more fierce the slaughter becomes. This makes sense if the individuals in question are engaged in criminal activities such as killing, stealing and raping. However, the Force of the Majority has a way of extending its function to those who rebel against the society in intellectual or spiritual ways.

Why would anybody want to exterminate a small group of people who do no one any harm, who are often hardworking, friendly, responsible citizens, but who meet in secret and study strange spiritual and religious teachings? What is their crime? This is one of the most perplexing questions of history. From the Cathars, to the Quakers to the Falun Gong, why does a society go to such draconian measures to persecute people whose only crime is harboring a different religious or spiritual belief?

At the foundation of every society are assumptions about the world, what the world consists of and what constitutes 'reality.' These assumptions are nearly always based upon some religious or philosophical belief system. Anyone who shares that belief system will automatically share those assumptions. And any leader who can manipulate those assumptions will automatically have control over the population. However, someone who doesn't share the belief system, or the assumptions that go along with it, is not subject to that control. The only measure of control left is to get rid of them as permanently as possible to prevent anyone else from following their example.

Leaders with the tremendous power of the Force of the Majority behind them often look upon people who disagree with them - even if they are not physically or emotionally preying upon the other members - as dangers to the community and will persecute them as such. Such a leader has secretly gained a certain amount of power over the people in order to gratify his or her personal desires (money, fame and sex being only the most common) and has constructed an intellectual and/

or religious rationale to justify it. Anyone who will not buy into this rationale and refuses to allow his or her energy and resources to be used for such purposes becomes a target for the leader's wrath.

Any person who takes steps to join a mystery religion of any kind runs smack into the fury of such a leader. The Majority in any society is concerned only with the self-preservation and self-gratification of its members. A small, harmless group of religious or spiritual dissidents rarely attracts their attention. It's only when a Shadowy demagogue finds them a personal threat that they become a target for demonization - often fabricating actual 'crimes,' particularly involving children, that these dissidents are supposed to have committed. With these accusations, the leaders are able to convince the Majority that the dissidents are threats to them personally and thereby justify persecution. The larger the society, the more power the Majority has and a ruler skillful in manipulating that Majority can effectively turn an entire society against a group of people whose only crime is that they won't buy into his personal agenda.

The seeker then, just by existing, risks not only the wrath of the Force of the Majority, but the persecution of the demagogue who wields it. However, this demagogue doesn't have to be the ruler of a nation with an army or police force at his or her command. It can be the person's own parent, boss, church pastor or anyone with any authority to determine his or her behavior and lifestyle. Banding together in groups of like minded people can alleviate the situation for awhile, but ultimately it is the seeker himself or herself who must decide often on a daily – sometimes hourly - basis whether to continue on the path of individual destiny or capitulate to the demands of the herd.

It takes tremendous courage to break away from the herd in order to pursue one's own individual destiny. One has to risk ostracism first and foremost from parents and siblings, most of whom are united in a group mind of their own. The son who wants to be an artist in a family full of doctors faces this kind of pressure head on. 'My father was a doctor, his father was a doctor, I'm a doctor, and you my son are damn well going to be a doctor." Worse, is the person who wants to pursue another religion or lifestyle from the one the family has followed for generations. The response is always 'How *could* you?' as though it is inconceivable that anyone born into that particular family would even think of deviating from the accepted way that the family's life has always been lived.

From dialogue such as this, it becomes clear that what is important to the members of the family is the family itself, not the individuals within it. As long as a family member is doing what he or she is 'supposed' to do, everyone is happy – except for the family member in question. A particular family often has many members who have been willing to submerge their own personal wants, needs and talents to 'go along' with what the family wanted in order to be loved, accepted and, in some cases, in line for an inheritance or other social advantages. The idea that one member would be willing to forego everything a family has to offer to pursue an individual path is inconceivable. It is the Herd Mentality on its most basic level.

So, the first hurdle a person must overcome is breaking compelling emotional ties to the family. It is not easy to turn one's back on people who've been loving and supportive – often physically as well as emotionally - for twenty or thirty years of one's life. The saddest part of this scenario is that the more close-knit and demonstrative the family is the stronger the pressure is to conform. If a person breaks out of this cocoon, he or she is literally 'out in the cold' and must do without not only affection and attention but financial support.

Even though a determined seeker is able to break free of family ties, he or she must then face the Force of the Majority in the workplace. Being 'out on one's own' invariably means working for a living - usually at a job which demands just as much conformity to a company's particular group mind as the family did. How much one is willing to 'fit in' depends on both the individual and the job, but for everyone a certain amount of discretion is required, particularly regarding such inflammatory subjects as religion and spirituality.

This is particularly a problem in the case of occult and psychic studies. The student of the occult is the ultimate rebel, challenging authority at its most fundamental level. Keeping one's pentagram hidden in one's shirt and keeping one's mouth shut when discussions turn to religion only works for awhile. Sooner or later, somebody will get wise and see beyond the protective coloration. A crisis will occur in which the seeker must either be true to his or her own inner truth or violate it by 'going along with the crowd.' Then, the jig will be up. The student must then 'walk the walk' rather than just 'talk the talk.' He or she must stand up for what they are and risk getting tossed out of the family, the job or the society and be utterly and completely self-sufficient.

This presents a problem. Biologically, we are herd animals. We have an instinctive need to be accepted by the herd. It is a most basic survival mechanism. We have been fed by others since infancy. We are hardwired to expect it and thrive on it. But the unhappy fact is that for some of us, feeding from other people simply doesn't satisfy. Granted, many of us grew up in families where genuine human love and acceptance was lacking. But even those of us who had this love as children, still often yearn for "something more" than just simple human community. We simply are not satisfied with what the herd has to offer. We want to be individual souls, not just units in the collective. But in order to do that, we must break away from the collective and strike out on our own.

And from there, our journey - and our trial - begins.

The Roebuck Way

The Roebuck is as much a process as a group - a process of initiation and transformation that goes beyond just membership in an organization. What began as a small experimental group made up of members of many different magical systems has evolved into a mystery tradition which has at its core the belief that through the process of personal transformation, humans can become as Gods.

Psychologist and seer Carl Jung called this process "individuation," the process by which the individual soul rises above the herd mentality and achieves "self-hood" or an identity as an entity independent of whatever environment in which it may find itself. This process, described by wise people from all ancient cultures, takes many lifetimes to complete. The soul must learn to understand and bring into balance all of life's processes within itself in order to be free of the excesses and imbalances which cause so much trouble.

To that end, we have dedicated ourselves not only to the purpose of rediscovering the wisdom and knowledge of our Anglo-Celtic ancestors that has been buried for many long centuries but also adapting this knowledge to our modern era. In our age of instant enlightenment, it is not easy to explain a system of magic that takes years of dedicated effort to pursue. But, we have found that the process of transformation does not happen overnight. The forging of the soul takes time. Then, we must take whatever knowledge and understanding we have gained and guide others who come into our circle so that they too, in time, can achieve that same understanding. So, it is not enough to merely achieve transformation for ourselves. We must reach out to others striving, however weakly, for the same goals.

Therefore, Roebuck initiation is a way of service to the Gods and humanity, not just of individual enlightenment. To be enlightened is a worthy goal, but it is only a means to an end, not an end in itself. We feel that the purpose of enlightenment is to be able to more effectively serve the people of the old Gods. By teaching, ministering and guiding, we hope to be able to give others the means by which they can, with the help of the Gods, escape from the morass of their own unhappiness and make their way towards harmony with the Gods.

It is for this reason that we do our best to put up with situations that don't please us and to take unhappy, troubled people into our company in the hope that they will find their way out of their troubles by the transformative influence of the Gods. When a candidate joins the Roebuck, even as a student, he or she puts himself or herself into a position of allowing the old Gods to begin this process of transformation. This means working through the process of karma ("fate" is the western term for the same thing) in order to achieve elemental balance in the person. Only if we are balanced ourselves, can we help others balance.

The heart of the Roebuck tradition is, and has always been, the Black Goddess, whose secret name means "Fate" or "Karma." The key to Her mysteries is the willingness to take responsibility for one's own fate, whether good or ill, and change it by transforming our actions and attitudes. Once we do that, the key is turned and the way is opened. We are then tempered in Tubal's Forge by learning to balance the elemental forces within ourselves and we emerge as Divine Heroes and Heroines who, in turn, must serve the needs of their people.

This is what Cochrane meant when he wrote "involvement is the prime duty of the wise. It is not just enough to see the Goddess, one must serve Her people by being involved in the process of fate."

But Heroes and Heroines must abandon any role of innocent victim. Power to affect change is truly a two-edged sword. We can't claim that we have no control over our own environment and then try to do magical rituals to make changes in that environment. If we wish to become empowered, that is, able to effect change in the world, we must take responsibility for our lives and accept that it is our mistakes that have messed up our own lives. We can't have it both ways. The implications of this are profound, both for the group as a whole and the people within it.

Over the twenty two years of its history, the Roebuck has differed from much of the mainstream Pagan community in a number of significant ways. We have maintained over the years that only a small percentage of Pagans have what it takes to study the mysteries. This is not a path for everyone and we only accept those who have shown that they can "pass muster." Therefore, not everyone who asks is given training or initiation. This is the source of the unpleasant connotations that have been associated with the perfectly reasonable word 'discrimination.' The Roebuck is discriminating in its choice of students and members, and many people consider this wrong. However, the criterion upon which the Roebuck discriminates goes much deeper than the surface differences of race, previous religious training and even sexual orientation.

Being basically an Anglo-Celtic tradition, we hold to the ancient concept of the Divine Right of Kings. The King (or in this case, the chieftain or Magister) holds his office by virtue of being chosen by the Gods and not through his own efforts or personal virtue. Indeed, all of us hold our Priesthood the same way. We do not choose this path — we are chosen for it. We can accept or reject it for a time, but when it comes down to it, we are not here through our own efforts or desires.

This is why we don't choose our members. They are chosen for us. The Gods, in sometimes quite dramatic ways, will accept one person into the group and not another for reasons known only to them. There were cases in which we could see no reason why a particular student shouldn't have made it through the training. They seemed to be just perfect for the group. But they didn't belong and so they didn't stay around. In other cases, a student just couldn't be made to leave no matter what we did. It wasn't until years later that we realized that he or she truly did belong, but needed to shed some emotional baggage first.

This issue is a hotly contested one, particularly in this country. In America, there is an attitude that everyone is created equal, no one is born "special" and if one tries hard and long enough and wants it badly enough, they deserve to have anything they wish and nobody has the right to refuse them. In the case of the Craft, if one is willing to do the work, one should automatically be initiated. However, the hereditary family traditions have always held that one must be 'of the Blood' or one is not a 'Witch.'

Traditionally, this meant that in order to be a Witch, one must either be born into the family, marry into it or be adopted in much the same fashion as Native Americans adopted 'blood brothers' into the tribe. If someone is not 'of the Blood' it doesn't matter how badly he or she wants to be a Witch, the Gods will not accept them as such. Desire doesn't do it, hard work and dedication doesn't do it either. It can't be earned. It must be conferred. And the Gods do the conferring by far different standards than we humans do.

This is a tough morsel to swallow. Many devoted people spend years in the Craft, teaching students, writing books, running groups, achieving in some cases, quite a bit of fame and notoriety. By all rights, they should have earned something. And they have: human respect and acknowledgement of ability and experience. But the otherworldly power that flows from the Gods is simply not there and eventually the person often resorts to ego trips, power games, petty jealousies, personal and political crusades or Witch wars to make up for the lack. Then, along comes someone who by all human standards hasn't earned the power, doesn't deserve it and might even abuse it. And yet, they shine with it and are able to do things effortlessly that another person has taken years to learn to do and still doesn't do well. It doesn't seem fair, and it isn't by human standards. But the old Gods play by different rules. They know their own. One is of the Blood or one is not, and wannabes just don't make it, no matter what their human friends might wish.

Another issue has been that of balance within the circle. The Roebuck has always striven for balance between opposite forces, especially male and female. There are a number of women in the Pagan community who don't approve of the equal status (for some, the mere presence) of men in our circle and object to the fact that we do not glorify women's (and, by extension, the earth's) fertility cycles in our rituals. However, we are a mystery tradition, not a fertility one. The point of our workings is to find the methods of personal transformation that apply to both men and women. While we do not denigrate women's mysteries, or men's mysteries for that matter, our focus is that of "person's mysteries" or those mysteries that men and women can relate to equally. A matriarchal, female only group, without even a token male God figure, is just as unbalanced as a patriarchal, all male group. The fact that the former is considered acceptable within the Craft community and the latter is not, constitutes a political issue rather than a magical one.

There are those who will argue that religion in western society has been patriarchal and exclusive of women for so many centuries, that it is not only desirable but necessary to swing the pendulum the other way, as it were, in order to eventually regain the balance. While this overcompensation towards the feminine may have merit for the craft movement as a whole, it may not be desirable for individual women - and individual men, for that matter, who may justifiably resent being personally held to blame for the abuses of the last two thousand years. We have discovered that patriarchal religion is just as abusive to men as it is to women and taking patriarchal Christianity and changing all the pronouns from He and Him to She and Her doesn't redress the balance. All it does is fly the same old prejudices under a new banner.

There are also a few feminists who delight in using Goddess religion to grind their own personal axes against men. They seek a kind of Divine Dispensation to justify blaming men in general for all of their problems rather than taking their share of responsibility for such problems and seeking to resolve them. This behavior isn't any more healthy and desirable for women as it is for men. It encourages a "victim" mentality that is incompatible with the goal of personal empowerment and responsibility that forms the basis of the mysteries for women and men alike.

All Roebuck circles have at their center a man and woman working together as Priest and Priestess. They are not expected to have physical sex and often they are both legally married to someone else in the circle. However, the pair must consist of a man and a woman in order to generate the energy needed to run the ritual. Two women or two men just doesn't work the same way. Many gays consider the Craft as a refuge from the strict Judeo-Christian culture and wish to express their gay lifestyle without censure. While this is understandable, some gays consider any limits set on their behavior, even when it's only in circle, as discriminatory. However, men and women have different ways of generating magical power, just as anodes and cathodes do inside a battery. This has nothing to do with sexual preference, but with hormonal makeup and other psycho-physiological factors. A gay man is not a woman any more than a lesbian is a man. Two anodes may love each other very much, but they aren't going to generate the electricity of an anode and a cathode.

This is one of the reasons why we have had so few gay people in the Roebuck over the years. We don't deliberately keep them out, but they tend to find our circle practices, with its emphasis on polarity between male and female energies, uncomfortable and don't stay around very long. If a gay man or a lesbian woman is willing to perform their ritual functions within the circle with a person of the opposite sex, they are welcome to give the training a try, regardless of their sexual orientation. If they are not willing to do this, then they will be unable to complete the training. The choice is theirs. However, we refuse to make exceptions to this fundamental principle of magic to accommodate them. Equal access is one thing - preferential treatment simply on the basis of personal preference is another.

One of the biggest issues has been our refusal to participate in the promiscuous sexual relationships that have permeated Pagan circles. We founded the Roebuck at the height of the 'free love' era in which the relations between men and women were undergoing an upheaval which has been dubbed 'sexual liberation' or 'polyamory.' A number of covens at that time were quite open about their sexual expectations of potential members and a few even went so far as to require sexual relations as part of their initiation.

Twenty years later, it has become increasingly clear that such 'liberation' wasn't all it was cracked up to be - with AIDS or other incurable sexual diseases being only part of the reason. We are certainly not advocating a return to the abuses of so-called "Christian marriage." However, more groups are destroyed on both sides of the Atlantic by their leaders thinking that they had the right to have sex with whichever member appealed to them, irregardless of who was legally married to whom. We decided from the very first that fidelity and self-restraint were Pagan virtues too. A coven is not a group marriage and individual marriage vows, like any other oaths, are important and binding.

Much of this is the result of the mysterious Right of Carnal

Access rules that began to sprout up in people's Books of Shadows in the early seventies. These strange rules spell out the responsibilities of the High Priest to meet the sexual demands of the women in his coven. Except under certain specified conditions, he must not refuse. Similarly the High Priestess can also demand sexual favors from the male members of her coven, who also must not refuse.

When we inquired of our original AmTrad coven regarding these rules, we were told that they came from a time when women were married against their will and were not sexually satisfied by their husbands. A trained High Priest, who is aspecting Pan or some other fertility God, presumably would make very sure the woman enjoyed the experience - theoretically at least. And for a young man to refuse to have sex with the High Priestess would be tantamount to refusing the Goddess herself. The potential for abuse of these 'rules' should be obvious. Not only are women more in touch with their sexuality now than in previous centuries, marriages are now entered into freely with the full consent of both parties. Even if there actually were such rules in medieval Witch covens, there was no reason to practice them now.

In the course of training students, it often happens that one member of a married couple is interested in pursuing their studies and the other is not. If the uninterested partner is tolerant and understanding of the situation, then all is well. However, this is rarely the case. Too often, the uninterested partner begins to resent the time the student spends in circle or circle related activities, does not feel welcome at open circles, and generally watches with growing concern as his or her partner becomes more and more deeply involved in something that he or she does not share. Even if the student does not become attracted to someone in the circle, the uninvolved partner will naturally become jealous and resentful. This can put a heavy strain on even a healthy marriage.

In the case where the student finds someone else in the circle more attractive and compatible than his or her spouse, things get even worse. In cases such as this, the student's first impulse is to seek to "have their cake and eat it too" by forming a circle liaison and still keeping the marriage intact for financial or social convenience. This is unfair to the spouse and needlessly hard on the circle. Even when the spouse is initially in agreement, the arrangement doesn't last very long and causes emotional upheavals. Neither is it fair to just "dump" the inconvenient spouse. If the marriage is not salvageable, then a clean break needs to be made taking care of all obligations to children in an honorable and responsible manner before the student can continue his or her studies.

With single people, the situation is different but no less complex. When people come into a group seeking the mysteries and find each other in the process all is well and good, but when people come in with the express purpose of looking for a mate, they are not going to be interested in anybody or anything else. Other people come into circle under the impression that ritual sex is more exciting and fun than ordinary sex, especially ordinary sex that carries with it emotional commitment and responsibility. These "thrill seekers" don't last long in the mysteries.

One of the most difficult things to do when studying the mysteries is to learn to 'walk between the worlds.' This means integrating one's magical life and one's mundane life – and not let one interfere with the other to the detriment of both. This isn't easy. Most of the people who come into the Craft have been forced by economic circumstances to work at boring, emotionally unfulfilling jobs which pay for basic necessities and very little else. Magic and Pagan spirituality can be a siren song tempting the newcomer to ignore his or her mundane affairs and devote every possible waking moment to Craft studies, with the justification that one is now being 'more spiritual.'

It takes a great deal of self discipline to deal with this temptation. While Craft studies can be a great way to balance the more depressing and frustrating aspects of the mundane world, they can also be problematical if they are allowed to gobble up time and energy that should be spent at the very least insuring one's survival in the mundane world. While we have never expected our students be wealthy or hold prestigious professions, we have always insisted that they at least be self-supporting and self-reliant.

The reasons for this should be obvious. Everyone has to eat, buy clothes and have a place to live. These things cost money. If the person himself or herself doesn't earn the money to pay for them, then somebody else has to do it. A person who goes on public assistance or lives with relatives for the purpose of avoiding having to deal with the mundane world by getting a job and earning a living isn't going to make a very good student of the mysteries.

One reason is a lack of discipline. Magical training is hard work. It involves doing a lot of things that aren't fun and immediately gratifying. Difficult and often boring books must be read and understood. Commitments must be made to show up to circles and meetings on time even when there is something else the person would rather do that evening. Often, merely showing up to a ritual is not enough. Time consuming preparation must be done ahead of time – lines learned in a script, props and equipment made or purchased, background material assembled, copied, etc. A person who doesn't know how to do such things isn't likely to stick with magical work once the novelty wears off.

Another reason is lack of grounding. Intense emotional and psychic experiences seem less urgent after doing something mundane. Being forced to deal with the ordinary world often puts psychic things in perspective. Questions like 'is this really happening or is it just a projection of my own fears' are much easier to answer in the cold, clear light of day after having been distracted from them by a cup of coffee and the morning newspaper.

Still another reason is tolerance and perspective. Magic seems so easy when one can devote all one's time and energy to it and such a person isn't always sympathetic to his or her circle mates when they come to circle tired and strung out from a long week at work. As one of our members once put it "any fool can be a Great Magus if that's all he does all day. It takes real moxy to still be a Great Magus after putting in a 40-hour work week."

Sometimes people, particularly those involved in fantasy role-playing and historical recreation groups, wish to dispense with their real names and adopt a 'magical' persona for use within Pagan circles. This is fine in a social setting where the name serves as an affectionate 'nickname.' However, too often it results in a number of people hiding their real identities behind elaborate and fanciful names and titles in order to appear to be something they are not. We acknowledge that in a few isolated cases a person must use a pseudonym when writing or appearing in a public forum. However, when someone is inquiring into joining our organization, we have always insisted on knowing the person's real name and where they live. After all, they know our real names and where we live. We can see no reason why such knowledge can't be reciprocal.

Much of this secrecy regarding names began with the Gardnerian movement in England. At that point in time, there were very real and serious social consequences that could result from being known as a Witch or even a Pagan. Not only were there family repercussions (which tend to be more serious there than they are here) but economic ones as well. One could be dismissed from a job with impunity if one's occult interests came to be known. Therefore, pseudonyms needed to be used in nearly all dealings, both public and private.

However in the United States at the present time, such secrecy no longer needs to be so stringent. There are laws in place in all states designed to prevent job discrimination on the basis of religion and those people who feel they have been so discriminated against have every right to pursue it in the courts just as people might for racial, gender or sexual preference discrimination. Granted, there are incidents, particularly in states other than California, where someone's craft involvement complicates a job or child custody dispute. In these sorts of situations, discretion is usually more useful in the long run than hiding behind a fanciful name.

Often, elaborate and fanciful pseudonyms are accompanied by a title to indicate that the person in question has some sort of rank within the Craft and should therefore be accorded deference and credibility. It has been the practice for the last thirty years for certain Wicca traditions to use the titles 'Lord' and 'Lady' to denote the ranks of High Priest or High Priestess. This is a peculiarly American practice and has its roots in the close connection discussed earlier between Wicca and historical recreation groups, particularly the SCA. While the Wicca Priesthood needs some designation other than Father, Mother or Reverend, the titles Lord and Lady (as titles of nobility) have always seemed to us to be a bit presumptuous. In any case, the more strongly a person insists on being called Lord or Lady, especially by people outside of their particular tradition who have no idea what they have done to earn the title, the more suspicious it becomes.

The most serious issue we have had over the years in dealing with the community at large has been our lack of political correctness. Our cultural exclusivity, strict entrance requirements and circle discipline, refusal to be involved as a group in political causes and our insistence on personal responsibility (not to mention our fondness for weaponry of various kinds) makes us unacceptable to those in our society who wish to resolve all social problems with one wave of a magic wand from some outside authority. We feel that people achieve enlightenment and spiritual maturity one person at a time, not in a mass movement. Therefore, we concentrate on individual growth and development rather than political issues.

There are those who will argue that it is the responsibility of Witches to make the world a better place to live. This argument is nearly always made by kind, tender-hearted souls who want to right wrongs and prevent bad things from happening to innocent people. However, we have not been convinced that getting involved in mundane political activities is the best way of doing that. Nearly all political issues have two valid points of view. If a law is passed mandating something or forbidding something else, there will always be someone who will suffer because of it. And saying that those people who suffer because of the law are 'bad' people who 'deserve' to suffer because they are displeasing to the Goddess in some way is making a value judgment worthy of a Bible thumper.

Modern Pagans often like to pretend that fanatics, bigots, self-righteous moralists and power hungry demagogues are part of somebody else's religion - exclusive to monotheistic religions, Christianity and 'The Patriarchy.' This attitude is not only untrue, but also deadly. Pagans are just as capable of persecuting the heretics in its ranks as the Holy Office was. For Paganism to project its shadow side onto the opposition rather than own it and deal with it only sows the seeds of its own destruction.

An unbiased look at history reveals that the rebels of one generation tend to become the tyrants of the next. The ideology behind the movement isn't important. It's just as wrong to spike a tree and kill a lumberjack as it is to bomb an abortion clinic and kill a doctor. Those in the Pagan community who insist otherwise might just be the ones holding the torch to the pyre in the next millennium while insisting that they're liberating us from the oppressors of the previous millennium. Either way, dissenters are toast.

The problem lies in a very human tendency to confuse a personal agenda with a religious one. For the religious zealot, the issue becomes not what "I" want but what "the Gods" want or what "the Goddess" wants as though any one person has the right to insist that he or she is privy to such a thing. They perceive a person or situation that disturbs them profoundly (often for purely personal reasons, such as a childhood trauma) and go on a crusade to change or eliminate it. Often, the situations are things that should be changed or eliminated, such as involving abuse of children or animals. Such situations should be stopped or prevented if it within an individual's power to do so. However the problems begin when the person in question desires not just to change that one particular situation, but all situations that resemble it in any way, using his or her childhood trauma as a template.

In such people, reason takes a back seat to emotion. A would-be crusader will scrutinize all situations and people with suspicion and examine them for any signs of the undesirable behavior – reflexively attacking them if they show any behavior that resembles it, no matter how remotely or superficially. Sometimes, such a person will even project signs of the unwanted behavior onto totally innocent situations and proceed to interfere despite reasonable and justified measures to prevent him or her from doing so. Any attempt at pointing out that a particular situation is not one that qualifies is branded as part of the problem and anyone daring to even broach such a question is demonized as a villain. It isn't long before the 'don't confuse me with facts, my mind is made up' mentality takes over whatever critical faculties the person may have had left and extreme measures are resorted to – measures often more destructive and hurtful than the behaviors they are supposed to prevent.

For people suffering from childhood traumas, it is extremely tempting to project that trauma onto external situations rather than doing the painstaking and painful work of confronting it within themselves. They seek to exorcise it from their own psyche by eliminating it in the outside world and justify the process with delusions of selfless altruism. Sadly, the goal of such 'altruism' is rarely to help another person but to relieve the crusader's own emotional distress. Therefore, any refusal of such 'help' is met with anger and coercion. With the cry of 'I'm doing it for your own good,' such a crusader will apply an amazing amount of coercion up to and including physical violence.

It is when the goals become religious rather than social that the activist turns into a zealot. "I'm doing this for other people" turns into "I'm doing this for God(dess)" and any attempt to question the person's motives is tantamount to blasphemy. It doesn't take much for someone with a personal problem to turn it into religious dogma. All it takes is to project it onto another group, race or gender and demonize them by inventing a spurious mythology that casts them into the role of 'usurper' or 'destroyer' of some idyllic society that embodies the zealot's view of a utopia. The zealot is now justified in ostracizing the unwanted ones which eliminates entirely the needs to come to terms with any personal issues involving them.

Once begun, this process takes on a life of its own. The zealot will gather together a sizeable group of people with similar problems who will not only reinforce each other's denial but reinforce the leader's as well. People who band together for the purpose of avoiding personal problems rather than resolving them do not take kindly to one of their own, particularly their leader, "breaking faith" and suggesting, with Shakespeare, "the problem is not in our stars but in ourselves." Such a person will be drummed out of the corps and branded anathema while the groups goes on under it's own momentum with a new member, or a new leader, that is more amenable to the party line. Any appeal to reason, or attempt to present another side of the issue is denounced as not being 'real' Witches or Pagans. And any group sufficiently large and loud-mouthed enough to offer significant opposition on some political or even personal issue can provoke an attack with the ferocity of a jihad.

Rescuing victims is not the work of Gods. It is the work of human despots who will feed off the energy of the herd to satisfy their own hungers. For whenever a human claims that he or she is somehow more enlightened than the rest of humanity, that is an illusion and illusions are only maintained by the energy of other people. The difference between reality and illusion is that reality is self-maintaining from the energy of the divine. Illusion needs feeding from the energy of other people or else it evaporates. Rescuer is as much an illusion as Victim ... and just as destructive. In order to be a rescuer, you have to have victims just as in order to be a victim you have to have a rescuer. You don't need to (and ultimately can't) rescue someone who is slowly but surely being guided to his or her own maturity by the grace of the Black Goddess.

This is the final test for would-be Gods. The power that we must claim is not the power over the fate of others but over our own fate. As soon as we are tempted to meddle in other people's lives, for whatever noble and selfless reason, we abandon our quest for godhood. The Gods are guides, not caretakers. If one wishes to join their company, one must learn how not to take care of others since that, ultimately, impedes their growth. We must step off the wheel of victim-rescuer and learn to be still and know. We must turn our face towards Her.

If we refuse to do so, another natural force comes into play.

along to the next generation. However, the process of plugging into the Divine Wall Socket is the process of working for the greater purposes rather than personal gratification. What is important in the universe transcends what we personally might want at any one time. It goes beyond human wants and often needs. It is even beyond human physical existence.

Some mystical writers call this the renunciation of ego. It is a process by which the human soul is refined, purified, matured and ripened to the point where it is the best it can be. Then, it is "plugged in" to divine power and does great things in this world. This merging of human and divine is the only force that works on the physical realm. The sword does nothing by itself, no matter what a fine sword it is. Even when placed in the hand, it causes nothing but chaos. It needs direction. The Gods provide the direction; we on the physical plane provide the force and the form. But first, one must prove oneself worthy (to oneself as well as to others) of the privilege of being plugged into the wall socket of otherworldly power and shining with divine light rather than flickering feebly on one's own batteries.

Some people will not do this. They insist that their personal purposes are more important than cosmic purpose. They feel that they know what's best for the people around them and will destroy whoever does not do what they say in the name of redemption. In order to maintain the illusion of being the chosen one to right the wrongs of the world, the person will ruthlessly attack innocent people with whatever means at his or her disposal and they will justify it by a rationalization process that convinces him or her of his or her nobility and virtue. One doesn't need to even oppose these people. One merely needs to exist and not conform to ignite the self-righteous wrath.

The key to unlock the door to the mysteries is to admit that we all want to be this person. We all want to be the saviors of humanity and rescue those we love from the Bad Guys because, of course, we will earn their undying gratitude, devotion and adulation thereby. People vilify you when you refuse to rescue them, when you quietly do your own thing and leave them to clean up the mess they make due to their own stupidity and excesses. But when you give them something they want without them having to work for it, even if it's an excuse to blame someone else for their problems, they give you affection, attention, money, sex, power and all sort of things that gratify hungers physical, emotional and spiritual.

Consequently, it becomes apparent that the driving force behind religious fanatics of all kinds is one of hunger. Such people feel disconnected from the divine energy that all souls feed on, so they have to feed on the energy of other humans. But first they have to maintain the illusion that they are not predators, but redeemers, saviors, avatars of God(dess) and that they are only doing what humanity really needs. But the secret of the Dark Mother is that each soul must be transformed one by one on its own individual merits. We must all mature separately at our own rates. No one can save us from ourselves. The purpose of godhood is not to redeem others, but to provide the signposts along the way that will help struggling souls grow, develop, mature and, if necessary, redeem themselves.

How does a student go about defeating the Shadow? In the first place, he or she needs to realize that there is nothing to "defeat." Every person is subject to being tempered, tested and, if necessary, culled by this force. There are certain behaviors and attitudes that various people in a group exhibit that serve to attract the Shadow. These are the illnesses of spirit that signal to the Shadow, as it does in the animal kingdom, that the herd is weak and can be attacked and that the herd needs to be culled. If people just eliminate these behaviors and attitudes, are they invulnerable? Not necessarily. For one thing, many of these behaviors and attitudes are part of being human. We can no more shed these completely any more than we can shed our bodies. What we can do is two things: call a spade a spade and own the spade.

Most of these problems are not "evil" or "bad," they are merely signs of spiritual and emotional immaturity. A baby screams when someone doesn't come and feed it because it is incapable to go get food for itself. This is appropriate for a baby. But, when an adult does it simply because he is too lazy, confused or self-damaged to feed himself, when he is perfectly capable of doing so, it is inappropriate.

People often revert to infantile behavior under stress. This can happen on the spiritual realm as well. People are tempted to give up the quest for godhood and long to return to the security of the herd like we did when we were helpless children. We want to be assured that someone more powerful than we will make sure that everything is okay and that all our needs and wants will be supplied without too much effort on our part. This isn't bad, it's just immature. This is behavior appropriate to a two-year-old, a four-year-old, an eight-year-old. This is not appropriate for an adult. It is especially not appropriate for a Priest or Priestess of the mysteries.

Besides that, it's a lie. There is no one more powerful to take care of us for the simple reason that there is no one more powerful than we are, not even the Gods. There. I've said it. Anyone who expects the Gods to take care of them is in for a rude shock. The Gods don't take care of you. They show you the best way of taking care of yourself. It's not that they don't want to take care of you. They can't take care of you - not on the physical realm at any rate.

Say, for example your little sister who still lives in your parent's house in another state calls you on the phone. She wants something that's in the house but she doesn't know where it is. You do, and you tell her as much.

"Come here and give it to me," she says.

"It's right there in the kitchen," you say.

"I can't see it," she says.

"That's because it's in the cupboard," you say. "Open the door and look."

"You don't understand," she wails. "I want it. I need it. I'll die without it. Why don't you just give it to me?"

"Because, I'm five hundred miles away talking to you over the telephone," you say. "But, I can tell you right where it is. Just go into the cupboard in the kitchen, the one over the sink, on the third shelf up, on the left, next to the wall."

"I want it, now." She's having a tantrum over the phone. "I want you to get it for me. I can't get it myself. It's up too high. I'm too short. If I climb up on something, I might fall and hurt myself. Besides, I'm not sure that it's even there, it may not be the right one, I might break it and then I won't be able to get another one, etc., etc., etc."

A human would hang up in frustration and walk away. The Gods don't. That's why they are Gods.

Since we are on the physical plane and they are not, we have to do whatever physical work needs to be done ourselves. They can give us hints, clues and suggestions. They can give us elaborate and detailed instructions, step by step. They can even arrange for serendipitous opportunities to appear. But they can't do it for us. We need to abandon the childish expectation that they can do anything physical for us and do these things for ourselves. If we don't, we just keep going around and around in circles, asking for something, pleading for it, not getting it, getting angry, asking, pleading, getting angry, etc.

So, how does this relate to the Shadow? Because this irrational, immature demand is precisely what signals the Shadow that it has something we want. Instead of saying, "I can't get it for you, you'll have to get it for yourself, but I'll show you how," it says, "There, there, you poor little thing. It's not your fault that you don't have it. That terrible person (those terrible people) just won't give it to you. You've been so abused. Of course, I'll get it for you, exactly where and when you want it. All you have to do is blame that nasty person (those nasty people) for being so mean to you. That's all." It's as though we were chumming the water for sharks. They taste the blood and come from miles around.

If we resist successfully, then the Shadow tries a more tempting morsel. It says, "You are too good for these people. They are weak, whiny and immature. You are strong and self sufficient. They are beneath you." If we show a flicker of interest in this, the Shadow goes on, licking its chops. "In fact," it says, "You are so strong, capable and highly evolved, so enlightened that they should follow your lead." If that sounds good, it gets better. "You are the chosen one of the God(dess). You are the one to rescue the poor souls who can't rescue themselves. They need you, they cry out to you to rescue them. They will love you, adore you, and proclaim your superiority. If they are wise, they will do what you tell them."

If you're still listening, then the Shadow sets the hook. "If they refuse to do what you tell them, then they are evil and must be destroyed. And any means to do so, no matter how irrational, dishonest, cruel and ignoble, is justified. Not for your own power and position. Oh, no! You are far too noble and honorable for that. You must do this for the sake of humanity."

Then, the Shadow has you in its clutches.

Those of us who join mystery traditions eventually have to make some very difficult and fundamental choices. Through sacred ritual and communion with the Gods, we receive divine power that can be used to produce changes in our world. This has been the purpose of the mysteries from the dawn of humanity. However, that power for change must first manifest in our own lives before it can manifest in the lives of anyone else. We must grow and change before the world around us can change. And therein lies the dilemma. We cannot claim the power to change our lives for the better without first admitting that we allowed our lives to be messed up to begin with.

This is why people who join mystery schools often experience such upheavals in their emotional and physical lives afterwards. By joining a mystery tradition, one declares before the Gods that one wishes to become the master or mistress of one's own spiritual destiny. However, we cannot choose to take charge of our life on the spiritual plane and insist on remaining a victim on the physical and emotional planes. It simply does not work that way. Nearly five thousand years ago, a man writing under the name Hermes Trismegistus inscribed upon the Emerald Tablet "As above, so below." And that is just as true now as it was then.

So, why do the very few choose to take the mystery path? Because, in all places and in all times, there have been those who refuse to be controlled by those who would exploit human weakness in order to keep a group of people under their spiritual, emotional or physical thumbs. There are those who instinctively know that they are not free if they remain dependent upon another for physical, emotional or spiritual sustenance. If you let someone else take care of you, then you must do as they tell you or they will withdraw their support. Take care of yourself and you become the master or mistress of your own destiny. It's as simple - and as difficult - as that.

Perhaps more than any other time in recent history, we live in a culture that has completely abandoned the notion of individual responsibility. We have become a nation of victims, encouraged by those in authority to blame everybody and everything else for whatever our circumstances happen to be. This attitude is directly antithetical to the purpose of the Roebuck, or, indeed, any other mystery school.

The bottom line of any mystery teaching is that each person is individually responsible for his or her own life, both spiritual and emotional. While we are not necessarily to blame for what others do to us, particularly in childhood, we are to blame if we allow those past experiences to mess up our current life. We can empower ourselves to overcome any obstacles that we wish to. The techniques are there and have been there for millennia for those who really desire to take advantage of them.

Human society will always exact its price from anyone who defies the status quo and insists on being an individual rather than just one more member of the herd. For most people, this price is too high to pay. They would rather fit in, belong and be accepted by their fellow humans. But for a few, the price for individuality is well worth it. Civilizations are ephemeral. They rise, fall and rise again, over and over in an endless cycle. At the beginning of the third millennium of the Common Era, our present society is in a downward spiral and will soon fall. But those who have chosen the mystery path don't have to fall with it. They will continue to survive as individual souls when their civilization is in ruins and its members are no more.

The choice is theirs alone.

Appendix I – Castle of the East

YOU STEP THROUGH THE MIRROR, AND IT IS SO DARK THAT YOU CAN SEE NOTHING AROUND YOU EXCEPT A VERY FAINT GLOW OF A SMALL LIGHT IN THE DISTANCE. YOU FOLLOW THE LIGHT AND AS YOU WALK, IT BEGINS TO GROW BRIGHTER AND BRIGHTER. SOON, YOU FIND YOURSELF IN A SECLUDED GROVE OF TREES THAT ARE JUST BEGINNING TO SPROUT TINY GREEN LEAVES. IT IS NOT YET DAWN. THE SKY IS PEARLY GRAY. THE MOON HOVERS GHOSTLIKE OVERHEAD AND THE SHADOWS STILL DANCE AMID THE TREE BRANCHES.

NEAR YOU IS A SPRING HALF HIDDEN BY VINES. IT EMERGES FROM THE BARE ROCK INTO A POOL SO DEEP THAT YOU CANNOT SEE THE BOTTOM. THE WATER IS ICY AND BUBBLES WITH LIFE. SCRAPS OF CLOTH ARE TIED ONTO THE OVERHANGING BRANCHES. THESE ARE THE OFFERINGS OF WOMEN FROM THE DAWN OF TIME WHO SEEK HEALTH AND FERTILITY. A STONE MARKS THE WELLHEAD AND ON THIS STONE IS A FLAME THAT BURNS WITHOUT BEING FED. THIS

IS THE LIGHT THAT HAS BEEN GUIDING YOUR WAY. YOU FIND THAT YOU HAVE A COIN IN YOUR HAND. RESOLUTELY, YOU TOSS IT INTO THE WELL AND IT SINKS DOWN OUT OF SIGHT.

YOU LOOK UP. BESIDE THE SPRING, THERE STANDS A WOMAN ALL BUT HIDDEN IN A DARK CLOAK AND COWL THAT REVEALS ONLY A FEW WHISPS OF BRILLIANT YELLOW HAIR. SHE HOLDS A LIGHTED CANDLE. THIS IS BRIDE, GODDESS OF FIRE, POETRY, HEALING AND SMITHCRAFT. THIS SPRING IS SACRED TO HER, THE WATERS HEAL AND INSPIRE. SHE BECKONS YOU TO KNEEL AND DRINK FROM THE SPRING.

(Pause)

NOW, SHE BIDS YOU TO FOLLOW HER. YOU TURN TOWARDS THE EAST, WHERE THE SUN IS JUST EMERGING OVER THE HORIZON. SHE LEADS YOU DOWN A ROAD PAVED IN BEATEN GOLD. THE BRILLIANCE ALMOST BLINDS YOU BUT YOU NOTICE FLAMES LIKE TUFTS SPROUTING UP ALONGSIDE THE ROAD, ONLY TO DISAPPEAR AS SUDDENLY AS THEY APPEAR. SOME OF THESE FLAMES TAKE THE FORM OF WRIGGLY SALAMANDERS THAT WATCH YOU WITH THEIR GLEAMING RED EYES AS YOU PASS BY. SHE LEADS YOU TO WHERE YOU CAN SEE IN THE DISTANCE A BRIGHT CASTLE SURROUNDED BY ROARING FLAMES THAT BURN BUT NEVER CONSUME. AS YOU DRAW CLOSER, YOU SEE THE GATES ARE OF WROUGHT GOLD, AND RED AND YELLOW BANNERS FLY ATOP THE TURRETS.

THE GODDESS LEAVES YOU BEFORE THE GATES, WHICH OPEN BEFORE YOU. YOU WALK DOWN A HALL ABLAZE WITH TORCHES. THE WALLS BRISTLE WITH SWORDS, AXES, MACES AND ALL MANNER OF WEAPONS MAGNIFICENTLY DISPLAYED AMID WAR BANNERS AND FLAGS. YOU ENTER A GREAT HALL TO THE NOTES OF TRUMPETS AND CORNETS OF POLISHED BRASS THAT ARE BLOWN BY NO MORTAL BREATH. THERE ON A GOLDEN THRONE BETWEEN TWO BLAZING BRAZIERS SITS LUGH, OR LLEW THE LONGHANDED, THE GREAT WARRIOR, LORD OF THE SUN AND MASTER OF EVERY CRAFT, KNOWER OF ALL THINGS. HE IS FAIR AND

STRONG, WITH FLAME-COLORED HAIR AND FLASHING EYES. HIS BREASTPLATE IS OF GOLD AND A GOLDEN CIRCLET SITS UPON HIS BROW. HIS SHIELD IS BESIDE HIM BEARING THE ARMS OF THE SUN IN CHIEF AND IN HIS RIGHT HAND HE HOLDS A SPEAR WITH A BLOODSTAINED TIP. YOU KNEEL BEFORE HIM. THE FLAMES SURROUND YOU BUT DO NOT BURN YOU AS ALL THAT IS BASE AND UNWORTHY IS CONSUMED BY THE PURIFYING FIRE. THE GOD RISES AND REACHES OUT HIS GLOWING HAND. YOU CAN FEEL HIS SEARING TOUCH ON YOUR BROW. YOU RAISE YOUR CLASPED HANDS, AND PLACE THEM IN HIS, AND HE GIVES YOU A MESSAGE THAT IS FOR YOU AND YOU ALONE.

(Pause)

YOU RISE, BID HIM FAREWELL AND FOLLOW THE LONG HALLWAY DOWN TO THE GOLDEN GATES WHICH OPEN AT YOUR TOUCH. BRIDE AWAITS YOU WITH THE EVER-LIT CANDLE AND THE BRILLIANCE OF THE CASTLE OF THE SUN DIMS AS YOU RETURN TO THE CIRCLE.

Appendix II — Castle of the South

AS YOU STEP THROUGH THE MIRROR, THE HEAVY, PUNGENT, SWEET AROMA OF FLOWERS SURROUNDS YOU. YOU FIND YOURSELF STANDING ON A GRASSY BACK SURROUNDED BY FLOWERING TREES AND SHRUBS IN EVERY COLOR OF THE RAINBOW, ALL MUCH MORE VIVID AND BRILLIANT THAN ANY FLOWERS YOU HAVE EVER SEEN BEFORE. BUT WITH ALL THE BEAUTIFUL FLOWERS AROUND YOU, YOU NOTICE A BUSH OF THE REDDEST, MOST BEAUTIFUL ROSES THAT YOU HAVE EVER SEEN. YOU ARE MYSTERIOUSLY DRAWN TO THE BUSH, AND REACH OUT YOUR HAND TO PLUCK ONE OF THE BLOSSOMS. A THORN PIERCES YOUR FINGER, DRAWING A DROP OF BLOOD. YOU WANT TO LET GO, BUT YOU CONTINUE TO PULL UNTIL THE STEM BREAKS, AND THE BLOSSOM IS YOURS.

IMMEDIATELY, YOU HEAR THE THUNDERING SOUND OF APPROACHING HOOFBEATS. A LADY APPEARS, RIDING A SNOW WHITE UNICORN WITH WILD EYES AND FLARING RED NOSTRILS. THIS IS NIAHM, HER GOLDEN HAIR RINGED BY A CHAPLET OF FLOWERS IS FLYING

UNBOUND BEHIND HER. SHE IS BEAUTIFUL, WITH FLAME RED LIPS AND GREEN EYES AND SHE WEARS A GOWN OF GREEN SILK. SHE DISMOUNTS, SMILES AT YOU, AND SITS YOU DOWN BESIDE HER UNDER A FLOWERING HAWTHORNE TREE. SHE HAS WITH HER A BASKET OF FRUIT AND A FLAGON OF SWEET WINE AND SHE FEEDS YOU WITH HER OWN WHITE HANDS.

(Pause)

NOW, SHE CALLS THE UNICORN TO HER SIDE. LAUGHING, SHE PULLS YOU UP BEHIND HER AND AWAY YOU RIDE DOWN A ROAD OF PAVING STONE THROUGH LUSH GREEN COUNTRYSIDE. THE ROAD WINDS AROUND BETWEEN TWIN PEAKS THAT RISE BEFORE YOU. AS YOU PASS BETWEEN THEM, YOU SEE THAT THEY ARE HONEYCOMBED WITH TUNNELS AND CAVERNS. SOON YOU CAN MAKE OUT TINY FIGURES SCURRYING INDUSTRIOUSLY IN AND AROUND THE MOUNTAIN. THEY ARE THE GNOMES, BENT AND GNARLED, BUSILY PICKING AT THE ROCKS AND LOADING THEIR CARTS WITH SPARKLING JEWELS -- RUBIES, EMERALDS, DIAMONDS AND SAPPHIRES.

YOU FEAST YOUR EYES ON THE VAST WEALTH, BUT THE GODDESS WHISKS YOU AWAY ALL TOO SOON AND YOU RIDE TOWARDS A DISTANT CASTLE BUILT OF GREY-GREEN STONE AND ENGULFED BY LUSH GARDENS AND DENSE FOREST. FLOWERS OF EVERY COLOR ARE IN FULL BLOOM AND TREES ARE LADEN WITH EVERY KIND OF LUSCIOUS FRUIT RIPE AND READY FOR THE PICKING. THE GODDESS LETS YOU DOWN AT THE GATE WHICH IS FASHIONED OF VINES AND HUNG WITH LIVING PURPLE GRAPES. IT OPENS AND YOU ENTER A HALL RICH WITH HANGINGS AND TAPESTRIES THAT DEPICT VIVID AND DETAILED SCENES OF THE PLEASURES OF HUNTING, FEASTING, REVELRY AND LOVE. AT THE END OF THE HALL IS A SUMPTUOUS THRONE LINED WITH VELVET AND COVERED WITH JEWELS.

BUT THE THRONE IS EMPTY, FOR CERNUNOS, LORD OF THE EARTH, HOLDS COURT IN THE LUSH GREENWOOD, AND WHEN YOU FIND HIM AMID THE FLOWERS AND TREES, HE LAUGHS HEARTILY AT YOUR SILLINESS.

YOU SOON FIND YOURSELF LAUGHING WITH HIM. HE IS HALF MAN, HALF BEAST. STAG'S ANTLERS CURL AROUND HIS HEAD AND HIS HOOVES ARE CLOVEN. AS HE SITS BENEATH A TREE, ALL MANNER OF ANIMAL AND BIRD CLUSTER ABOUT HIM, FROM THE FIERCE WOLF TO THE GENTLE MOUSE, FROM THE OWL TO THE SPARROW, ALL PAY HOMAGE TO THE LORD OF THE ANIMALS. SO YOU, TOO, KNEEL AT HIS FEET.

HE HOLDS IN HIS HAND AN EARTHENWARE CUP AND GIVES YOU A DRAUGHT OF THE INTOXICATING LIQUOR. YOUR HEAD BEGINS TO SPIN, AND YOU FIND THAT YOU ARE GIGGLING UNCONTROLABLY AT HIS ANTICS AND HIS JOKES. ALL THE CARES OF THE WORLD ARE LONG FORGOTTEN AND YOU FEEL SO GOOD THAT YOU DON'T WANT TO LEAVE. BUT SOON IT IS TIME FOR YOU TO GO. CERNUNOS SMILES, GIVES YOU A KISS AND WHISPERS SOMETHING SPECIAL IN YOUR EAR.

(Pause)

YOU RISE, AND SEE THE GODDESS WAITING AT THE GATE, HER UNICORN PAWING THE GROUND IMPATIENTLY. YOU CLIMB UP BEHIND HER, AND SHE FERRIES YOU QUICKLY BACK TO THE MIRROR THAT LEADS BACK TO THE SOUTHERN QUARTER OF THE CIRCLE.

Appendix III ~ Castle of the West

YOU STEP THROUGH THE MIRROR AND JOURNEY TOWARDS THE SETTING SUN TO THE SEASHORE. YOU WALK OUT ONTO A RICKITY WOODEN PIER. THE BOARDS CREAK BENEATH YOUR FEET. IT IS DARK AND VERY, VERY FOGGY. YOU CAN ONLY HEAR THE WAVES CRASH ONTO THE PIER. YOU WALK OUT PAST THE BREAKERS, FEELING ONLY THE HEAVE OF THE TIDE PRESSING AGAINST THE WOODEN PILLARS.

AT THE END OF THE PIER, A SMALL BOAT WAITS. AN OLD MAN DRESSED IN A COWL THAT IS TATTERED WITH AGE IS SITTING IN THE BOAT. HE LOOKS UP AT YOU. HIS BLUE EYES ARE SAD, HIS FACE IS MARKED BY SUFFERING AND HIS DARK BEARD IS STREAKED WITH GREY. WORDLESSLY, HE MOTIONS YOU INTO THE BOAT. YOU GET IN, AND HE ROWS OFF INTO THE FOG. THE MIST COMPLETELY SURROUNDS YOU, DAMPENING YOUR HAIR AND CLOTHING AS THE OLD MAN ROWS. THE FOG GETS THICKER AND THE SWELLS GROW CLOSER AND CLOSER UNTIL YOU FINALLY REALIZE

THAT INSTEAD OF BEING ON TOP OF THE WATER, YOU ARE TRAVELING BENEATH IT.

DOWN, DOWN YOU GO INTO THE BLUE WATER UNTIL YOU SEE A CASTLE EMERGE FROM THE ROCKS AND CRAGS OF THE OCEAN FLOOR. THE HIGH TURRETS ARE MADE OF CORAL. SEAWEED CREEPS UP THE WALLS LIKE IVY AND FISH SWIM UNCONCERNED THROUGH THE TOWERS. THE BOAT PULLS UP ALONGSIDE THE OPEN DRAWBRIDGE AND YOU CAREFULLY CLIMB OUT. YOU TURN TO THANK THE OLD MAN, BUT HE IS GONE. SO YOU WALK THROUGH THE GATE INTO THE CASTLE. THE UNDINES GREET YOU, GRACEFUL BEINGS WITH FINS INSTEAD OF LIMBS AND BRIGHTLY-COLORED GILLS ALONGSIDE THEIR FAIR FACES. THEY LEAD YOU INTO A GREAT HALL RICHLY ADORNED WITH TAPESTRIES. THEN, THEY LEAVE YOU ALONE.

SUDDENLY, TRUMPETS BEGIN TO SOUND. A SQUIRE STEPS INTO THE HALL, CARRYING A SPEAR WITH A DROP OF BLOOD AT THE TIP. FROM THE END OF THE HALL APPEAR TWO MAIDENS, ONE IN BLACK AND ONE IN WHITE, EACH HOLDING A SILVER CANDLEABRA. THEN, CERRIDWEN, THE GRAIL QUEEN, APPEARS, CLAD IN A GOWN OF THE DEEPEST BLUE. SHE CARRIES A VESSEL FROM WHICH POURS THE AQUA VITA OF INSPIRATION AND WISDOM. HER ENTOURAGE HALTS AND SHE STANDS BEFORE YOU. IN YOUR INNOCENCE, YOU ASK WHY THIS IS HAPPENING. SHE SMILES IN ANSWER AND HANDS YOU THE VESSEL, BIDDING YOU TO DRINK.

(Pause)

SHE NOW TAKES YOU BY THE HAND AND LEADS YOU THROUGH AN IMMENSE CARVED DOORWAY INTO A THRONE ROOM. THERE, ON A DIAS AT THE FAR END OF THE ROOM, IS A THRONE CARVED OF BLACK CORAL AND MOTHER-OF-PEARL. ON THE THRONE SITS NODENS, GOD OF WISDOM AND LORD OF THE SEA. HE IS A MATURE MAN WITH GOLDEN LIGHT PLAYING FROM HIM, AND A DOLPHIN AT HIS FEET. HE BIDS YOU WELCOME, RISES TO HIS FEET AND WALKS TOWARD YOU. YOU SEE THAT HE LIMPS. AS HE DRAWS CLOSER, YOU RECOGNIZE THE SAD, BLUE EYES AND

SORROWFUL FACE OF THE MAN IN THE BOAT. YOU KNEEL BEFORE HIM, BUT HE RAISES YOU TO YOUR FEET AND LOOKS DEEPLY INTO YOUR EYES AS HE SPEAKS TO YOU.

(Pause)

YOU THANK THEM AND BID THEM FAREWELL. THE UNDINES LEAD YOU OUT THROUGH THE OPEN DRAWBRIDGE WHERE THE OLD MAN IN THE BOAT AWAITS YOU. UP AND UP YOU GO, BACK THROUGH THE BLUE WATER INTO THE MIST ABOVE. THE PIER LOOMS BEFORE YOU IN THE FOG. BACK YOU COME, BACK TO THE WESTERN GATE OF THE CIRCLE.

229

Appendix IV ~ Castle of the North

YOU STEP THROUGH THE MIRROR AND A CHILL WIND BLOWS AROUND YOU FROM THE NORTH. IT IS TWILIGHT. YOU LOOK AROUND AND FIND YOURSELF STANDING IN THE MIDST OF WHAT WAS A BATTLEFIELD. SKELETONS WEARING ARMOUR AND CARRYING SWORDS AND SHIELDS LIE SCATTERED ON THE GROUND AND SKULLS GRIN FROM BEHIND THE VISORS OF HELMS. THERE IS NO SOUND BUT THE MOANING OF THE WIND. THEN A LARGE RAVEN APPEARS, CIRCLING ABOVE YOUR HEAD, SCREETCHING FOR YOU TO FOLLOW.

YOU FOLLOW THE RAVEN ACROSS THE BARREN TERRAIN TO A CAVE CARVED INTO THE ROCK OF THE SIDE OF A HUGE MOUNTAIN. YOU ENTER THE CAVE AND LOOK AROUND FOR THE RAVEN. BUT BEHIND YOU NOW STANDS A BEAUTIFUL BUT STERN WOMAN WITH FIERCE EYES AND BLACK HAIR. SHE HOLDS A BLOOD-STAINED DAGGER IN ONE HAND. FOR THIS IS THE MORRIGAN THAT YOU HAVE BEEN FOLLOWING. SHE STERNLY BIDS YOU TO COME FORWARD, HOLDING

THE HILT OF THE DAGGER OUT TO YOU.

(Pause)

NOW SHE CHANGES BACK INTO RAVEN FORM AND SCREETCHES FOR YOU TO FOLLOW HER ONCE AGAIN. BESIDE THE CAVE IS A STEEP AND ROCKY PATH THAT LEADS UP THE SIDE OF THE MOUNTAIN. AS THE RAVEN CIRCLS OVERHEAD, YOU BEGIN TO CLIMB. THE MOUNTAIN RISING BEFORE YOU IS SO HIGH THAT THE SUMMIT IS HIDDEN FROM SIGHT IN THE CLOUDS. THE WAY IS SLOW, BUT YOU KEEP CLIMBING HIGHER AS THE COLD NORTH WIND WHIPS AROUND YOU UNTIL YOU CAN NO LONGER SEE THE GROUND. YOU ARE SUSPENDED NOW BETWEEN EARTH AND SKY, BUT THE RAVEN STILL CIRCLES ABOVE YOUR HEAD AND YOU CONTINUE TO CLIMB. THEN YOU NOTICE THE WIND WHISTLING IN YOUR EARS BECOMES MORE LIKE VOICES.

THE WHISPS OF CLOUD HAVE NOW TAKEN FORM. THE SYLPHS NOW FLIT ABOUT YOU WHISPERING INTO YOUR EARS, TELLING YOU THEIR SECRETS AND CAUTIONING YOU TO BEWARE. FINALLY, ABOVE YOU, YOU SEE A GREAT CASTLE NESTLED IN THE CLOUDS. IT IS DARK AND HAUNTING WITH EBONY TURRETS AND COLD IRON GATES. BUT THE RAVEN BIDS YOU ONWARD AND SOON YOU STAND BEFORE THE GATE. IT CREAKS OPEN AND YOU HESITANTLY ENTER A STONE HALL, BLEAK AND AUSTERE LIT ONLY BY SMOKING TORCHES THAT SMELL LIKE MYRRH. ON A GRANITE THRONE SITS AN OLD, OLD MAN ANCIENT AND WITHERED WITH A WHITE BEARD CASCADING DOWN HIS BREAST AND A SHARPLY HOOKED NOSE BENEATH CLEAR SHARP EYES. HE IS CLAD IN A GRAY COWLED ROBE.

HE IS TAUTES, DARK LORD OF THE NORTH, GOD OF PROPHECY AND KNOWLEDGE. YOU KNEEL BEFORE HIM, BUT HE LIFTS A BONY HAND AND RISES TO HIS FEET. YOU FOLLOW HIM THROUGH A SMALL DOORWAY WITH A GRINNING SKULL OVER IT, INTO A LARGE LIBRARY WITH FLOOR TO VAULTED CEILING FULL OF BLACK VOLUMES ALL WITH GOLD LETTERING ON THEIR SPINES. TAUTES HOLDS OUT HIS HAND AND ONE OF THE VOLUMES FLOATS DOWN INTO HIS PALM.

HE WORDLESSLY GIVES IT TO YOU. IT IS YOUR NAME THAT IS SPELLED OUT ON THE SPINE. THIS IS THE BOOK OF YOUR FATE, KARMA, PAST LIVES AND DESTINY. YOU ARE ALLOWED ONE LOOK, AND ONE LOOK ONLY.

(Pause)

NOW, THE DARK GOD PLUCKS THE BOOK FROM YOUR FINGERS AND SENDS IT BACK UP TO ITS PLACE ON THE SHELF. YOU AGAIN BOW, BUT HE STERNLY POINTS YOU TO THE DOOR. THE RAVEN IS THERE TO MEET YOU AND GUIDES YOU BACK DOWN THE MOUNTAIN TO THE MIRROR AT THE NORTHERN QUARTER OF THE CIRCLE WHERE SHE DISAPPEARS INTO THE CHILL, NORTH WIND.

APPENDIX V – THE SPIRAL CASTLE

YOU STAND IN THE CENTER OF THE CIRCLE AND SLOWLY BEGIN SPIRALING MOONWISE UP AND UP TOWARDS THE BRIGHT STARS ABOVE YOU. AS YOU SPIRAL UPWARDS THE STARS BECOME CLOSER AND CLOSER AND BRIGHTER AND BRIGHTER UNTIL YOU BEGIN TO SEE, IN THE CENTER OF A RING OF STARS, A CASTLE, BRIGHT AS THE STARS AROUND IT, TURNING, TURNING TO THE FOUR CARDINAL POINTS. YOU MATCH YOUR SPIRALING TO THE TURNING OF THE CASTLE.

SOON, A BRIGHT SHIMMERING GATE OPENS TO YOU AND YOU ENTER THE SPIRAL CASTLE. AS YOU WALK YOU FIND THE FLOOR BENEATH YOU AND THE WALLS AROUND YOU BATHED IN LIGHT AND THE HIGH, VAULTED CEILING ABOVE YOU IS LOST IN A SHIMMERING GLOW.

THERE ABOVE YOU, ON A HIGH THRONE SURROUNDED BY THE BLACKNESS OF SPACE AND THE BRIGHTNESS OF STARS, IS GODA, THE HIGH GODDESS IN A

SHIMMERING ROBE AND CROWNED WITH A CIRCLET OF SEVEN STARS. BEFORE THE THRONE IS A SPIRAL STAIRCASE LEADING UP TO THE GODDESS. SHE RAISES HER HAND AND BECKONS YOU TO APPROACH.

YOU BEGIN TO CLIMB THE SPIRAL STAIRCASE. BUT THE MORE YOU CLIMB THE FARTHER YOU SEEM TO BE FROM THE TOP. YOU SEE AN ALMOST ENDLESS NUMBER OF STEPS BEFORE YOU. BUT NOW A VOICE WHISPERS TO YOU TO CLOSE YOUR EYES AND KEEP CLIMBING, FEELING, ONE BY ONE, THE STEPS BENEATH YOUR FEET. SOON, YOU LOSE COUNT AND EACH STEP BECOMES ISOLATED FROM THE OTHERS AS YOU TAKE EACH STEP AT A TIME.

THEN, THERE ARE NO MORE STEPS. YOU OPEN YOUR EYES AND YOU ARE ON A PLATFORM SUSPENDED ABOVE THE BLACKNESS OF SPACE BEFORE THE GREAT GODDESS. SHE SMILES AT YOU IN KINDLY AMUSEMENT, AND YOU SEE THAT HER SHIMMERING GARB IS ONLY A NET WOVEN OF FIBERS OF LIGHT. LAUGHING, SHE UNWRAPS IT FROM AROUND HER BODY AND FLINGS IT OVER YOUR HEAD, DRAWING YOU TO HER. YOU KNEEL, BOUND AND HELPLESS IN THE SHINING THREADS, STRONG AS ANY CABLE, BEFORE HER THRONE. AND YET, SHE IS KIND. TENDERLY, SHE LAYS HER HAND ON YOUR BROW, KISSES YOU AND GIVES YOU HER SECRET NAME BY WHICH YOU CAN CALL UPON HER FOR AID IN THE TRIALS THAT ARE TO COME. BUT IT MUST BE USED BY YOU ALONE AND BY NO ONE ELSE LEST ITS MAGIC BE LOST.

(Pause)

THEN IT ALL FADES INTO BRILLIANCE; THE GODDESS, THE THRONE, AND THE SPIRAL STAIRCASE, AND YOU FIND YOURSELF KNEELING ON THE FLOOR, ALONE. IT IS TIME TO GO. YOU RISE AND TURN AWAY FROM THE SPIRAL CASTLE, AND SLOWLY DESCEND TO THE GROUND IN THE CENTER OF THE CIRCLE.

Appendix VI – The Forge of Old Tubal

AS YOU STAND IN THE CENTER OF THE CIRCLE, SUDDENLY THERE IS A RUMBLE AND THE EARTH SHAKES BENEATH YOU. YOU HEAR A SHARP CRACK AND A CHASM OPENS UP AT YOUR FEET. SMOKE AND FUMES BILLOW UP OUT OF THE CREVICE NEARLY CHOKING YOU, AND THE SOUNDS OF METAL STRIKING AGAINST METAL ASSAULT YOUR EARS. A VOICE CALLS OUT TO YOU TO DESCEND, AND YOU DO, PICKING YOUR WAY CAREFULLY DOWN THE ROCKY SIDES OF THE CHASM. AT THE BOTTOM, YOU FIND A PATH AND YOU FOLLOW IT BETWEEN THE WALLS OF ROCK, DEEPER AND DEEPER INTO THE EARTH FOLLOWING THE SMOKE AND THE SOUNDS OF BANGING METAL.

THEN THE PATH OPENS OUT INTO A CHAMBER. FLAMES BLAZE OFF THE WALLS AND THE HEAT AND SMOKE ARE NEARLY UNBEARABLE. YET YOU PRESS ON AND SOON YOU SEE A HUGE ANVIL BESIDE A MONSTROUS, BLAZING FORGE. BEHIND THE ANVIL STANDS A HUGE FIGURE WITH A GLEAMING, MUSCLED CHEST AND ARMS AS BIG AS TREE LIMBS SWINGING THE

HAMMER AND WIELDING THE TONGS AS HE HAMMERS THE RESISTING METAL. CURVED RAM'S HORNS CURL FROM HIS HAIR AND CLOVEN HOOVES EMERGE FROM HIS STAINED APRON.

HE LOOKS UP AS YOU APPROACH, BUT HIS LOOK IS STERN. HE POINTS TO THE WALL TO HIS LEFT. ON IT HANGS ALL MANNER OF WEAPONS, SWORDS, KNIVES, DAGGERS, GUNS AND BAYONETS. HE BIDS YOU COUNT THEM. HE POINTS TO THE WALL ON HIS RIGHT. ON IT HANGS ALL MANNER OF TOOLS, HAMMERS, NAILS, PLOWSHARES, WAGON WHEELS, WATER MILLS. HE BIDS YOU TO COUNT THEM. THE TWO NUMBERS ARE THE SAME. HE POINTS TO THE FLAMES OF THE FORGE AND AS YOU LOOK AN IMAGE TAKES FORM. IT IS AN IMAGE OF YOU IN THE ONE SITUATION THAT WILL BURN AWAY THE DROSS AND TRANSFORM YOUR SOUL.

(Pause)

YOU LOOK AWAY, AND FIND HIM WATCHING YOU WITH COMPASSION AND UNDERSTANDING. HE BIDS YOU HOLD OUT YOUR HAND. THEN HE PICKS UP SOMETHING FROM THE ANVIL AND PLACES IT INTO YOUR OUTSTRETCHED PLAM. THIS IS YOUR SPECIAL TALISMAN, A SYMBOL OF THE PROTECTION OF THE BLACKSMITH GOD. YOU MUST FIND IT NOW ON THE PHYSICAL PLANE WHEN YOU RETURN. YOU BID FAREWELL TO THE BLACKSMITH GOD AND MAKE YOUR WAY BACK TO THE PATH THAT LEADS TO THE OPENING TO THE UPPER WORLD. AS YOU CLIMB OUT OF THE CHASM AND WATCH IT SHUT BEHIND YOU, YOU DISCOVER THAT YOUR CLOTHES AND HAIR ARE SINGED, AND YOU NEVER EVEN NOTICED THE HEAT.

Appendix VII — The Black Goddess

A DOOR OPENS TO THE NORTHEAST AND A PATH APPEARS. THE MOON IS FULL AND HER PEARLY LIGHT SURROUNDS YOU AS YOU WALK ALONG. SOON, YOU HEAR PEOPLE LAUGHING AND DANCING, AND SOUNDS OF MUSIC, PIPES AND DRUMS. YOU COME UPON A BEAUTIFUL GARDEN WITH A CIRCLE OF BRIGHTLY DRESSED PEOPLE ADORNED IN GARLANDS OF FLOWERS AND COLORFUL JEWELS.

IN THE CENTER IS A FOUNTAIN FLOWING WITH BLOOD RED WINE THAT THE DANCERS ARE DRINKING OF FREELY. AS YOU WATCH, THE DANCING BECOMES MORE AND MORE ABANDONED AND FRENZIED. A YOUNG BULL HAS BEEN SACRIFICED, AND ITS BODY, DRAPED WITH FLOWERS, LIES ON A STONE ALTAR. ITS BLOOD RUNS IN RIVULETS DOWN TO A SHALLOW TROUGH AT THE BASE. ONE BY ONE, THE DANCERS FLING THEIR WINE TO THE GROUND AND FILL THEIR EMPTY GOBLETS FROM THE TROUGH. LEADING THE DANCE IS A WOMAN OF UNEARTHLY BEAUTY, NAKED AND GLEAMING, HER HAIR THE COLOR OF FLAME.

SHE SMILES ENTICINGLY AT YOU AND REACHES OUT TO DRAW YOU INTO THE CIRCLE OF DANCERS. THE SCENT OF THE FLOWERS AND THE WINE IS HEADY, BUT YOU REFUSE, SHAKING YOUR HEAD. SHE FROWNS, AND TURNS HER HEAD AWAY FROM YOU AS YOU CONTINUE ON THE PATH PAST THE GARDEN.

THE MOON BEGINS TO WANE AND IT GROWS DARKER. AS YOU WALK, THE PATH BECOMES MORE AND MORE NARROW, ROCKY AND TREACHEROUS. THE VEGETATION GROWS THIN UNTIL THERE IS NOTHING BUT BLACKENED TWIGS. A CHILL WIND BLOWS AROUND YOU, MAKING YOU SHIVER. YOU CAN HEAR THE HOWLING OF WOLVES, FIRST FAINT AND FAR AWAY, BUT THEN LOUDER AND NEARER. AS YOU CONTINUE DOWN THE PATH, YOU BEGIN TO HEAR THE SOUNDS OF RUSHING WATER, AND SOON YOUR PATH CURVES AROUND BESIDE A STREAM. YOU FOLLOW IT ALONG, BUT IT IS DARK, AND YOU CANNOT SEE IT, BUT ONLY HEAR IT. IT IS LIKE NO WATER THAT YOU HAVE EVER HEARD. IT SOUNDS THICK AND SLUGGISH, AND YOUR NOSE PICKS UP A FAINT, SALTY SMELL. THEN YOU COME TO A PLACE WHERE THE STREAM WIDENS, AND YOU CAN BARELY MAKE OUT AN ISLAND LOOMING IN THE DISTANCE. BEFORE YOU IS A NARROW WOODEN BRIDGE, DANGEROUSLY RICKITY, THE DARK TIMBERS ROTTING WITH AGE. THE BLEACHED SKULL OF A HORSE IMPALED UPON A STAKE STANDS A SILENT SENTRY AT THE ENTRANCE. YOU STEP UPON THE BRIDGE AND PAUSE. THE WOLVES HAVE STOPPED HOWLING, AND ALL YOU HEAR ARE THE SOUNDS OF THE STREAM. A SUDDEN TERROR GRIPS YOUR HEART, BUT SLOWLY, HESITANTLY, YOU CROSS THE BRIDGE TO THE MOST DESOLATE SPOT THAT YOU HAVE EVER SEEN.

THE MOON NOW IS ONLY A FAINT RING. YOU COME TO A GATE OF IRON WITH HUMAN SKULLS ON EITHER SIDE. ONE OF THEM SPEAKS AND CHALLENGES YOU. YOU ANSWER AS HONESTLY AS YOU CAN. THE GATE SWINGS OPEN, AND YOU CONTINUE ALONG THE PATH. AROUND YOU ARE THE SHADES OF THE PEOPLE WHO HAVE RECENTLY DEPARTED LIFE, FLOATING ABOUT, OBLIVIOUS OF YOU, ABSORBED IN THE RECOLLECTIONS OF THEIR PAST. SOME SMILE,

SOME WEEP, OTHERS CRY OUT IN PAIN. BUT YOU DARE NOT STEP TO SPEAK WITH THEM, SO YOU CONTINUE ON. THE PATH STOPS ABRUPTLY AT A DOLMEN ARCH BUILT INTO THE MOUTH OF A HUGE BURIAL MOUND. YOU REACH OUT YOUR HAND BUT YOU ARE BLOCKED. YOU MAY NOT ENTER WHILE STILL IN MORTAL FORM. BUT A DARK, VEILED FIGURE EMERGES, SHROUDED IN A BLACK CLOAK. THIS IS THE NAMELESS GODDESS OF WISDOM, FATE AND DEATH. SHE LIFTS HER VEIL ONLY FOR A MOMENT.

(Pause)

SHE DROPS HER VEIL AGAIN, BUT HER FACE WILL HAUNT YOUR DREAMS UNTIL THE TIME COMES WHEN YOU LEAVE YOUR MORTAL FRAME BEHIND AND FOLLOW HER THROUGH THE DOLMEN ARCH INTO THE BURIAL MOUND. BUT NOW YOU MUST TURN FROM HER AND EXIT BY THE GATE THROUGH WHICH YOU ENTERED. YOU PASS THE GARDEN, BUT IT IS EMPTY AND SOON YOU FIND YOURSELF AT THE NORTHEASTERN GATE OF THE CIRCLE.

Index

Symbols

1734 9, 22, 23, 25, 26, 27, 28, 29, 38, 43, 47, 48, 50

A

ABCs of Witchcraft 44
Admission Criteria 115
Airts 44
Aleister Crowley 101
Alexandrian 18, 19
Alexandrian Tradition 26
Alex Saunders 26
American Craft traditions 40
American Trad 19, 22, 23, 38
American Tradition 18, 19
AmTrad 202
Anglo-Celtic 8
Animal pathworkings 80
apprenticeship 59
Arthurian 13
Athena 8
autohypnosis 64
Aztecs 10

B

Beltaine 46, 59
Bill and Helen 28
Bill and Helen Mohs 18, 19, 22, 23
Bill Gray 55
Bill Mohs 19
Black Goddess 47, 49, 197, 208
Blodewedd 46
Book of Shadows 17, 20, 21, 22, 23, 25, 26, 27, 29, 35
Books of Shadows 32
Bridget 45
By Elder Tree and Standing Stone 54

C

Cabala 22, 54
CAER SIDI 137

Carenos 43, 44
Carroll "Poke" Runyon 40, 41
CASTLE OF THE EAST 218
CASTLE OF THE NORTH 230
CASTLE OF THE SOUTH 222
CASTLE OF THE WEST 226
Celtic 13, 44
Celtic Myth and Legend 70
Ceremonial Magic 22, 39, 54, 77
CERNUNNOS 138
Cernunnos 44
CERRIDWEN 138
Cerridwen 46
Chalice Well 53
circle 39, 42, 46, 79, 138, 149
Circle Casting 38
Circles 35
Clan 74, 75, 110
Clan Oath 74
Clan of Tubal Cain 8, 9, 46, 58, 59, 111
Closing 160
Coal Black Smith 47
Cochrane 25, 26, 27, 45, 48, 49, 52, 53, 55, 197
Cochrane's cord 55
Cochrane's death 59, 111
Cochrane's letters 24
Cone of Power 183
Consecration 160
Contact 163, 165
Contacts 167
coven 19, 20, 26, 35, 42, 202
Covenant of the Goddess 19
covens 108
Craft 10, 12, 15, 16, 17, 19, 20, 23, 26, 30, 60, 112, 113, 199, 203
Crowther 48
Crystal Well 20

D

Dark Mother 209, 210, 212
Demonology 22
Deosil 55
Dion Fortune 10, 68
Doreen Valiente 44
Dungeons and Dragons 14
Dweller on the Threshold 210

E

Earth Religion News 25
eclectic traditions 20
Ed 15, 16, 17, 18, 19, 20, 21, 22, 23, 28, 39, 112
Ed Fitch 12
elders 112
Elfame 46
England 52, 57
Evan John Jones 55, 56
Experimental Psychology 63

F

FFF 27
First Degree 18, 19
Flags Flax and Fodder website 27
Fred and Martha Adler 19, 26
Full Moon 76

G

Gardner 16, 48
Gardnerian 12, 16, 18, 19, 20, 22, 25, 26, 27, 34, 38, 48, 53, 161, 204
Gardnerian Craft 24
Gardnerian hierarchy 19, 20
Gardnerians 17, 23, 28, 33, 35, 44, 101
Gardnerian tradition 22
Gerald Gardner 17, 25
Gerald Noel 9
Glastonbury 53
God 66
Goda 46, 47
Goddess 9, 15, 17, 19, 23, 31, 40, 41, 42, 49, 64, 65, 66
Goddesses 45
Godiva 46
Goetia 40
Goibniu 47
Graal 49
Grail Queen 46
Grandmother 24
Great Rite 30
Great White Brotherhood 87
Grinding the Mill 55, 56
Group Mind 68, 69, 71, 72, 73
group mind 127
guided meditation 143

244

Gundustrup Cauldron 44
Gwyn ap Nudd 44

H

healing 78
Healings 77
Hereditary Witches 25
Herman Slater 25
Herne 44
High Priest 26, 31, 202, 205
High Priestess 17, 19, 20, 31, 32, 34, 205
HIO 48
Hypnotherapy 63
hypnotic techniques 28
hypnotism 28

I

initiation 117
Inquisition 67, 69, 107
instructor 133
Invocation 130

J

J.R.R. Tolkein 13
Joe 24, 27, 29, 45, 48, 52, 53, 103
Joe Wilson 9, 39, 55, 111
John 56, 57, 59, 111
Joseph Wilson 23
Jung 128, 196

K

King of the Witches 26

L

Lady Sheba's Book of Shadows 25
Lammas 18
Light Bringer 43
Llawereint 44
Llew 43
Llewellyn 25
Lucet 43
Lucifer 43
LUGH 137

Lugh Samildanach 43

M

Magic 180, 203
Magical training 203
Magister 58, 74, 198
Magus 204
manifestation 130
Man in Black 55
Mara 45, 53
Marion Zimmer Bradley 13
Masonic 47
matriarchal 200
Mayans 10
meditation 146
Mistletoe 55
Mohsean Tradition 18
Morrigan 45

N

Native American 10
Neurolinguistic Programming 63
New York 17, 19
Niamah 45
Nietzsche 128
Nimue 46
Nodens 43, 44
Norman 23, 52, 53
Nuada 44
Nudd 44

O

Odin 44
Old Dorothy 17
Old Gods 15
One True Craft 25
Opening 159
Order of the Temple of Astarte 40
OTA 40
Otherworld 46
Outer Court Grimoire 20
Outer Court material 21

P

Pagan 13, 33, 203
Pasadena Training Coven 19
pathworking 142
pathworkings 130, 140, 154
patriarchal 200
Pentagram 9, 25, 55
Poke 40, 41
Possession 163, 165
Possessions 173
Priesthood 67

Q

Queen of Elfame 46
Quintella 19

R

Ray and Rosemary Buckland 17
Rede 103
Rex Nemorensis 25
Ritual 162
Ritual Planning 158
ritual sex 35
Robert Cochrane 9, 23, 50, 103, 111
Roebuck 12, 15, 29, 30, 34, 35, 36, 57, 58, 59, 60, 62, 64, 67, 68, 69, 74, 75, 76, 77, 78, 93, 104, 106, 107, 108, 109, 110, 111, 114, 115, 127, 129, 147, 158, 160, 161, 173, 196, 197, 198, 199, 200, 201, 215
Roebuck Tradition 8
Rogues Gallery 86
Rollrights 53
Roy Bowers 9

S

Sacred Masks, Sacred Dance 111
Sacred Ritual Dance Step 32
SCA 12, 13, 205
Second Degree 19
Shadow 209, 210, 214
Shape-shifting 80
Sight 132
Silent ritual 80
skyclad 35
Smell 132
Society for Creative Anachronism 12
speiring 67

Spell casting 16
Spiral Castle 136
Spontaneous possessions 42
Star Trek 13
Stuart and Janet Farrar 26
Substance abuse 31
swords 96

T

Taliesin 24
Taste 132
Tautates 65
Tettans 43, 44
Teutates 44
theatricality 162
THE BLACK GODDESS 238
the Craft 8
THE FORGE OF OLD TUBAL 236
The Pasadena Training Coven 19
The Rollright Ritual 54, 55
THE SPIRAL CASTLE 234
The White Goddess 29
Third Degree 19, 30
Touch 132
Traditional Craft 19
training 36, 114, 120, 127
trance 140
Tubal Cain 45, 46, 47

U

unscrupulous teacher 20

V

vendetta 98

W

walk between the worlds 203
Wayland 47
Western Inner Workings 55
Whispering Knights 53
White Goddess 46, 47, 70
Wicca 9, 65, 205
Wiccans 96
widdershins 55

William G. "Bill" Gray 54
Witch 199, 205
Witchcraft 8, 9
Witchcraft: A Tradition Renewed 111
Witchcraft laws 24
Witches 24, 100, 102, 103
Witch gurus 20

Z

Zeus 8

www.ingramcontent.com/pod-product-compliance
Lightning Source LLC
Chambersburg PA
CBHW070347120426
42742CB00054B/1881